C000096905

Academies and Educational Reform

Full details of all our publications can be found on http://www.multilingual-matters.com, or by writing to Multilingual Matters, St Nicholas House, 31–34 High Street, Bristol BS1 2AW, UK.

Academies and Educational Reform

Governance, Leadership and Strategy

Elizabeth Leo, David Galloway,
Phil Hearne

MULTILINGUAL MATTERS
Bristol • Buffalo • Toronto

Library of Congress Cataloging in Publication Data
A catalog record for this book is available from the Library of Congress.
Leo, Elizabeth
Academies and Educational Reform: Governance, Leadership and Strategy/Elizabeth
Leo, David Galloway, Phil Hearne.
Includes bibliographical references and index.
1. Academies (British public schools) 2. Youth with social disabilities--Education
(Secondary)--Great Britain. 3. Educational change--Great Britain. I. Hearne, Phil.
II. Galloway, David, 1942- III. Title.
LA635.L46 2010
373.41--dc22 2010026210

British Library Cataloguing in Publication Data
A catalogue entry for this book is available from the British Library.

ISBN-13: 978-1-84769-316-7 (hbk)
ISBN-13: 978-1-84769-315-0 (pbk)

Multilingual Matters
UK: St Nicholas House, 31–34 High Street, Bristol, BS1 2AW, UK.
USA: UTP, 2250 Military Road, Tonawanda, NY 14150, USA.
Canada: UTP, 5201 Dufferin Street, North York, Ontario, M3H 5T8, Canada.

The policy of Multilingual Matters/Channel View Publications is to use papers
that are natural, renewable and recyclable products, made from wood grown in
sustainable forests. In the manufacturing process of our books, and to further
support our policy, preference is given to printers that have FSC and PEFC Chain
of Custody certification. The FSC and/or PEFC logos will appear on those books
where full certification has been granted to the printer concerned.

Typeset by Techset Composition Ltd., Salisbury, UK.
Printed and bound in Great Britain by Short Run Press Ltd.

Contents

Note on Methodology vii

Acknowledgements ix

Abbreviations xi

Part 1: Background

1   Why Academies? 3

2   Socially Divisive Gimmick, or Political and Moral Imperative? . . . 22

3   Opposition: Dogma or Legitimate Concern? 37

Part 2: Innovation, Governance, Leadership, Teaching and Learning

4   'It's Really Down to the Sponsor' (Academy Principal) 63

5   Schools for the Future: Trophy Buildings or Learning
    Environments? 86

6   Distinctive Features of Academies: 1. Independence,
    Accountability and Pressure 109

7   Distinctive Features of Academies: 2. Innovation. 125

Part 3: Futures

8   A Coherent Policy? 153

9   Designed to Deliver? 175

10 The Future of Academies: Consolidating a Beachhead? 191

References 210

Index 217

Note on Methodology

Academies have been controversial and as a result have been relentlessly evaluated, both by the government's own evaluators and by independent groups. These evaluations suffer from two failings. First, there is a lack of sharp focus on the different, often conflicting, perspectives of key players, notably sponsors, architects responsible for design of new buildings and principals. Second there has been too much attention to unanswerable questions about whether academies are more 'successful' than their predecessor schools or comparable schools in their neighbourhood, and too little to what policy makers and practitioners can learn from their distinctive features.

The fieldwork for this book aimed to fill these gaps. It was based on 26 in-depth interviews:

- Seven academy leaders (six principals and one deputy principal).
- Nine sponsors or their representatives at seven academies, for example an academy's chair of governors and chair of governors at an independent school sponsoring an academy. (At two academies two key players were interviewed separately.)
- Four architects and/or professionals with extensive experience of design of academies.
- Three teacher union officials.
- One former deputy head and head teacher of primary schools close to an academy.
- One former Director of Education in a local authority.
- Lord Andrew Adonis, former Minister for Schools.

With one exception all interviews were carried out with an undertaking of anonymity and confidentiality, both for the individuals and for their institutions. The exception was Lord Adonis, who agreed to be interviewed on the record. All interviewees were sent a transcript with sections used in quotations in the text highlighted. They were offered an opportunity to correct, clarify or veto any section. We received some helpful clarifications but no requests to delete any section. Only one academy we approached declined to take part, though we did not see the sponsor and the principal at every academy.

The sample of academies included some from the first two years of the programme, some more recently opened academies and two that were still in preparation. Sponsors and their representatives included business entrepreneurs, an independent school, two universities and two of the largest 'chains' with multiple academies.

Almost all interviews lasted 50–70 minutes. With one exception, permission was given to use a digital recorder, with the undertaking that recordings would be deleted on completion of the project.

Note on Authorship

The first rough draft of this book was written by David Galloway. The final version incorporates corrections, comments and additions by Phil Hearne and Elizabeth Leo.

Note on Nomenclature

Government departments sometimes change their names. The Department of Education and Science (DES), the Department for Education and Employment (DfEE), the Department for Education and Skills (DFES), the Department for Children, Schools and Families (DCSF), and the Department for Education (DfE) have each, at different times, had responsibility for schools.

Acknowledgements

The people who agreed to be interviewed did so subject to a strict undertaking of anonymity and confidentiality for their institutions, but we want to record our appreciation of their willingness to talk candidly and openly about their experience. One interview, with Lord Andrew Adonis, former Minister for Schools in the DCSF and widely seen as lynchpin of the academies programme until his transfer to the Department of Transport, was on the record and we record our appreciation of his willingness to see us.

Abbreviations

ARK:	Absolute Return for Kids
AST:	Academies Sponsors Trust
BBC:	British Broadcasting Corporation
BCSE:	British Council for School Environments
BSF:	Building Schools for the Future
CABE:	Commission for Architecture and the Built Environment
CACE:	Central Advisory Council in Education
CBI:	Confederation for British Industry
CSE:	Certificate of Secondary Education
CTC:	City Technology College
DAS:	Durham Achievement Services
DASH:	Durham Association of Secondary School Head Teachers
DCSF:	Department for Children, Schools and Families
DES:	Department of Education and Science
DfE	Department for Education
DfEE:	Department for Education and Employment
DfES:	Department for Education and Skills
EAZ:	Education Action Zones
ERA:	Education Reform Act (1988)
FE:	Further Education
FSM:	Free School Meals
GCE:	General Certificate of Education
GCSE:	General Certificate of Secondary Education
GM:	Grant Maintained (school)
GNVQ:	General National Vocational Qualification
HMCI:	Her Majesty's Chief Inspector of Schools
HMI:	Her Majesty's Inspector of Schools
IB:	International Bacalaureat
ICT:	Information and Communications Technology
LA:	Local Authority

LAPP:	Lower Attaining Pupils Project
LEA:	Local Education Authority
LEP:	Local Education Plan
NCSL:	National Council for School Leadership
NEET:	Not in Education, Employment or Training
NLS:	National Literacy Strategy
NPQH:	National Professional Qualification for headship
NUT:	National Union of Teachers
PFI:	Private Finance Initiative
PfL:	Partnerships for Learning
PSHE:	Personal, Social and Health Education
PWC:	PriceWaterhouseCoopers
RIBA:	Royal Institute of British Architects
SAT:	Standardised Assessment Tasks
SEN:	Special Educational Needs
SIP:	School Improvement Partner
SSAT:	Specialist Schools and Academies Trust
TUC:	Trades Union Congress
UCST:	United Church Schools Trust
ULT:	United Learning Trust

Part 1

Background

Chapter 1

Why Academies?

Introduction

The academies programme was launched by the Labour government in 2000 'to replace seriously failing schools' and to break 'the cycle of under-performance and low expectations' (Blunkett, 2000). Starting with three academies in 2002, the programme grew almost exponentially over the next six years. The growth coincided with a notable dilution of the independence granted to the first academies, and with inclusion in the programme of schools that were probably underachieving, but were certainly not 'seriously failing'. Following the Labour party's defeat in the 2010 general election, the incoming Conservative–Liberal Democrat coalition introduced a radical shift of focus. Whereas previously academy status had been reserved mainly for underachieving schools, the new government encouraged 'outstanding' schools to apply for fast track procedures to become academies and indicated that all secondary, primary and special schools would eventually be able to apply. Our book is concerned with experience gained before this radical shift of focus. Did it justify the new administration's proposed expansion of the programme? If so, what are the cornerstones of its success, and can we identify the quicksands into which it could sink?

Background

> There was a yearning in the early years of the Blair government for a bold and credible program of secondary school improvement beyond simply employing more teachers and putting more money into the system. (Andrew Adonis)

Writing in 1997, Adonis and Pollard had argued that money buys a good education – not only in the independent sector, but also in the state sector. In the mid-1990s he saw a state education system that suffered, he

3

believed, from under investment and flight of the middle class from schools in the inner cities:

> Those who can afford to flee the system desert it for the private sector; those who have the money to escape to a leafy middle class catchment area leave the inner cities; and those who can't are left behind to pick up the pieces. (Adonis & Pollard, 1997: 61)

This situation was compounded by the emergence of the 'educatholics' (Adonis & Pollard, 1997: 53): families whose devotion to the catholic church was closely linked to their anxieties about British education. These families considered themselves lapsed until they reached child-bearing age and then brought themselves to the attention of the priest to ensure that their child had a chance of a place at a 'good' catholic school. Adonis described run down comprehensive schools, overcrowded with poor facilities, high rates of vandalism and frustrated teachers. With some exceptions they constituted a failure of egalitarian policies.

Another key player in the education reform agenda that the incoming Labour government was to establish in 1997 was Michael Barber (1996). He claimed that a minimum of 1 in 14 schools was providing its pupils with an inadequate education; although some schools were successful, and some local authorities (LAs) had succeeded in leading interventions, far too often deep-seated problems were not being addressed:

> ... imagine the public outcry if an air traffic controller tried to justify a crash on the grounds that the other nine planes landed safely. (Barber, 1996: 123)

For Barber (2007), the central concern of the government's education policy in 1997 was to:

> ... solve the real problem that teachers face in tough inner city areas ... and to make schools in these locations more attractive to those parents who would otherwise abandon them. (Barber, 2007: 36)

He regarded policy at this time as a blend of Prime Minister Blair's emphasis on aspirant parents and David Blunkett's emphasis on equity. Blair saw LAs and the education establishment as actively placing barriers in the way of radical educational agendas.

Michael Levy (2008) was another influence on Blair and a key player in the development of the academies movement. He was clear that the academies programme was central to Blair's reform agenda. The person most closely associated with the academies programme itself in the Prime Minister's Policy Unit in Downing Street was Andrew Adonis. Levy was a kindred spirit with Adonis, Barber and Blair in his views on and experience of education in the period leading up to 1997. He described the time when he and his partner were looking at secondary schools for their children. On visiting their nearest secondary school, his partner pronounced it 'awful, absolutely awful' (Levy, 2008: 58).

Charles Leadbetter (1999) also influenced the Labour government around the turn of the century. He wrote of the need to:

> make it easier for people to create and open new schools. (Leadbetter, 1999: 241)

With Will Hutton (1995) he reflected both a commitment to education and a commitment to rethink current practice and do things differently. Against this background of the need to do something that would make a difference, the Labour government launched the Academies initiative, originally called City Academies, in 2000.

What This Book Tries to Do: And Does Not Try to Do

The above summary shows that a political head of steam had built up by the time Labour came to power in 1997. The incoming prime minister's often quoted priorities of Education, Education, Education were based on a conviction that the secondary school system required urgent attention. He believed the problem was most acute in impoverished inner city areas, and a major contributory factor was the inadequacies of LAs. There was nothing particularly original in this conviction. As we see later, it was shared by John Major's outgoing Conservative administration in 1997 and by David Cameron's incoming government in 2010. In opposition, the Conservatives always gave the academies programme their broad support and their manifesto for the 2010 election committed them to extending it. We are not principally interested in this book in discussing the political analysis of the failings of schools and LAs, though in Chapters 2 and 3 we do try to show how it affected the development of the programme.

The lack of significant discord between the two main parties influenced the focus and shape of the book. It would have been quite possible to write a book challenging the concept of academies and the premises on which the programme was based. Others have already done that (e.g. Beckett, 2007). Our underlying questions were:

- What can be learned from the academies programme?
- What are the implications for education policy and practice?

Subsidiary questions arising from these were:

• What have been the programme's main achievements?
• In what circumstances and under what conditions are academies most likely to be successful?
• What have been the programme's main problems?
• In what circumstances and under what conditions is an academy likely to run into serious difficulties?

We hoped that these questions would appeal to the general reader with an interest in education as well as specialist policy makers, teachers and governors. Our starting point was that the political consensus will prevent the programme's numerous opponents from derailing it for the foreseeable future. The opposition to academies seemed to us important only insofar as it would help us throw light on the above questions.

For three reasons, therefore, we were not principally interested in asking whether academies are more successful than LA schools. First, and unsurprisingly, some are and some are not. As we see later, the variation between academies is as great as between LA schools. Second, since there is no prospect of them being phased out, demands for their closure or return to the LA fold are at best unrealistic. At worst they betray a closed mind: Can the programme really have achieved nothing useful from which other parts of the education system should learn? Third, academies represent the most decisive shift in school governance since the 1944 Education Act introduced a tripartite system of grammar, technical and secondary modern schools. We note later that LAs that have retained this system have exceptionally high numbers of low achieving schools and argue that the existence of grammar schools has contributed to the difficulties they face. Yet the limitations of many secondary moderns did not lead anyone to demand a return to the *status quo ante*. Nor, in the 1970s did the limitations of some comprehensive schools lead any open-minded people to demand a return to secondary moderns. In both cases the questions for policy makers were: What can we learn from the achievements of the new system? And what can we do when things go wrong? That is our starting point in this book.

Developing the idea

Academies can be seen as a development from the Grant Maintained (GM) schools of the late 1980s and 1990s and from the City Technology Colleges (CTCs) created by the 1996 Education Act. A key feature of these schools was that they were independent of their local education authorities

(LEAs). This independence included holding their own budgets, with freedom to commission their own support services and to arrange their own professional development programmes. GM schools were rightly seen by the incoming Labour administration in 1997 as a Tory initiative, which had done little to raise standards in areas where both main parties thought it was most needed, namely schools in inner city and socially disadvantaged areas. More seriously, GM schools almost always replaced successful schools. A failing or underperforming school would have been deemed unable to manage its own budget or to take responsibility for maintaining and raising standards. Hence, the incoming government did not believe that GM schools provided a model for the incoming government to follow in its drive to raise standards throughout the country's schools. (There were exceptions. One of the authors worked in a poor performing secondary modern school in a highly selective area. Within two years of becoming GM, its results had improved, as had the numbers seeking admission. Ironically, it undermined two neighbouring non-GM schools and later became the lead school in a federation with the two schools in an attempt to transform their fortunes. The federation is now an academy.)

Nevertheless, every government since the 1980s has shared the Conservatives' view that LEAs lacked the single-minded determination required to improve the quality of education in the schools that Ofsted identified as failing or underperforming. Moreover, the inevitable inertia, as the government saw it, in local authority bureaucracy was compounded by a system of school governance that impeded rapid change rather than helping it.

CTCs were seen as having the necessary commitment to raise standards but for four reasons could not be seen as a model for a wider programme of reform. First, they were mostly new schools, opened in the face of local opposition, and thus could not replace the existing failing or underperforming schools that the government saw as its greatest challenge. Second, a more extensive programme of reform would need to work with LAs rather than in opposition to them, however reluctant the initial cooperation might be. Third, it was seen as essential to focus on areas of disadvantage and underachievement. Fourth, any extensive programme would need sponsors for chains of academies rather than a single sponsor for each school.

Academies can also trace part of their ancestry to the thinking behind the Reconstituted School programme in the United States, which developed in the United Kingdom as Fresh Start. As part of their agenda to raise standards, the New Labour party had considered the notion of Fresh Start while in opposition. In 1995 David Blunkett proposed drawing on the (rather mixed) US experience of Reconstituted Schools, and this became official government policy following Labour's election success in 1997. Fresh Start relied on leaders of the highest calibre, soon to be referred to in the media as 'superheads', creating an ambitious sense of purpose in failing schools.

The Fresh Start programme began in 1998 and by early 2000 some 15 secondary and primary schools were involved. However, it was a constant target for the media. A poorly judged decision by one 'superhead' to allow a television production company to make a prime time fly on the wall documentary of her Fresh Start school, and the high profile resignations of three 'superheads' in March and April 2000, led to inevitable headlines:

> Third Superhead quits fresh start school. (*The Guardian*, 15th March 2000)
>
> Fresh start school will be closed for good. (*The Independent*, 9th May 2000)
>
> Fresh start turns sour. (*Times Educational Supplement [TES]*, 12th May 2000)

And finally:

> Ministers admit defeat in 'fresh start' policy for failing schools. (*TES*, 12th May 2000)

The basis of this headline was a speech from the then Secretary of State for Education, Estelle Morris, suggesting that LAs were not playing a full role in the Fresh Start programme. Given the search for a radical approach to raising standards, it is unlikely to be a coincidence that the academies programme, known originally but briefly as City Academies, was announced as Fresh Start was making the headlines for not raising standards. While there are similarities between Fresh Start and academies, the latter went further by cutting out the LAs that Estelle Morris had identified as not playing a full part in Fresh Start. Academies also offered more security from the potentially destabilising closing and reopening of schools that had occurred under Fresh Start. For example, in July 2000 the BBC reported that Dr Jill Clough was to start as the new head of East Brighton College of Media Arts in the coming September. This school had already been closed and reopened twice. It was originally called Stanley Deason School, judged to be failing and reopened as Marina High School, closed again and reopened the previous September as East Brighton College of Media Arts. Fresh Start required none of the changes in governance that were to become defining features of academies.

The academies programme was announced by David Blunkett, then Secretary of State for Education, in a speech at the Social Market Foundation in March 2000 on transforming Secondary education:

> Over the next year we intend to launch pathfinder projects for new City Academies. These Academies, to replace seriously failing schools, will be built and managed by partnerships involving the government, voluntary, Church and business sponsors. They will offer a real challenge and improvements in pupil performance, for example through innovative approaches to management, governance, teaching and curriculum, including a specialist focus in at least one curriculum area. They will also be committed to working with and learning from other local schools... The aim will be to raise standards while breaking the cycle of underperformance and low expectations... They will take over or replace schools which are either in special measures or underachieving. (Speech to Social Market Foundation, 15 March 2000).

The first three academies opened in 2002. In 2003 there were 12, 17 in 2004, 27 in 2005, 46 in 2006, 83 in 2007 and 133 in 2008, with 'up to 80' scheduled to open in September 2009 and another 100 in 2010 (DCSF, 2009). On 30 November 2006 Tony Blair announced a commitment to 400 by an unspecified date.

The Department for Children, Schools and Families (DCSF) Standards site explained the Labour government's view of academies.

> Academies are all-ability, state funded schools established and managed by sponsors from a wide range of backgrounds, including high-performing schools and colleges, universities, individual philanthropists, business, the voluntary sector, and the Faith communities. Some are established educational providers and all of them bring a record of success in other enterprises which they are able to apply to their Academies in partnership with experienced school managers.
>
> Sponsors challenge traditional thinking on how schools are run and what they should be like for students. They seek to make a complete break with cultures of low aspiration which affect too many communities and their schools. We want this to happen, which is why we entrust the governance of Academies to them. On establishing an Academy, the sponsor sets up an endowment fund, the proceeds of which are spent by the Academy Trust on measures to counteract the impact of deprivation in their local communities.
>
> Academies are set up with the backing of their local authority, which also has a seat on the academy's governing body – Academies that are

co-sponsored by their local authority will have two seats in the governing body. Academies are not maintained by the local authority, but they collaborate closely with it, and with other schools in the area. Academies are funded at a level comparable to other schools in their area.

The governing body and head teacher have responsibility for managing the Academy. In order to determine the ethos and leadership of the Academy, and ensure clear responsibility, the private sector or charitable sponsor always appoints the majority of Governors. This is the case even if a local authority is acting as a co-sponsor for wider purposes. The number of governors on an Academy is not prescribed, but the expectation is for them to be relatively small.

All Academies are bound by the same School Admissions Code, SEN Code of Practice and exclusion guidance as all other state-funded Schools. All new Academies are required to follow the National Curriculum programmes of study in English, Maths, Science and ICT. All Academies – like the majority of Secondary Schools – have specialist schools status, and have specialisms in one or more subjects. (DCSF, 2008a)

Governance, 'turnaround', independence, leadership and standards

Five points arise from this overview. The first is governance. Sponsors were seen as a central feature of all academies and appointed a majority of the governing body. In the early academies they were successful business people and entrepreneurs who were willing to contribute £2 million of their own money towards the building and/or other costs. For reasons we discuss further in Chapter 4, the number of people with the time, energy and money to act as sponsors was limited. As the programme developed, the DCSF encouraged sponsorship from business, faith communities, independent schools, universities and other charitable organisations. 'Chains' of academies with a single sponsor were encouraged. Instead of each academy having a single sponsor with a direct, personal interest in it, an academy might be one of several academies, led by the same sponsor or sponsoring body, and answerable to them. Some of these 'chains' provide the services previously delivered by LAs, such as payroll and human resources. While the emphasis remained on sponsors challenging 'traditional thinking on how schools are run and what they should be like for students', this necessarily raised questions about the relationship between the sponsor and governing body, and hence about policy and practice within each academy. Nevertheless, the challenge to traditional thinking was backed up by a new approach to school governance, with closer ties to business methods than LA schools and an explicit expectation that change would be both faster and more far reaching than was normally possible in LA schools.

Second, academies were expected to achieve 'turnaround' in standards of behaviour and educational achievement. The DCSF statement referred to the low aspiration afflicting too many communities as well as schools. This was not just an implied acknowledgement of the link between educational achievement and poverty, unemployment, and indeed all indices of social exclusion. It also signalled a clear expectation that academies should contribute to regeneration of such communities. An immediate and visible indication of the government's commitment to them would be new buildings, signalling a new start from the often dilapidated premises of the predecessor schools. Changes in behaviour and educational standards might be less immediately visible, but no less important.

Third, their independence became a matter of continuing concern to academies. The somewhat oblique reference to 'new' academies being required to follow the national curriculum in English, Maths, Science and information and communications technology (ICT) merits comment. It probably had little or no relevance for the curriculum provided in any academy. Nevertheless, it represented a weakening of the independence given to the early sponsors. This could be seen as part of a wider pattern. In the early academies, LAs had little, if any, influence on the commissioning process, nor on the design and procurement of new buildings. For reasons discussed in Chapter 5, they became central to commissioning and to the design and procurement of buildings for new academies.

Fourth, leadership was seen as a defining feature of academies, and improvement in educational standards was often seen as the key evidence of effective leadership. The rather bland statement that the 'governing body and the head teacher have responsibility for managing the Academy' skated over an important point. The sponsor appointed the majority of governors and some sponsors chaired the governing body themselves. The obvious question about the relationship between sponsor and principal, (most academies have principals rather than head teachers) was given added force by the very high expectations, both of sponsors and of the DCSF, which saw academies as the flagship programme in its reform of secondary education. The problem is simple: A sponsor and the DCSF may have a vision of transforming aspiration and underachievement in underperforming schools in depressed areas, but they have to rely on a principal to lead the only people who can convert that vision into reality: a team of teachers, assisted by support staff. That requires exceptionally strong and effective leadership. Problems arise when a principal fails to deliver the improvements expected. Resolving them by finding a new principal is reasonable provided the sponsor's expectations were realistic, and the principal is given freedom in leading and managing the academy. However, sponsors may have their own views on how an academy should be run, and this could conflict with the strong leadership that an academy needs. We discuss this further in Chapters 4–7.

Fifth, and underpinning everything else, academies played an important part in the Labour government's 'standards agenda', the aim of which was to raise standards across the country's schools, but particularly in schools where they were lowest. While this is curiously understated in the above quote from the DCSF Standards site, Blunkett (2000) gave it prominence when launching the programme, and evidence for its continuing centrality is overwhelming.

Origins

Before saying more about the academies programme, we need to understand the origin of what Andrew Adonis described to us as the 'yearning in the early years of the Blair government for a bold and radical programme of secondary school improvement'. Similarly, it is important to understand what lies behind the cross party consensus on education. It is no surprise that both the largest political parties are committed to increasing the number of academies, albeit for different reasons and with different emphases on the sort of schools that should become academies.

The Downing Street website used to credit James Callaghan's (1976) speech at Ruskin College, Oxford with 'kick-starting modern debate on education'. In this speech Callaghan insisted on society's right to have an influence on what was taught in schools, and on the need to establish a 'so called "core curriculum" of basic knowledge'. Today, those views seem too obvious to be worth mentioning. It is hard to remember – or to credit – that in the 1960s and early 1970s the curriculum was known as a 'secret garden', entry to, and management of, which were jealously guarded by professional educationalists. Schools controlled the curriculum, with advice from LEA advisors or inspectors. The General Certificate of Education (GCE) and the Certificate of Secondary Education (CSE) at 16 and 'A' Level at 18 provided an external syllabus and assessment. Except for these, there was no control over the curriculum apart from very rare inspections by Her Majesty's Inspectors of Schools (HMI), whose reports were not normally published. The plants in the secret garden (children, presumably) were to be nurtured by teachers, not kicked around by clumsy-footed politicians. Callaghan felt obliged to say:

> I must thank all those who have inundated me with advice: some helpful and others telling me less politely to keep off the grass, to watch my language and that they will be examining my speech with the care usually given by Hong Kong watchers to the China scene. It is almost as though some people would wish that the subject matter and purpose of education should not have public attention focussed on it: nor that profane hands should be allowed to touch it. (Callaghan, 1976: 1)

Never again would a prime minister feel the need to justify intervention in education. Yet it was not for another 12 years after Callaghan's speech that Kenneth Baker, Margaret Thatcher's Secretary of State for Education and Science, finally ploughed up the flowerbeds of the secret garden with the 1988 Education Reform Act and the introduction of the National Curriculum.

Callaghan's Ruskin College speech was based on a clear recognition that changes in the economy were having a profound effect on what society could legitimately expect of schools. Labour governments raised the school leaving age to 15 in 1947 and 16 in 1973 without vigorous opposition. Those moves were seen as necessary in light of changing circumstances. Education became a subject of intense controversy only when changes in the economy started to have major implications for the knowledge and skills required of school leavers.

The late 1960s and early 1970s were a time of rapid and exciting change in schools, but with little intense political or media controversy. The second half of the 1970s can now be seen as a period of calm – if not before the storm, then certainly before the successive waves of reform in the Thatcher, Major, Blair, Brown and Cameron years. Yet most of these, including academies, had their origins in growing anxiety about the reforms of the late 1960s and early 1970s and the consequent ability of teachers and schools to adapt to new requirements. What were these reforms?

Publication of the Plowden Report (Central Advisory Council in Education, 1967) triggered what remains one of the most rapid and most remarkable periods of change since education in England became free and compulsory. That is neither an evaluation of those changes, nor an endorsement, merely a statement of fact. Successive governments have ignored, to their detriment, how they were achieved. Five years earlier, children in most primary schools sat in rows. The curriculum and pedagogy were formal, geared to the 11+ exam for secondary school selection. Primary teachers were less well qualified than secondary and tended to see themselves as poor relations of secondary teachers. Within five years of the Plowden Report's publication, children in almost all primary schools were sitting around tables. A new and supposedly 'child-centred' approach to the curriculum was based, at least in theory, on learning through topics rather than 'artificial' divisions into separate subjects. Primary teachers had acquired a pride in their professional identity, separate and distinct from secondary teachers that, amazingly, remains intact today even though successive reforms have largely removed the differences between methodology in primary and secondary schools. Three things made the transformation of primary education possible. First, the Plowden Report called for and legitimised a more child-centred curriculum. On its own, though, that would have had little impact. Second, change was made possible by abolition in most areas of the 11+, with the replacement of grammar and secondary modern schools by comprehensives. Primary schools were no longer judged by the number of children 'passing' into grammar schools. This had a liberating effect on the curriculum and on pedagogy – how teachers taught the curriculum. Third, the James Report (DES, 1972) led to an all graduate profession with the introduction of B Ed and BSc Ed degrees. The idealism of the primary dream led countless foreign visitors to admire a new way of teaching young children. The important thing, however, is not that the changes were indisputably beneficial – we shall see that they were not – but they were essentially a grass roots movement, led from within the primary sector. They were not driven by external pressures. Government acquiesced, but they were not government-led reforms. We return to this point in Chapter 10 when discussing what the academies programme may achieve.

Secondary education, too, was transformed in the late 1960s and early 1970s with the introduction of comprehensive schools in the large majority of LEAs. Unlike the Plowden reforms in primary schools, this was initiated by the then Labour government. The overriding motivation was public anger at 70–88%, depending on the LEA, of children being consigned to what was widely perceived as a second class education. That the 12–30% of children winning a place in a grammar school came disproportionately from more affluent and socially privileged families strengthened the Labour government's resolve. Research showed the 11+ to be an imperfect predictor, with too many pupils who obtained a place failing to benefit from it, and others who might have benefited failing to obtain one. Yet, as so often in education policy, research was used to legitimise a decision rather than to formulate it. The comprehensive utopia of opportunity for all was difficult to challenge.

In opposition the Conservative party had opposed comprehensive reor-ganisation, but with little of the rancour that characterised other debates. The political debate was perhaps muted by reluctant recognition of the inequity in the 11+. And, as her critics enjoyed pointing out with ill-con-cealed *schadenfreude*, the Secretary of State who approved the largest number of LEA proposals for comprehensive reorganisation was the Conservative Margaret Thatcher. (In electing her as leader to replace Edward Heath, the party was influenced less by this than by her courage in withstanding the very vocal and personalised protests at the government's decision to abolish free milk in primary schools. It is ironic that cutting her teeth as a cabinet minister on milk – by surviving the 'milk snatcher' jibe – was what convinced her colleagues that she had the backbone to lead the party.) Nevertheless, the absence of serious opposition to comprehensive reorganisation maintained a broad cross-party consensus that is still evi-dent today. The consensus has seldom been acknowledged, though explicit cross party support for academies are a notable exception, but without it the reforms since 1979, when Thatcher won power, would have been immeasurably more difficult.

The Stimulus for Policies Leading to Academies: Realities Behind the Primary Dream and the Comprehensive Utopia

It was not long before critics of the Plowden reforms made their voices heard. Right wing commentators of the 1970s attacked the standards and behaviour in both primary and secondary schools (e.g. Cox & Boyson, 1977). In the case of primary schools the problems were not hard to see (e.g. Alexander, 1992; Galloway, 2001). Although children sat around tables, they worked individually, with little evidence of the interactions that Plowden's committee had anticipated from collaborative group work. Especially in English and maths there was often heavy reliance on unimag-inative schemes of work, the monotony which was broken only by occa-sional visits to the teacher's table. The chronic problem of too many pupils achieving too little – what Alexander *et al.* (1992) were later to call, inele-gantly, 'an extended tale of distribution' – was all too obvious to second-ary teachers receiving pupils from primaries at age 11. An influential study at the time showed that while progressive methods could yield outstand-ing results, for the majority of teachers more formal methods tended to be more successful (Bennett, 1976).

The position in secondary schools was similarly bleak, though seldom recognised as clearly. There was never much evidence that the top 20–30%

on national norms were harmed by reorganisation from a selective system to comprehensive schools. There was no reduction in well-qualified graduates from the state sector applying to universities, nor in overall GCSE and A levels results. Claims that pupils who had done well in grammar schools were held back by the mediocrity of the comprehensives were always hard to substantiate. The problem was not that the top half was suffering, but rather that the other half was showing no sign of benefiting. In 1979, the year of Thatcher's election, and the start of the unrelenting reforms and initiatives that have faced teachers ever since, about 30% of leavers left school with no higher level GCSE grades after 11 years of compulsory education.

Nevertheless, the 30% of leavers with poor or no qualifications was nothing new. Whatever we may now believe to have been the case, it had never aroused strong political passions – on either side of the political divide. The reason was straightforward: Unemployment was low; the country's traditional industries such as coal mining, shipbuilding, car manufacturing, readily soaked up the pool of unqualified leavers. Had this unqualified pool not been available, the Confederation for British Industry (CBI) would doubtless have complained that the education system was failing.

The concern underpinning Callaghan's speech was equally clear: Recognition that the economy was moving into a post-industrial stage, in which employees would no longer need a large minority of unqualified, semi-literate leavers. Without employment, however, they would not just become a burden on society; they would become an active threat to it.

Sir Keith Joseph's Bottom 40% and Why They Started to Matter

The recession of 1981–1982 – then the deepest since the war – tipped the economy undeniably into a post-industrial phase. Unemployment rose to above 3 million. Margaret Thatcher was for a time the most unpopular and mistrusted Prime Minister of post-war years. Her position was precarious. Her own political reinstatement in the Falkland Islands conflict and the government's economic recovery with the help of revenues from North Sea oil are irrelevant to this discussion. The 1981 riots in Toxteth, Liverpool, however, had a profound effect on government ministers, by transforming the way they saw unqualified school leavers. Far from being necessary to the economy – albeit a creaking, antiquated economy in need of reform – unqualified *and unemployed* young people were becoming a burden on society. Worse, Toxteth implied that they had become an active threat to its stability. Since the recession of the early 1980s the economic prospects for school leavers with no qualifications have remained bleak.

The fact that Britain was not alone in facing this challenge merely underlined its urgency. Thus, Hong Kong was already starting to move towards a service rather than a manufacturing economy, with consequent demands for extension of the school system. Similarly, in Barbados a secondary school model inherited from the British provided high-quality education to the elite destined for the professions and the civil service. For most of the rest it provided little more than was required for manual work in the sugar cane fields (Galloway & Upton, 1990). That met the economy's needs as long as sugar attracted high prices on the world commodity markets, but created huge problems with mechanisation and the collapse of sugar prices. The unqualified workers in sugar fields faced unemployment, with few prospects of finding work in the growing tourist industry. Although on a larger scale and more complex, this was essentially the problem facing the UK in the early 1980s.

For the political left, unqualified school leavers represented a waste of opportunity, caused by avoidable weaknesses in the country's educational system. For the right it represented a burden on the taxpayer and an obstacle to much needed reform in the workplace. For both, the solution was to reform the school system.

Academics, too, had the secondary school system in their sights. A series of vivid and critical ethnographies had revealed the lack of opportunity to fulfil human potential in the secondary schools studied (e.g. Burgess, 1983; Corrigan, 1979; Hargreaves, 1967; Willis, 1977). In an excoriating critique, Hargreaves (1982) asserted that:

> Our present secondary school system, largely through the hidden curriculum, exerts on many pupils, particularly but by no means exclusively from the working class, a destruction of their dignity that is so massive and so pervasive that few subsequently recover from it. (Hargreaves, 1982: 17)

It was in this climate that Thatcher appointed her mentor, Sir Keith Joseph, to be Secretary of State for Education and Science. Joseph was convinced that the core problem lay in the less than inspiringly named 'bottom 40%'. In the wake of the worst recession since the war he wrung funds from a reluctant Treasury for the equally uninspiringly named Lower Attaining Pupils Project (LAPP). Joseph was unusual among Education Secretaries, in having the intellect and energy to contribute to think tanks rather than just rely on them. Certainly, he gave more and deeper thought to the ills of the English education system than most of his predecessors, or successors. His legacy was his verdict that education in England required root and branch reform, from pre-school to university. Whether or not they agreed with him, each of his successors has been in the grip of his legacy ever since.

Tory Governments Preparing the Ground for New Labour's Academies?

Thatcher is remembered for her radical policies, not just in education but in the economy, industrial relations and foreign affairs. Looking back on her first two administrations, her talent lay in her strategy of gradualism. There were modest reforms in the 1980 Education Act, requiring schools to make more information available to parents, including examination pass rates, on special education in the 1981 Education Act and on school governors in the 1986 Act. In addition parents were given new powers in choosing their children's schools. Each was seen as radical at the time, though today teachers would be baffled that they were ever contentious. In retrospect they can be seen as the start of a process. For example, parental powers to express a preference in selecting a school anticipated the gradual erosion of LAs' powers. This also anticipated the manner in which specialist secondary schools were presented as a way of extending parental choice. Similarly, the rather limited information available to parents from the 1980 Education Act prepared the way for the much more extensive information that is currently available.

If the Government's early education reforms can now be seen as modest, that cannot be said of the 1988 Education Reform Act (ERA). The preparatory Bill was sent out for public consultation during the summer holiday, when teachers were presumably expected to have other things on their minds. Disconcertingly, 18,000 replies were received and of these almost all from teachers and from related professionals were hostile (Haviland, 1988). Having consulted, as they were required to do, the Government took a largely unchanged Bill through Parliament.

The ERA introduced a legal entitlement to a national curriculum for all pupils. The highest attaining 30–40% were probably already receiving at least an adequate curriculum in most schools. The national curriculum aimed to ensure that pupils in all schools would receive a broad, balanced curriculum. Hence, it aimed to raise seriously low attainments in a minority of schools. In prescribing curriculum content, though not methodology, it also aimed to raise standards by freeing teachers from the burden of curriculum design and development. The main impact though, was on Joseph's 'bottom 40%'. For the first time, *all* pupils, including those with special educational needs (SEN), would have a legal entitlement to the full range of a national curriculum.

Moreover, the ERA ensured results would be visible by proposing the programme of national testing that came to be known as SATs (Standardized Assessment Tasks). Together with publication of each school's GCSE results, this ensured that the 30% of Joseph's 40% who left school with no useful qualifications would become starkly and increasingly visible. Schools would be accountable for these students as well as for their high flyers.

The ERA also introduced changes to school funding. Schools were to be funded on the number, and ages, of their pupils. This, too, was seen as a way of making schools more accountable to parents and extending parental choice. It was expected to increase Head Teachers' motivation to show parents of lower attaining pupils that they were valued and receiving high quality education.

The Labour-opposition voted against the ERA, and indeed against most of the Conservative educational reforms from 1979 to 1997. Yet just as Conservative opposition to Labour's encouragement of comprehensive schools had been muted, the same applied to Labour's response to Conservative reforms. To the irritation of colleagues on both the left and right, Galloway (1990) argued that the Tories' 1988 Education Reform Act could logically have been proposed by a government of the hard, Marxist Left. It gave the most disadvantaged children the same rights to the curriculum as the most privileged. National testing and publication of results ensured that they could never again be overlooked. School funding arrangements meant that LEA's could no longer channel funds away from schools in disadvantaged areas and into those with a higher profile publicly and politically. While most education academics, and certainly almost all in the field of SEN, were opposing the ERA, Galloway argued that it was an overdue reform that could bring substantial benefits to the most disadvantaged pupils. Unfortunately, the evidence of the next nine years, until the election of a Labour Government, showed that he was only partially right.

Joseph's 40% referred to the lowest attaining pupils, not to individual schools. Yet unsurprisingly they were found disproportionately in schools located in or near areas of poverty and social disadvantage. This mattered because the early school effectiveness studies were showing that lower attaining pupils tended to make less progress when they were in a large majority in their school. In other words, a mixed intake seemed to help (Rutter *et al.*, 1979).

Unfortunately, three policies of the Thatcher and Major years contributed to a polarisation in which some schools became increasingly socially divided. First, publication of Ofsted reports ensured that criticisms were well-aired in the local press. Second, publicity of SATs results ensured schools at the foot of the performance tables were identified, as well as those at the top. Third, as the result of the first two, middle class parents started to compete for places in what they deemed to be the better schools, and to avoid the others. This transformed the rhetoric of parental choice of school into the reality of a successful school's choice of the child. The result was the flight of the middle class to what they perceived as better schools or, failing that, to the independent sector.

Andrew Adonis, former Schools Minister with responsibility for academies, told us:

> to my mind the chronic weakness of the English education system was the bottom half of the state secondary schools, which were between poor and very poor in their absolute and relative performance. And in the cities they were in many cases offering an unacceptable standard of education, that was creating a very segregated society. And I saw this only too strongly myself where I live in North London, where basically the middle class had opted out of the local state secondary schools completely, and the choice was whether to go private (and where I live more than 20% go private at secondary level,) or whether they sought to get out of Inner London entirely and transport their children to state schools in the suburbs, which, of course, a large proportion do. (Andrew Adonis)

There is in fact a substantial body of research showing the importance of a balanced social intake. Rutter *et al.* (1979) showed that children receiving free school meals (FSM) tended to do better when they were not in a large majority in their school. More recently, Whitty (2008) has argued that a balanced social intake raises the aspirations and expectations of low attaining students. The effect on learning behaviours can be particularly important by enabling students who may not have developed high aspirations and effective learning habits to learn from those who have. Attending the same school as other young people in the neighbourhood can also be beneficial in establishing cohesive relationships and shared experiences.

The low attainments and behaviour in a significant minority of schools was compounded by neglect of infrastructure. Perhaps inevitably, this was worst in areas where parental pressure was least well organised, in estates characterised by high levels of crime, vandalism and graffiti. We see in Chapter 4 that this was a prime motivator for academy sponsors.

This, then, was the position when Labour came to power in 1997, led by a Prime Minister who had committed his government to three priorities: Education, Education, Education. In making this commitment he was acknowledging that education had become a topic of heated debate across the country. For children of the working class the confident expectation of a safe job on leaving school no longer existed. For the middle class the notion of a job for life was becoming a folk memory. In his Ruskin College speech James Callaghan started a debate that had been pursued enthusiastically throughout the Thatcher and Major years. From inner city estates to elite public schools it became an article of faith that employment depended on more advanced educational qualifications, and higher level skills. Never had so many parents from all sectors of society regarded education as so important. In the next chapter we examine the evidential and moral basis for the academies programme.

Chapter 2
Socially Divisive Gimmick, or Political and Moral Imperative?

Introduction

By the time of Labour's election victory in 1997 the groundwork for educational reform had been completed. There was no question of repealing the Conservatives' legislation on the national curriculum, national testing and inspection of schools. Yet the incoming government was committed to retaining previous levels of public expenditure. In theory an excuse to avoid major additional expenditure on education might have seemed attractive. Moreover, academic research was starting to cast doubt on the belief that *schools* were underachieving. The emphasis on schools is crucial, because if it could be shown that differential levels of attainment were the result of poverty and other socio-economic factors, expecting schools to compensate for these would be unrealistic. If that were indeed the case, it would undermine the whole basis of the academies programme, and indeed raise questions about the need for a further period of reform in state schools. This chapter starts by examining that possibility. It then examines the view that educational reform requires a change in culture and aspiration in schools facing the most challenging circumstances.

Was School Reform Necessary?

Seminal school effectiveness studies by Rutter *et al.* (1979) and Mortimore *et al.* (1988) had convinced ministers that schools could make a difference to their pupils' life chances. These studies certainly showed that choice of school mattered, but careful reading also showed that prior attainment was by far the strongest predictor of subsequent attainment. The issue was not that the qualities of a school made no difference to the all-important qualifications that its pupils obtained at age 16, but that their attainments on entry were four or five times more important. In their evidence to the

House of Commons Select Committee on Education and Skills, Gorard and Smith (2003) claimed:

> At the level of comparison between schools (department or teachers), school effectiveness work has attempted to describe the characteristics of a successful school in a way that could form the basis for a blueprint for school improvement. Ironically, the major undisputed outcome of all this work has been the reinforcement of non-school context (Coleman *et al.*, 1966; Gray & Wilcox, 1995). National systems, school sector, schools, departments and teachers combined have been found to explain approximately 20 per cent of the total variance in school outcomes. In all studies this effect is small, and the larger the sample used, the weaker is the evidence of any effect at all (Shipman, 1997) ... The remainder of the variance in outcomes is explained by student background, prior attainment and error components. (Gorard & Smith, 2003: 8)

In other words, league tables of children's performance on SATs or public examinations would largely be measuring differences in the attainments that secondary school children brought from their primary schools, and *these* would largely be reflecting differences in family income or social background. Gorard and Smith continued:

> To expect a school with many students in poverty to gain the same kind of exam success as a school with nearly no poor students at all, is ridiculous. Yet this is what raw score comparisons (such as league tables) do. Once levels of poverty, and other background factors, are taken into account in regression equations, then there is no evidence that any type of school performs better than any other. State funded schools in the UK are also rapidly catching up the exam scores of fee paying schools (Gorard & Taylor, 2002). So the question is not about the underachievement of schools or regions. Rather it is about why there is this link between poverty and attainment and what can be done about it. (Gorard & Smith, 2003: 8–9)

On this evidence there would be a powerful case for caution before introducing an expensive reform programme such as academies. A new government committed to not exceeding its predecessor's expenditure, as was the incoming Labour administration in 1997, could legitimately have said: If it (the school system) ain't broke, don't fix it! There may well be better and worse performing schools of all types and in all areas, but if, as Gorard and Smith argued, most of the variance in school results was attributable to student intake, the temptation could have been to concentrate scarce resources on reducing poverty rather than improving the school system. That, however, was never an option for at least seven reasons:

(1) The correlation studies on which Gorard and Smith relied take insufficient account of outlier schools that do not conform to the general pattern. If low performing outliers with exceptionally poor performance were to be concentrated in inner cities and estates with multiple social problems, their importance for public policy would be greater than if they were distributed more generally across the country. There are two reasons. The first is that early research in developmental psychopathology showed that when the number of stressors increase, they interact with and aggravate each other (e.g. Rutter, 1978). Hence, a failing school in an area with many social problems is likely to have a more damaging impact on its pupils' life chances, and on their psychosocial behaviour, than a failing school in a more settled, stable area. Second, the high correlation between poverty and poor educational outcomes is strong evidence that schools with exceptionally low performance are found disproportionately in areas that are exceptionally high on multiple indicators of social disadvantage, from poor housing to delinquency and mental health.

(2) Evidence from Ofsted reports consistently identifies a minority of schools with poor student behaviour and educational attainments well below the level expected from the students' backgrounds.

(3) Returning from visits to schools in their constituencies, MPs reported badly maintained, dilapidated buildings, compounded by litter and graffiti. That these were frequently consistent with the surrounding neighbourhood made them no more acceptable. No government with a professed commitment to reducing social exclusion could ignore the evidence of sub-standard infrastructure. Even if GCSE results could legitimately be attributed to poverty or other indicators of social malaise, the quality of too many school buildings could not.

(4) The annual process of allocating secondary school places in response to parents' applications was becoming an acute political embarrassment. It was not just that constituents were overwhelming MPs with requests for help, though that certainly contributed. Locally and nationally, the media relished the weeks of anxiety while parents and children waited to hear whether a place could be found in their preferred school – and the anguish when it could not. The process highlighted the flight from schools that were perceived as failing, and the difficulty in obtaining places in those perceived as successful. Whether or not the schools were indeed failing or successful was not the point. Politically, the perception was what mattered.

(5) Although research showed that the strongest predictor of students' GCSE grades at age 16 was their level of attainment on entering the school at age 11, the same could not be said of behaviour. Rutter *et al.* (1979) showed that: 'the secondary schools with worst behaviour in the classroom and on the playground were not necessarily those the "worst" intake of difficult pupils at the age of ten years' (Rutter *et al.*, 1979: 74). Subsequently, Galloway *et al.* (1985a) found no relationship between measures of social disadvantage and exclusions for unacceptable behaviour from 39 secondary schools in Sheffield. Hence, while poverty and social disadvantage are reliable predictors of educational attainments, they are *not* reliable predictors of behaviour within the school. This is the case whether we consider general behaviour within the classroom or the numerically much smaller number of children whose severely disruptive behaviour leads to exclusion (Galloway, 1995). The strongest influences on behaviour lie within the school itself. Stable behaviour and positive relationships are a necessary condition for good educational progress, though not in themselves sufficient. Poor behaviour and relationships tend to have a more damaging impact in schools in socially disadvantaged areas, where there is likely to be less compensatory support from home than in more affluent areas. Consequently, poor behaviour and relationships at school will drag pupils down further.

(6) A rather obvious limitation in studies of the relationship between poverty and educational attainments is that not even a perfect correlation would tell us anything about the *potential* of students living in less privileged areas, let alone of those in the least privileged. Psychologists have argued endlessly, and inconclusively, about the effect of the environment on measured IQ. No political party would dare to attribute the low attainments of pupils living in poverty to low IQ, nor would they wish to do so. Politically and morally, hoping that, in the fullness of time, alleviation of poverty would solve the problem of low attainments was simply unacceptable. The question for the new government had to be: How can we demonstrate the potential for substantial and sustained improvement in the most difficult areas?

(7) Finally, Ministers were conscious of another rather obvious point: Changes in the economy and employment market required young people with new and more advanced qualifications. On some estates, the parents of many pupils had never been in full time employment. Unemployment is associated with poor physical and mental health. While there is debate about the causal relationship, there is general agreement that the longer people remain out of work, the less likely

they become ever to return to work. Schools cannot solve the problem of an unemployed underclass, but they have an important role to play in increasing the opportunities open to school leavers.

Inaction, therefore, was never an option. Gorard and Smith's (2003) evidence to the House of Commons Select Committee indicated the challenge that government faced in reforming the school system. Schools could not compensate for society, but the government had to seek ways to enable pupils in the most problematic areas to break out of the cycle of poverty and disadvantage. Hence, the statistical link between poverty and low attainment was irrelevant to the case for reform.

Further, academies represented more than another school improvement initiative. They represented a sustained attempt to turn around failing and under-performing schools. They differed from previous initiatives in four crucial ways:

(1) The sponsor, and the sponsor's nomination of a majority of the governing body, represented a decisive break with the governing bodies of LA schools. It introduced a business model into governance, and hence into the management of schools.

(2) In a large majority of academies, the sponsor was involved in the appointment of a new principal. Murphy and Meyers (2009) note the opportunities open to a new leader when leading 'turnaround' of an organisation.

(3) The new principal was held personally accountable for achieving an improvement in standards, and failure to do so within a year or two could lead to a search for a new post. Similarly, with the governing body's support, the principal was able to hold teachers and members of the school's management team to account. Academies can be quicker and more decisive in replacing poorly performing staff.

The new buildings stood in stark contrast to the often dilapidated estates that academies served, and thus symbolised possible regeneration.

Cultural Reform in Schools: What it Could Mean and What it Could Look Like

Walter Doyle (1986) makes the interesting observation that teachers and students are too often in a symbiotic relationship in which each has a vested interest in driving down the cognitive demands of a task. We have seen examples at all levels, from pre-school to doctoral classes in universities for school leaders and inspectors. In pre-school settings, we have seen children staying in their comfort zone of tasks they understand and can complete without difficulty. Their teacher, preoccupied with other children and anxious to maintain classroom harmony, is happy to let them. The message, never articulated but clearly understood on both sides, is: 'Don't make trouble for me and I won't make trouble for you!' In a doctoral class students were required to propose their own assignment title. Each year some titles would be rejected because they required little more than regurgitation from standard texts. Again the subliminal message was clear: 'If you don't expect too much independent thought from us, we'll be sure to provide an acceptable assignment, so there won't be any problems when it comes to assessment!'

Doyle's symbiotic relationship is particularly evident in failing and low achieving schools. It is illustrated in Lupton's (2004) vivid study of four inner city schools. She identified distinctive features of the schools that contributed to an unpredictable working environment. Two features concern us here. First, each school had pupils with a wide range of abilities and prior attainments:

> A tendency towards less challenging tasks was noted when controlling the classroom was difficult. Some teachers admitted that it was easy to slip into feeling that a good lesson was one in which most of the pupils had been on task for most of the time, and major disruption had been avoided. The quality and challenge of the task could be seen as secondary. Worksheets and copying exercises were used more commonly with lower classes. Subject content was simplified and discussion was limited. These findings add to a substantial body of research (see Hallam, 2002 for a review) suggesting that teaching for groups with many lower ability pupils may be insufficiently challenging. (Lupton, 2004: 9)

The second point relates to the emotional climate of the school:

> ... possibly most distinctively, all the schools had a charged emotional environment. The number of pupils who were anxious, traumatised, unhappy, jealous, angry or vulnerable was reputed to be much greater than in schools where parents were materially better off, less stressed themselves and more able to secure a stable, comfortable environment for their children.
>
> In each school there was a minority of children (probably no more than about twenty) who had severely disturbed behaviour. These pupils were disruptive in lessons, found it difficult to concentrate, were sometimes aggressive towards other pupils and staff, found it hard to

accept rules, and struggled to get through the school day smoothly on a regular basis. (Lupton, 2004: 9–10)

Lupton noted three implications. First, teachers had to develop classroom strategies for dealing with pupils' emotional needs. Second, non-contact time was spent on 'pastoral issues'. Third, the pupil welfare issues could be rewarding but the atmosphere could easily become draining and energy sapping. Her description may be familiar to teachers in many inner city schools with well below average attainments. If so, it raises two important questions about the dominant professional culture in such schools.

First, it is clear that high levels of problem behaviour are not inevitable in inner city schools. We have already noted evidence that school climate has a profound effect on behaviour (Rutter *et al.*, 1979). Galloway (1983) found no evidence of the draining, energy sapping atmosphere that Lupton describes in his account of four urban schools with exceptionally low rates of disruptive behaviour. It was, however, evident in other schools with similar pupil intakes. We therefore have to look at leadership, teaching and learning, and pastoral care rather than accept behavioural and pastoral problems as an unalterable fact of low achieving urban schools.

Second, the teachers in Lupton's study seemed to be attributing the problems they experienced to factors in the pupils and their home backgrounds. In the short term, this will have reduced feelings of pressure by externalising their causes. In the longer term it is likely to have resulted in chronic feelings of stress because the individual teacher could do nothing to resolve the problem. This is a long term problem in English schools. Croll and Moses (1985) found that more than 90% of teachers attributed behaviour problems to factors over which they had no control. The percentage for learning difficulties were only slightly less. This belief is part of an entrenched staff room culture in many schools. Yet in every school there are likely to be some teachers who succeed in creating a businesslike, orderly atmosphere. Following a child or group of children through the day can be instructive. With some teachers they are alert, interested, and eager to take part in the lesson. Behaviour is excellent. With others there are high levels of inattentiveness and minor behaviour problems, such as talking out of turn and distracting other children. The switch in behaviour and motivation from lesson to lesson is instant and effortless. Nothing could better illustrate the fallacy that factors in the child, the family and the local neighbourhood is responsible for problem behaviour and lack of commitment to school work.

The 'cultural reform' implied in the heading of this section should now be clear: Heads with an uncompromising, evidence-based belief that they are responsible for the behaviour of pupils in their schools, with teachers who share that belief in the classroom. If ministers saw a need for a radical shift in the beliefs and attitudes of heads and teachers in the country's lowest achieving schools and most multiply disadvantaged areas, no mere change in government *policy* would be likely to achieve it. Something more radical would be needed, such as what Woods *et al.* (2007) called cultural entrepreneurialism:

> ... Innovation, driven by a vision to bring meaning, which mobilises resources to advance values and understanding of the deepest importance to personal and social development. (Woods *et al.*, 2007: 242)

Except, of course that the values and understanding would be of deepest importance, first and foremost, to *teachers'* professional development, and through teachers to pupils. Woods *et al.* (2007: 243) argue that cultural entrepreneurialism 'breaks new ground and mobilises resources in order "to imbue a more entrepreneurial culture with a higher work ethic" (Woods, 2005: 32), by bringing "values and a conceptual understanding of the world (grounded) ... in some sense of ultimate meaning and purpose or guiding ethical position"' (Woods, 2000: 234). The academies programme can be understood as an attempt to trigger cultural shift by introducing an ethos of cultural entrepreneurialism into some of the country's most problematic schools. If these schools could be transformed, ministers believed, so could others.

The academies programme was based on a political imperative: to make changes in the country's most troubled schools, and to make the necessary changes quickly. This political imperative was based on a moral, social and economic imperative: to reduce the increasing social divisiveness of schools. The details and technicalities of the programme, however, can be seen in light of research on turning round failing organisations (e.g. Boyne & Meier, 2009). The extent of 'turnaround' an organisation can attain is dependent on four key factors: Retrenchment – focusing on core business, which for academies is students' educational progress and achievements; Repositioning, which can include re-branding the organisation; Changes in human resources; and High investment. Until 2010 academies had the last of these and, because they were new organisations, they also had an opportunity to redefine themselves and to make changes in staffing. High investment , or rather the lack of it acquired additional importance with the global recession of 2010 and the government's announcement that new academies were unlikely to continue to receive it.

Planning Academies: Key Features

Academies were widely seen as the government's flagship policy in the secondary education sector (although all-through academies for pupils aged 3–18 were also encouraged). Equally important, arguably, was the encouragement given to every school to offer a specialist subject. This was a reaction to a perception of unproductive uniformity among comprehensive schools – the prime minister's press secretary's notorious reference to 'bog standard' comprehensives. Moreover, the argument that specialist schools would extend parental choice was always hard to defend outside the largest cities. Parents continued to be more concerned with a school's overall quality as reflected in GCSE and A level results than with its specialism. Nevertheless specialist school status signalled at least an aspiration to high standards in the specialism, and that could potentially benefit the rest of the curriculum. Specialisms, though, were a more generic initiative covering the whole secondary school system. Academies had a narrower but more challenging remit.

They were closely linked to another government initiative, launched in June, 2008: National Challenge (DCSF, 2008b). The challenge for schools was to achieve a minimum of 30% of students gaining five GCSE passes at A*–C including English and Maths. In 2007, 638 secondary schools failed to reach this benchmark. In 2008 the number had dropped to 440. The Labour government's challenge to itself was to provide support that would enable all schools to reach the benchmark by 2011.

The 'support' proposed for these schools included the LA replacing the governing body with an 'interim executive board'. Long-term solutions included conversion to academy status, and the DCSF committed itself to use National Challenge to accelerate the academies programme. This was somewhat ironic as several existing academies had failed to meet the target and were thus threatened with transformation into – academies! Yet failure to meet the National Challenge target may seem less surprising in view of the range of challenges facing academies.

Schools and communities with the greatest problems

A few academies were new schools, generally in areas of high social disadvantage. An even smaller number were created from successful independent schools wishing to join the state system. This was contentious even within the academies programme and is discussed further in Chapter 8. Until 2010, though, most replaced failing or underperforming schools in areas with multiple social problems, and there is little dispute that predecessor schools were among the most challenging in the country. Academy status was automatically considered when a school with an 'Unsatisfactory' Ofsted report failed to make rapid progress. Any school with fewer than 30% of students gaining at least five A*–C grades at GCSE – well below the National Challenge benchmark since there was no obligation that English and Maths be included – was eligible for consideration for academy status. Unlike the Grant Maintained schools of John Major's government, for which good results and effective governance were key requirements, most academies replaced the least successful and most problematic 10% of schools, generally in the most problematic communities. Where that was not the case, they sought to create additional access to high quality schooling in areas where it had been lacking

Infrastructure

Until 2010, when approving an academy project, the DCSF made a commitment to replace buildings of the predecessor school where these were inadequate, or to refurbish or extend the existing buildings. Especially with the earlier academies, the new buildings were often dramatic. Some of the early sponsors insisted on their own preferred firm of architects, with a view to the academy buildings being seen as a public statement of commitment to excellence, contrasting with a predecessor school that was characterised by the lack of it. The National Audit Office (2007) gave the mean cost of academy buildings as £27 million.

Independence

Successive governments convinced themselves that although LAs might not hold back successful schools with strong leadership, they were unsuited to transformation of failing schools with weak leadership. This was largely because a LA bureaucracy was inevitably more concerned with maintaining harmony and stability in its constituent parts than with the friction and upheaval necessarily involved in challenging poor performance. Andrew Adonis argued in his interview with us:

> Bureaucracies are not by and large good at running schools. The schools that were running better in 'local authority control' weren't in fact controlled by them. They were doing their own thing. But where you needed local authorities most, or rather someone to reform and change the system, local authorities were at their weakest. They did not have a body of expertise, or good managers, or

good processes that could systematically turn round weak and failing schools in those areas where they most needed to be improved. And indeed often they were obstacles to reform in these areas (Andrew Adonis).

This was probably unfair to some LAs, though by no means all. Moreover, bureaucratic inertia was also evident in Australia, where Gonczi (2008) noted dryly that:

> The Federal parliament has held major reviews of many aspects of school education and the professional development of teachers during the last ten years . . . . . In the area of teacher education there have been more than 100 reports in the last twenty years, which have recommended literally thousands of reforms. Yet very little has changed. (Gonczi, 2008: 7)

In Australia, the federal government is frustrated by the constitutional autonomy of the states in running schools. In England successive governments have seen LAs as a source of inertia. New governance arrangements, removing power from LAs, were seen as the obvious solution.

Yet while doubting the ability of LAs to run schools successfully, the government recognised that significant expansion of the academies programme would require their cooperation. LAs were therefore required to identify potential academies under the Building Schools for the Future programme (DfES, 2004) (see Chapter 5). Further, LAs were given a central role in procurement of academies, and it is the LA that signs off new buildings to the sponsor. Sponsors now had to work closely with the LA.

Governance

Independent sponsors with an implacable determination to succeed were seen as the solution to the perceived inadequacies of LAs. Sponsors of the early academies were mostly successful entrepreneurs who donated £1.5–£2 million towards the cost of the buildings. This was soon modified to permit a trust fund that could be used to provide pupils with opportunities that would otherwise not have been available. Sponsors always appointed a majority of governors, and were able to exert a powerful influence. It is likely that the government saw these sponsors as bringing two main benefits to the new programme: First, they would use their contacts to establish a much closer relationship between the academy and the world of business. This would benefit students and ensure that the curriculum became more sensitive to the world of work. Second, and far more important, they would bring their business and entrepreneurial skills to governance of the academy. Problems would be identified and decisive action taken, more quickly than was ever possible in a LA.

For reasons discussed in Chapter 4, the early model of a single sponsor for each academy was soon broadened. As well as chains of academies, universities were also welcomed as sponsors. Even LAs were encouraged to co-sponsor academies, though they were not permitted to be the lead sponsor, and thus to appoint a majority of the governing body. Chains were seen as a way of expanding the programme quickly. Thus, in mid-2009, the United Learning Trust (ULT) had 15 academies open, with more in preparation, Absolute Return for Kids (ARK) had six open with three in preparation, Oasis had nine open with five in preparation, the Harris Trust had seven open with five in preparation. There appear to be two reasons for the growth in chains. First, they facilitated quick action when it was deemed necessary to replace a failing school with an academy. Second, the government saw academies as a national initiative to replace failing and underperforming schools. With 638 schools identified in the latter category for failing to meet the National Challenge target, the proposed expansion to 400 academies could be seen as relatively conservative. There was never any prospect of finding 400 entrepreneurs to contribute the time, money and energy to sponsor an academy. By spreading the net, the target of 400 academies became more realistic. Nevertheless, this raised significant questions, to which we return in Chapter 4.

Standards Driven and Market-Driven Reforms

Academies represent an interesting combination of the market-driven and standards-driven approaches to educational reform in England. Charter schools in the United States have been an influence, and often, controversially, an inspiration, to their development. Charter schools are independent but publicly funded, charge no fees, operate open enrolment policies and take part in state assessments. Writing about the influence of Charter schools in the United States on the 12% of children whose special needs were recognised under the Individuals with Disabilities Improvement Act, McLaughlin and Rhim (2007) noted that:

> Standards driven reform required assessments that measured the degree to which students met performance expectations, and a system of accountability based on results of assessments. Standards driven reform sought to close the achievement gap between students disadvantaged by poverty and their peers. (McLaughlin & Rhim, 2007: 27)

It was based on the twin assumptions that: (1) performance, even of the most disadvantaged, could be raised if schools were sufficiently rigorous in their expectations and in the quality of teaching; (2) *all* students' educational attainments would improve if schools were held accountable for the standard students reached. In contrast, market-driven reforms relied on:

> ... traditional market forces, such as competition and choice, which in theory serve as incentives for performance. A key assumption of market driven frameworks is that if consumers (i.e. students and their parents) can choose a school, as opposed to having to attend the school in the neighbourhood zone, then schools will compete for students by striving to offer a superior educational product. (McLaughlin & Rhim, 2007: 27)

In England, the standards model had long used SATs and GCSE and A level grades to hold schools publicly accountable. Parental rights to express preference for a school, together with *per capita* funding represented the market model. Although choice of school was restricted by availability of places, it did not prevent a flight from a school perceived as having unacceptable standards of work or behaviour.

Academies extended the standards- and market-driven models in two ways. First, the new and often iconic buildings with the latest state of the art resources represented a public commitment to education, and it is hard to imagine this not giving them an advantage over surrounding schools when parents made their choices. Second, pressure to raise standards quickly was probably higher in academies than anywhere else in the school system. It came from the sponsor and the DCSF, and from a media that greeted evidence of positive progress with interest, and the reverse with glee. For principals, failure to deliver rapid improvement led to a search for a new job.

There were three tensions, each linked to the single-minded standards- and market-driven accountability models, at the heart of the academies programme:

(1) McLaughlin and Rhim argued that:

> ... both frameworks could also introduce incentives that further marginalise already underserved populations, such as children with disabilities, minority students and economically disadvantaged students. (McLaughlin & Rhim, 2007: 28)

In theory this should not have been a problem with academies, provided they followed the DCSF Admissions Code and did not change their admission procedures or their catchment area to recruit higher attaining children from more affluent homes. We argue in Chapter 3 that the case for this happening is unproven. A more serious and better documented problem was a tendency towards higher rates of permanent exclusion than other schools (PWC, 2008).

(2) The concept of a low- or under-performing school is notoriously opaque and became even less transparent when an academy was sponsored by a high performing school, whether in the state or independent sectors. An example from Kent County Council can illustrate this. Kent remains wholly selective, effectively with grammar and secondary modern schools (though the latter term is seldom used). It contained 33 schools on the government's first National Challenge list of 638 underperforming schools, more than any other LA. At Skinner's school in Tunbridge Wells 99% of students met the benchmark of five A*–C GCSE passes, including English and Maths. The Skinner's school sponsored Tunbridge Wells High School, with 21% of pupils meeting the benchmark. Two points can be made about this sponsorship. First, given the highly selective intake of the Skinner's school, it would have been underperforming if 99% of students had not reached the benchmark. Second, under the then head, Tunbridge Wells High School had improved from 5% gaining five A*–C GCSEs in 1998 to 43% in 2007 (though not necessarily with English and Maths) and was top of the local value-added league table. Neither market- nor standards-driven models give parents sound data with which to interpret the achievement of the two schools. Obviously, further improvement was possible in each case, (and at Skinner's School might presumably have consisted of a target of 99% gaining five passes at A*–B). The early signs were encouraging (Garner, 2008), but it remains to be seen whether the proposed arrangement will help Tunbridge Wells High School to achieve sustainable change. The concern must be that the market model will simply deepen the problems of other schools for 11 plus failures by encouraging the best informed and most articulate parents to seek places at Tunbridge Wells High.

(3) Academies were under huge pressure to achieve improvement quickly. It is clear that significant improvements have been achieved since Callaghan's (1976) speech, not least that fewer pupils are now leaving with no useful qualifications. Changes in GCSE criteria may have contributed, but they cannot be the sole explanation. There is nevertheless a difficult question about the sustainability of improvements achieved under pressure of standards-driven reform. The drive to raise standards in primary schools, notably the National Literacy Strategy (DfEE, 1998) and National Numeracy Strategy (DfEE, 1999)

preceded the opening of the first academies. The government claimed dramatic improvement from these high-profile initiatives, but it is not clear that the improvement has been sustained nor even that it exists at all when assessment instruments are used that were not designed by a government agency (Tymms, 2004).

Conclusions

In our critique of Gorard and Smith (2003) we argued that the crude determinism of studies showing high correlations between poverty and educational performance provides no grounds for complacency about the performance of schools serving areas with multiple social problems. Disruptive behaviour is not inevitable and the frequent variation in standards between departments in the same school suggests that some departments are underachieving. Yet merely throwing money at the problem, for example, by providing a new building and better resources, is unlikely to solve it. No solution leading to sustainable improvement will be possible without a frontal assault on the underlying culture in failing or underperforming schools. An academy principal argued:

> Let's spend a bit of time thinking about the characteristics of a thoroughly failing school. The first thing is it absolutely will not accept that its children are like any others. The staff don't believe the data; they don't believe any comparators. That goes along with an increasingly inward looking culture, where some very good work trying to deal with the needs and difficulties faced by the children, in a humane way, is prized way and above anything to do with their achievement .... But the second thing that happens is that anyone whose practice is good – anyone who can manage the children and wins the golden door stop award because as you walk past the classroom it's fantastic – is seen as a heroine or hero, not as someone whose practice can be analysed and then systematically replicated. So there's a complete lack of faith in systems and procedures. (Academy principal)

The consequence of this sense of inevitability is as bleak as it is clear: at best marginalised children and young people, poorly prepared for employment, and at worst an increasingly polarised, divided and unequal society. Academies represent an explicit challenge to a culture of failure and underachievement in a significant minority of schools. Using CTCs as a model, there was a belief in government that a determined sponsor working with a strong principal could change that culture. To those who argue that academies are not the way to do it, the answer was: Show me a better way. But, as we see in the next chapter, academies were intensely controversial.

Chapter 3

Opposition: Dogma or Legitimate Concern?

Introduction

Opposition to academies was widespread, often acrimonious and from a wide range of sources. It was based on ideology – that power over a publicly funded service should not be transferred to the private sector, let alone to individual entrepreneurs or faith groups – and on pragmatism, that the results of academies were no better, allegedly, than the schools they replaced. Opposition had many different voices, calling from different rooms. The politically active and campaigning Anti-Academies Alliance, sceptical journalists and university academics all lent their voices and keyboards in a wide-ranging and often bitter critique of the programme. Their commentaries coalesced around a number of core issues.

Specifically, it was alleged that academies:

- Did not offer value for money compared to ordinary LA schools operating in similar circumstances. They had not raised standards sufficiently to justify the investment.
- Were created following an unfair and clandestine consultation process.
- Were involved in re-engineering their student populations through manipulating the SEN protocols and general admissions criteria.
- Had a negative impact on neighbouring schools.
- Had inadequate links with neighbouring LA schools and are distant from their local communities.
- Had not demonstrated significant improvements in teaching and learning.
- Were inequitably funded.
- Excluded disproportionate numbers of students, thus throwing problems back on the LA.
- Removed schools from the control of LAs, parents, staff and community representatives.

- Had sponsors who were not local (indeed appeared to pick and choose the academies they wanted to sponsor and were imposed by the DCSF) and did not offer local solutions to local issues.

The programme was relentlessly evaluated, not only by the evaluators commissioned by the DCSF (PWC, 2003, 2005, 2006, 2007, 2008), but also, for example, by the National Audit Office (2007), the TUC (2007), the House of Commons Committee of Public Accounts (2007) and the Sutton Trust (Curtis *et al.*, 2008). The government claimed that the programme was a remarkable success. If that claim could be substantiated, it would perhaps be an adequate answer to the ideological objections. We shall return to the evaluation data in subsequent chapters. Our aim here is to illustrate and consider the main grounds for concern about the programme, and to provide a critique of them.

Pragmatism and Ideology

Raising standards?

Gorard's (2005) early paper on the first three academies remains of interest because it set the scene for what was to become an increasingly familiar picture. The first three academies opened in 2002, and Gorard compared GCSE results in their first two years with those of their predecessor schools from 1997 onwards, using the number of students receiving FSM as the most reliable available measure of social disadvantage. In two of the three academies there was a decline in FSM relative to other schools in what was then the LEA, implying that those academies were taking a decreasing share of local disadvantaged students. For example, in 1998 the predecessor schools for the Unity Academy in Middlesborough had 62% of pupils receiving FSM, but by 2003 the figure had fallen to 49%. In contrast, the predecessor school for the Business Academy in Bexley was the most disadvantaged in the area, and that academy continued to take nearly four times the average for the area.

Turning to GCSE results, two of the three academies claimed dramatic improvement in their first year. Thus, Greig City Academy in Haringey reported 35% of pupils obtaining five A*–C passes. This was indeed an improvement over the 30% of passes in 2001, but it merely continued the steady year-on-year progress that had been made since 1997. There was nothing to suggest that academy status had accelerated the improvement. Moreover, while two academies had a noteworthy drop in the number of pupils leaving with no qualifications, for example, from 17% in 2001 to 5%

in 2003 at Greig City Academy, at the Unity Academy the number increased from 4% in 2001 to 13% in 2003.

Two points can be drawn from this early study, as from all subsequent investigations. First, there was substantial variation between academies, both in the pupils they admitted and in their examination results. Gorard interpreted the data as suggesting that some academies might be using their independence to secure a less disadvantaged pupil intake, a point to which we return. Second, this had implications for the interpretation of GCSE results. Gorard commented:

> Sleight-of-hand school improvement involves schools changing the nature of their intake . . . . And then claiming that an ensuing rise in test scores is due to an improvement in teaching and management. The early academies show signs of already doing this. (Gorard, 2005: 376)

On the basis of his data, Gorard's argument seems illogical. Intake figures refer mainly to students aged 11–12 in Year 7, but GCSE results refer to students aged 15–16 in Year 11, after a two-year course. To substantiate his claim, Gorard would need to show that the change in numbers of children receiving FSM was not only due to change in admission policies for children entering the academy at 11, which we consider below, but also to a sudden rise in the number of middle class children taking a two-year GCSE course, and therefore presumably admitted more than half way through their secondary school career. Another point from this early study is that it illustrates how averaging data across academies can be misleading. For example, the Business Academy at Bexley showed no sign of the 'sleight-of-hand school improvement' that Gorard criticises (as indeed he acknowledges). The substantial differences in performance between academies in this early study have been confirmed in every subsequent investigation. The average is of limited value, denying credit to those who rise above it, while throwing no light on the nature of problems experienced by those who do not.

It is also worth pointing out that the DfES could legitimately have argued that GCSE results in two of the first three academies gave grounds for *cautious* optimism. They could also legitimately have pointed out that school improvement is a complex process, and expecting an immediate sharp rise in performance is unrealistic. They could also have argued that sustainable improvement in educational achievement generally comes after improvement in behaviour.

Gorard (2009) returned to the same theme four years later, with a broadly similar methodology. He considered each cohort of new academies from 2002 to 2006, and concluded that there was no evidence of academies obtaining better results than LA schools with equivalent intakes (though surprisingly Paddington Academy in the 2004 cohort appears to have been omitted). Unsurprisingly, this second paper showed the same large variations between academies as the earlier one.

Admission policies

A consistent and unfortunate tendency since the first academies opened was the DCSF's relentless determination to 'spin' all evaluation data in the most favourable possible light. Gorard (2005) noted the selective use of statistics in the publicity given to the initial data on the first three academies, and that, too, set a pattern for the future. This is unfortunate because the debate could easily have been more rational, as illustrated with reference to the proportion of children receiving FSM. Gorard made two points: first, that of the first three academies, two did not replace the most disadvantaged schools in their LEA; second, two of the three reduced the proportion of children with FSM, which he interpreted as indicating a declining commitment to admitting pupils from disadvantaged backgrounds.

The first point can be disposed of quickly. The government's original commitment was 'to replace seriously failing schools' with academies that would 'take over or replace schools which are either in special measures or underachieving' (Blunkett, 2000). The original criteria for academy status were that a qualifying school must have FSM above 30% and fewer than 25% of students gaining five GCSE passes at grades A–C. If schools with the most disadvantaged students were not failing, there would be no grounds for turning them into academies. (The expansion of the programme raises different questions, which we discuss later.) The second point is more complex and is illustrated by the experience of a retired primary school head teacher. She had been deputy head of an inner city primary school just outside the catchment area of a new academy. When parents from this primary school applied to the academy they were rejected on grounds that they lived outside the catchment area. She then became head of a different school, also just outside the same academy's official catchment area, but in a much more affluent middle class neighbourhood.

> The children I was teaching in the inner city were turned down .... But when I became head of a leafy suburb school they applied too. The difference in the way the academy regarded the children from these different areas was quite an eye opener. (Former primary school head)

This former head teacher did not object only to the fact that the same academy rejected all applications from her inner city school but welcomed those from her new school in a 'leafy suburb'. She also objected to the way they selected the children:

> The parents were interviewed .... They claimed they were not selective, but interviewing parents in terms of their attitude to education and the support they are likely to give their children – that's selection in anyone's terms. (Former primary school head)

This head recognised that the DCSF Code of Practice on Admissions now prevents parental interviews as part of a selection process. However, the acceptance of children from the more privileged areas *could* still be interpreted as 'sleight of hand school improvement': an attempt to improve the academy's reputation and the all important league tables of exam results by skewing the intake towards more middle class students. On the other hand, it could also be seen as an indication of the academy's success in bridging the socially divisive split between working and middle class schools. Whitty (2008) argued that working class children are likely to do better in a socially mixed school. The catchment areas in many academy predecessor schools had indeed become skewed by the flight of better informed and more ambitious parents to higher attaining schools. As a result, they had become distorted as the school catered increasingly for children from estates and other areas with multiple social problems. Thus parents in middle class suburbs adjoining the academy sent their children to other schools even though they lived closer to it than the estates served by its predecessor school. One academy in our sample reduced its catchment area in response to growing numbers of applications from children living closest to it.

Seen in this light, the return of the middle class could be an important achievement, representing success in reducing the damaging polarisation between high and low achieving schools that Whitty (2008) regarded as a key improvement strategy. Crucially, though, we found no evidence that this academy, or any others, were admitting fewer pupils eligible for FSM than their predecessor schools and the reason for a decline in the proportion of pupils receiving free meals was that they were admitting more pupils overall than their predecessor schools. Whether or not this is a legitimate argument can only be determined by looking in detail at the admission policies and – more important – practices of individual academies and the geographical spread of pupils they admit. In doing so we should consider where the children actually live, and the impact of distance on socio-economic distribution.

It is worth adding, also, that sleight of hand with admissions policies is not peculiar to academies. Certainly, admissions should be monitored in academies, but it is also an issue that LAs should monitor more rigorously through their Admissions Forums. In doing so, it is important to recognise that the catchment area of any school is likely to be affected by any number of variables, including new housing, shift in public perception of the school, for example, when it acquires specialist school status, the availability of grammar or single sex schools and so on. But again, this is not an issue specific to academies.

Exclusions

As with educational progress, large differences between academies have also been reported in their use of permanent exclusion of students (e.g. PWC, 2008). Overall, academies have consistently excluded more students than comparison schools, or schools in England as a whole. Some academies, though, did not conform to the general trend. Thus, 12 of the 24 academies reviewed by PWC (2008) reported three or fewer exclusions in a 12-month period and six reported none. In contrast, permanent exclusions were very high in five academies – 13 in two, 17 in one and 20 in one. It has been known for years that there are large differences between schools in exclusion rates and also, counter-intuitively, that these are not strongly associated with differences in the proportion of pupils from disadvantaged backgrounds (Galloway *et al.*, 1985). Nevertheless, the evidence that some academies, though by no means all, are consistently more likely to resort to permanent exclusion leaves them open to criticism from LAs and other agencies that have to pick up the pieces. The critical point here is the evidence that some academies appear consistently to exclude significant numbers. In any one year a higher than usual number of exclusions may be entirely appropriate, due to the actions of a student or group of students. In addition, the troubled nature of predecessor schools makes it unsurprising that this should occur in an academy's early years. Concern is legitimate only when it becomes a year-on-year pattern. Thus, a student bringing a knife to school requires swift, decisive action; but if students continually bring knives to school, undeterred by the exclusion of previous students, one has to start asking hard questions about the school's social climate and culture.

PWC (2008) suggested that some academies might have needed to exclude larger than average numbers of students to restore order after inheriting a disorganised, undisciplined predecessor school. Three arguments can be made against that argument. First, only a minority of academies made heavy use of exclusion, albeit a substantial minority, and no evaluation has shown that they faced unique problems not experienced by others. Second, the evidence on general behaviour in school, unlike that on educational attainment and progress, shows that the school itself is the dominant influence, and not the level of disadvantage in the pupils' home backgrounds (Galloway, 1995). Third, the evidence also suggests that policy and practice within the school are the dominant influence on exclusion rates (e.g. Galloway *et al.*, 1982) with some schools consistently having high rates until or unless there is a change of policy.

The Justification for Expansion

Based on the 'success' of the early academies, the government proceeded to develop the programme, with a target set in 2006 of 400. Gorard's (2005) analysis of the early years of the first three led him to conclude:

> To expand the programme on the basis of what has happened so far, is so removed from the evidence-based policy that is a mantra of government today that it is scarcely worth pointing out. (Gorard, 2005: 376)

It is easy to see the justification for his conclusion. It is nevertheless worth considering six counter arguments:

(1) Delaying introduction of a new policy until academics have got round to carrying out a full evaluation – and the PWC evaluation took five years – would be interpreted by the media as reducing progress to the speed of coal formation; governments are not elected to sit in armchairs waiting for evaluation data. That is *not* an argument against detailed, rigorous evaluations. It is just a statement of the obvious.

(2) It is not clear how an evaluation of just three academies could guide future policy. Even if all three could have been shown to have been outstandingly successful in every respect – which was manifestly not the case – it would not have solved a familiar and intransigent problem: How to apply the experience of one, or even three, academies to failing or under performing schools in other situations. This has been the holy grail of school improvement, and it remains elusive.

(3) The culture of low aspiration and low achievement in a minority of schools, with the consequent flight of more ambitious parents from them, and the consequent polarisation of higher and lower achieving schools in too many parts of the country, was something that required immediate attention.

(4) In the government's view, LAs were large, complex bureaucracies and, like all bureaucracies, were better at resisting change than introducing it where it was most needed, namely the schools in which

parents were least likely to be sufficiently well organised and influential to make successful demands for action.

(5) By expanding the programme, first to 200 and eventually to 400 academies, the Labour government was still extending it only to a small proportion of secondary schools. Certainly, it represented a higher proportion of failing or underachieving schools but these had already been shown not to respond to encouragement or support available from LAs. Some scientists would see that as a reasonable size for a pilot project. It certainly did not require root and branch reform of the LA system throughout the country. The new Conservative–Liberal Democrat coalition government's proposals to expand the programme *are* likely to require this – a point to which we return later.

(6) The distinctive features of academies, for example, a sponsor, independence from the LA and new or refurbished buildings could reasonably be expected to help in raising performance. Whether they actually do so must, of course, remain a matter for future evaluation and research, but the expectation was not unreasonable. More important, checks and balances were in place, in the form of Ofsted and the funding agreement for each academy, to protect children's interests in the event of failure to deliver improvement in work or behaviour. Again, how those checks and balances actually worked would be a matter for future investigation.

In light of these arguments, the decision to expand the programme seems, at the very least, defensible. Andrew Adonis argued that a replicable formula for secondary school reform was needed:

> What I needed to do was find a way of establishing the academies predominantly as replacement schools, not as new schools, though some new schools would be needed . . . to replace failing schools which were becoming a really serious embarrassment to (LAs). And doing it in this way made it much easier, too, to take on the critics at large. Because it was a replacement model particularly in respect of weak or failing schools in deprived areas, I was able to say to people: 'Well, you may not like this idea of more independently managed schools, and sponsors and all that, but could you please tell me what you think is going to do it better'. (Andrew Adonis)

For a government committed to choice, testing whether diversification could play a part in raising achievement would need a large scale programme with up to 400 academies. They were seen as a way of changing perceptions of what could be achieved in areas of multiple disadvantages by challenging the LA monopoly over schools. Obviously, independent evaluation would be essential, and the government could claim to have put this in place with the five year PWC evaluation. Yet, although, a coherent case could be made out, questions remained, including about the impact of academies on other schools.

Impact on other schools

The final PWC (2008) report found no *clear* evidence (our italics) that academies had a negative effect on surrounding schools. Yet the proportion of children receiving FSM in academies had declined substantially (though as usual with large differences between academies,) relative to the decline in schools nationally (six percentage points compared with two nationally). At first sight this is disturbing: however hard it may be to demonstrate from the figures in surrounding schools, the children eligible for FSM who were no longer in academies must have gone *somewhere*. However, we saw above that this argument is based on a misunderstanding. It is clear from the final PWC (2008) evaluation that academies were actually admitting at least as many children eligible for FSM as their predecessor schools. The reason for the drop in the *proportion* was that most academies were admitting *more* pupils overall than the predecessor schools. Hence, as well as their historic intake, academies were admitting other pupils who were less likely to be receiving FSM.

It is true that a relatively minor change in the balance of intake can have a significant effect on a school's ethos and performance. The possible justification for academies admitting more middle class children is irrelevant to this argument. Yet in a market-driven economy, what happens in one school has consequences for others. Academies did not appear to be admitting fewer pupils in socio-economic hardship. They did appear to be admitting more pupils than their predecessor schools who were not living in such conditions, and that must have had some implications for other schools. From a policy perspective the aim must be to make all schools less socially divided, not to prevent any existing schools from achieving that aim (Whitty, 2008). It is also possible that this is just about redressing an imbalance arising from other schools having eaten into an academy's catchment area, either by selection or by their success in attracting applicants. Most academies do not select and base their admissions policy on proximity to the academy. In such circumstances, their admissions criteria will not impact on other schools other than by redressing the imbalance that has arisen in previous years.

The capital sums spent on academies are a powerful but potentially mis-leading symbol of their prestige relative to other schools. The National Audit Office (2007) cited the mean cost of new academy buildings as £27 million compared with £20–22 million for ordinary schools. The figures are not strictly comparable, due to location and size. A large number of academies are in London, where building costs can be up to 50% higher than in some other parts of the country. The funding agreement covering recurrent expen-diture is in line with other schools, though it is not so clear that that was the case with the earliest academies. Contrary to widespread belief, therefore, academies are not better off than neighbouring schools in terms of recurrent expenditure on teachers, equipment, resources and running costs.

Reflecting the turnaround strategy adopted by the DCSF, new acade-mies received a start-up grant though this was dropped in 2010 in response to the global economic recession. Until 2010, start up funds took two forms. The first, Start up A, was a formula led amount, based on the number of students in the academy on opening. A large majority of this budget was paid in the first year, with the remainder spread equally over up to the next six years. This grant was intended to enable the academy to acquire a basic stock of teaching and learning materials such as library books, textbooks, software, science equipment and stationary. For acade-mies with no predecessor school, this grant was higher. The second grant, Start up B, was intended to cover the current student numbers and the eventual expected roll. It therefore included costs that the academy could not meet from funding based on current student numbers, for example, transitional costs such as development of new curricula and provision of uniform and provision of a dual curriculum to support the integration of students from closed schools. Entitlement here was partly formulaic and partly based on bids submitted to DCSF by the academy. This element of the start-up grant usually lasted up to three years. When these two grants were finished the academy's funding was similar to that of a LA school, with the exception of the LA top slice, normally around 8%, for centrally provided services, which academies retained (though these services still had to be provided and paid for, and some chains deducted their own top slice).

Clearly, the trust funds created by some sponsors are not available to other schools. They can be used in powerfully symbolic ways. For exam-ple, an established academy had already used the allocation for students' uniform in its start-up funding. When a new principal was appointed fol-lowing a period of turbulence trust funds made it possible to give every student a new uniform and school bag as a way of demonstrating a turn-ing point in the academy's fortunes. Important though they can be, the trust funds do not change the underlying point about broad equivalence in recurrent funding. That said, the often iconic buildings of the earlier academies must have had some effect on how they were seen by parents, and by local schools for whom such largesse was beyond reach.

True to Mission?

When people were angry about academies getting all this investment (in new buildings) I would look them in the eye and say: 'Why shouldn't you do the worst first?' It doesn't mean you won't do everybody else and, of course, we hope the DCSF in time still will .... You give to the neediest schools the best tools to get the changes their communities need. (Academy principal)

The DCSF (2008a) said that 'All academies are located in areas of disadvantage'. They might not have been located in the *most* disadvantaged in their LA, at least as measured by the number of pupils receiving FSM, but that is irrelevant to the aim of improving the quality of education in the weakest schools. Nor is it necessarily relevant that the predecessor schools of some academies had won awards for school improvement. That is neither inconsistent with the possibility, nor with the need, for further improvement given the advantages that academy status might offer.

Coherence in approach?

It quickly became clear that successful entrepreneurs with philanthropic motivation would not be found for the projected expansion in the academies programme. The final blow to recruitment of business entrepreneurs as sponsors came with a police inquiry into allegations of the Honours system being used as an inducement, known to the media as the 'cash for peerages' inquiry. For the first time, a serving prime minister was interviewed as a potential witness in a criminal inquiry, and senior members of his office were arrested and interviewed under caution. The press besieged the homes of some of the early sponsors. One sponsor's representative commented that the sponsor had been so badly upset by the publicity that he said it had made him feel like a paedophile. The inquiry resulted in no prosecutions, but it was clear that the programme would be stalled without a change of emphasis in the arrangements for sponsorship.

Blunkett's (2000) speech launching the programme envisaged a wide range of sponsors, including faith organisations, successful schools and business. That vision was realised only as the programme started to expand and it became clear that business entrepreneurs would not meet the demand. Blunkett's original list of potential sponsors was extended to include universities and successful schools in both independent and state sectors. There are two ways of thinking about this. First, it could be dismissed as simply incoherent: A panic-driven attempt to find new sponsors who would expand the programme beyond recall before Tony Blair handed over to a successor who might not share his vision of academies as 'the future of schooling' (at a speech at the opening of the Business Academy, Bexley). Second, it could be seen as entirely coherent, and consistent with the original vision of independence and strength of governance as key characteristics. Within these very broad constraints, it could be argued that imposing one kind of sponsorship would be irrational. To take independent schools as an example, the sector is strengthened by including schools with a range of approaches, from the late A.S. Neill's Summerhill to Eton College. Different sponsors could be seen as bringing different ideas and strengths to the programme.

Chains of academies

Some sponsors were encouraged to open several academies, for example, ULT, ARK, Oasis, EduTrust and the Harris Trust. This was not without controversy. It provoked an exasperated outburst from the representative of a sponsor at one of the early academies:

> The problem with the multi sponsors is that often all of their academies are failing – none of them you could actually say: 'They're the leading light, leading this programme'. They're all blooming failing, so what do they do? They just add another one! They open one; oh well, results aren't great; never mind, we'll open another one! And they end up with four, five, six, all on the National Challenge list, and they've all got terrible problems. They're losing heads left, right and centre, yet it's a model that's being replicated countrywide. What's going to happen? Another tranche of failing schools, presumably! And the Conservatives will come in and change the whole thing again! (Sponsor's representative)

We shall see in Chapters 4–7 that there have indeed been problems in some academies. Can the speed with which chain sponsors have expanded be justified? The answer is obviously no, if one believes in the traditional approach of a carefully evaluated pilot project, followed by a carefully graduated expansion. That is a legitimate view, but not the only one. The starting point for a counter argument would have to be the long-standing inadequacies of the existing system in spite of repeated attempts from governments on the left and right to reform it. Another argument is that the people behind chains of academies wanted to see results in their own lifetimes, and the longer term approach favoured by many academics could have made significant systemic reform impossible. In addition, some sponsors, such as ARK and Oasis were already heavily involved in charitable work overseas, and had to be convinced that there was a genuine opportunity to make a significant contribution in England. In addition, they had ideas, derived for example, from the Charter schools in the USA, and a group of academies would facilitate faster learning from each other's successes and problems than a pilot project with just one or two academies. A chain would also increase the chances of their experience becoming known outside the chain, to the benefit of other schools and academies. To the objection that rapid expansion was a high-risk strategy, ministers could have replied that the same applied to the status quo.

Sponsors pursuing their own agenda with public money? One of the academy programme's most vocal critics claimed that:

> The Christian churches, with falling attendances and a crisis of confidence have grabbed the chance massively to increase their importance in British education. The city academy programme is making Christian churches vastly more powerful ... This is a huge leap in the control Christianity has had on our education system ... There may be arguments for it, but no one has bothered to make those arguments. It has been done by stealth, by a Prime Minister who is himself a very religious man and a supporter of faith schools. (Beckett, 2007: 68).

There is no doubt about the influence of faith organisations in the academies programme. The largest sponsor, ULT, is an off-shoot of the United Church Schools Trust (UCST), an Anglican trust that runs a chain of fee paying independent schools. Other significant players are diocese of the Church of England, and evangelical groups. The latter include Oasis, run by Steve Chalke, a Baptist minister who firmly resists any suggestion that Christians should have any preference in Oasis admission policies. They also include Sir Reg Vardy, sponsor of the Emmanuel Schools Foundation, with three academies in which there has been persistent controversy over the alleged teaching of creationism alongside the Darwinian theory of evolution in science lessons. This was the subject of an Ofsted (2002) inquiry, which concluded that the teaching of science met the requirements of the national curriculum.

Ministers have always appeared relaxed about the influence of faith organisations in academies.

I saw my role as not to be for or against faith sponsors, but to facilitate what local communities wanted themselves. Where a local authority said it did not want a faith sponsor, that was always fine by me ... If, because of the nature of the local community or their views on the interface between religion and education, they did not want a faith sponsor, then that's fine. A lot of local authorities did want faith sponsors and that was fine too ... And as a matter of fact there isn't a single academy open at the moment which has been set up with the local authority refusing to endorse the sponsor. (Andrew Adonis)

There appear to have been three justifications for the number of academies sponsored by faith groups. First, most academies were oversubscribed, so presumably this was not a problem for parents. Second, the same checks and balances applied as to any other school. The Secretary of State could issue a warning notice on one or more of three grounds: That standards were unacceptably low, that safety of staff or pupils was threatened; or that there had been a serious breakdown in management. There is no reason to argue that stricter procedures should apply to academies than to other schools. Third, if parents were not happy with an academy they could ask Ofsted to carry out an inspection. This happened at one academy in the north west of England, and Ofsted identified it as needing 'special measures' in order to improve. Of course, it is possible to argue against the existence of *any* faith schools in a state funded system, but given their existence it is difficult to see reasons for preventing faith organisations from sponsoring academies.

Strong Government or Over-Confident Ambition?

Governments would achieve nothing if deterred by vocal protests. That does not mean that protests should be ignored. There were nevertheless occasions when determination to 'drive through' the academies programme came disturbingly close to railroading opposition.

Beckett described a proposal to replace two schools in Merton with an academy. Four matters particularly concerned him. First, although just coming out of special measures, one school was in fact improving rapidly and the head had received an award from the Mayor of London and Lord Adonis as the most improved school in the area. Second, the sponsor of one academy did not want to inherit a Public Finance Initiative (PFI) that the council had entered into, and the council had to pay to withdraw from the contract. It is hard to envisage other circumstances in which a government would encourage a council to withdraw from a PFI contract, at substantial cost to council tax and/or tax payers. Third, both academies were permitted to have sixth forms, although this appeared inconsistent with the reorganisation of secondary education in the borough. Fourth, dubious methods were used to generate public support. The local MP sent parents a questionnaire in which each question had a box requiring a tick or cross. The questions were: *Yes, I am in favour of raising standards at Mitcham Vale and Tamworth Manor High School by getting academy status,* and *No, I am against these changes to Mitcham Vale and Tamworth Manor Schools, designed to improve examination results.*

Beckett commented dryly that parents were asked either to be in favour of academy status *and* raising standards, or to be against academy status and to want low standards. When teaching research methods to university students we ask them to spot bias in questionnaires. This one, based on Beckett's account, would be no use. The bias would be obvious at the level of GCSE Grade E. Unsurprisingly, the replies received, (we don't know how many went straight to the bin,) were overwhelmingly positive. Perhaps equally unsurprising, the council's own inquiry showed parents voting four to one against academies, but Beckett did not give details of that one.

Transparency of sponsorship funds

The early sponsors gave their own money. With sponsorship trusts and chains of academies, the position is not so clear. Beckett and Evans (2008) quoted Christine Blower, acting general secretary of the NUT.

> The names of those who give money for academies ought to be publicly available in the same way as the names of political donors. (Beckett & Evans, 2008: 2)

The reason is that some sponsors, such as religious organisations, depend on donors, and donors could therefore have considerable influence. Just as there would be legitimate public concern about the tobacco industry funding an inquiry into the effects of smoking, or the arms industry funding one into the wars in Iraq and Afghanistan, the public has a legitimate interest in what lies behind independent state funded academies. Beckett and Evans cite documents obtained from the DCSF under the Freedom of Information Act. In one memo, a senior official said that the department did not conduct 'due diligence' checks on donors, only on sponsors. Sponsors themselves were expected to carry out due diligence checks on donors. The authors noted that the DCSF appeared relaxed because charity rules did not require the identity of donors to be made public. While that is doubtless true, it seems likely in the long run that lack of transparency about the origin of funds provided by donors could undermine the academies programme. On the other hand it has to be noted that academies are popular with parents and, in a majority of cases, are oversubscribed – in striking contrast to predecessor schools.

Local Representation

In his interview with us, Andrew Adonis did not see a problem in parental representation on the governing bodies of academies being less than on LA schools:

> I lost count of how many terrible conversations I had with parents (as Minister for Schools) about the quality of their local schools. I never had a single conversation with an ordinary parent saying that they regarded an answer to the problem of their local school as being more elections for parent governors. I only ever got that from local politicians who came at it from the political end, not the quality of education end. (Andrew Adonis)

We doubt whether any parent ever chose a fee-paying independent school because it had parents on its governing body. Nor, presumably, did many parents reject one because it did not. Adonis' argument was that there was room for a variety of school governance arrangements, provided:

> All the different and competing models of governance are geared towards producing more good schools, which are fully accountable to parents for their results, and which parents want to send their children to. (Andrew Adonis)

Local authorities

Unsurprisingly, LAs have had varied reactions to academies. Although Andrew Adonis could say that no academy existed in which the LA had not endorsed the sponsor that did not necessarily reflect warm and cooperative relationships. An academy principal had attended a meeting at which the Director of Education, unaware of her presence, said:

> There will be another academy in this local authority over my dead body!

(There is, but the Director is still alive.) When the first academies opened, DCSF's lack of confidence in LAs was palpable. Within five years the rhetoric had changed, with talk of partnership within a 'family of schools'. There seem to have been four reasons.

(1) The DCSF proved itself, at best, not very competent, in its oversight of the design and procurement of buildings for the early academies. It is no answer that this was the sponsor's problem. The DCSF had representatives on every relevant planning group, and if any government department had responsibility for the spending of this public money it had to be the DCSF. We explain this in Chapter 5, and need only note here that PWC (2006) in their third annual report raised serious questions about the fitness for purpose of some buildings. Given the costs involved and high political profile, this could have been hugely damaging. The obvious and logical solution was to include academies in the largest school building and renovation programme for 30 years. Contracts under the Building Schools for the Future programme (DfES, 2004) were to be run by LAs. This meant that LAs would have to pick up the bill for cost overruns and, as important, take the blame when things went wrong.

(2) By linking academies to LA proposals under Building Schools for the Future (BSF), government was able to give them a stark message: Include academies in your proposals, or you will be unlikely to get funds for any other schools. As the task of LAs was to commission schools, they could commission academies too.

(3) The White paper on the education and skills required for students aged 14–19 (DfES, 2005) proposed '14 sets of specialised diplomas, at three levels up to advanced level, covering the occupational sectors of the economy' (DfES, 2005: 5). It was immediately clear that no single school or academy, and indeed no single FE college, would be able to cover all 14 diplomas. It would require much closer cooperation between all schools, academies and FE Colleges than had previously taken place in most LAs. This required a change in the relationship with LAs. When the first academies opened the government explicitly saw them as a response to the perceived inadequacies of LAs. Now, they were to become valued partners, with a key role in coordinating provision in the local 'family of schools'.

(4) Under Gordon Brown, and with Ed Balls Secretary of State in the DCSF, the government became less hostile to LAs. This was probably just a personal ideological matter. A more cynical interpretation is that it could have represented long-term planning. After a few years, the political party in power in government generally starts to lose control of marginal local councils. That certainly happened with Conservative

administrations from 1979–1997, and with the Labour administrations from 1997–2010. If Labour had anticipated losing power in 2010, it would have made sense to strengthen cooperation with local branches, who might be expected to gain control of marginal councils as the incoming Conservative government became less popular. (It will also be interesting to see whether the Conservative rhetoric of academies being at the heart of their local community (DCSF, 2010b) survives loss of power to Labour in local elections – as the new coalition government becomes less popular.)

LAs reacted in different ways to rhetoric of academies as part of the local family of schools. The chairman of governors of an independent school with approval to sponsor an academy said:

> With the local council, our relations are very good; and with the local primary schools. The county council is trying to encourage business to come to (Name of town) and the relationship is very good indeed. In fact they are giving us a temporary office base. (Governor of independent school sponsoring an academy)

Difficulties in the relationship with LAs are well illustrated in Maurice Smith's (2008) independent evaluation of bids from potential sponsors of academies in Durham LA. Interest in the possibility of sponsoring academies is evident from the fact that there were 10 bids for the three proposed academies. One proposal was from a consortium of Durham LA's own school improvement service (DAS) and from the Durham Association of Secondary School Head Teachers (DASH). Referring to the LA, Smith noted dryly that under BSF:

> ... academy proposals can lever in additional funding more quickly. This is undoubtedly a significant motivation to Durham County Council for creating an academy programme. For many councillors it is the sole motivation. (Smith, 2008: 6)

In rejecting the proposal, Smith wrote that it:

> Focussed too much on the niceties of a representational model and too little on the rigour of an effective model. (Smith, 2008: 9)

He continued:

> Officers of DAS and the majority of head teachers in DASH are direct employees of the County Council; add this to the proposal to enter into a formal co-sponsorship agreement with Durham County Council

for all three academies and the distinction between an academy as an 'independent' school and a Durham County Council school becomes very blurred. This is largely an ideological matter dependent on what one's view is along the continuum of the independence of academies and how far they should be part of the local authority's family of schools. (Smith, 2008: 9)

Unions

All unions are on record opposing academies. They have six broad arguments. First, academies are, at best, unnecessary. All the things for which they use their much publicised independence are in fact already being done by LA schools. Second, sponsorship of all academies opening until 2011 gives power over state-funded schools to people whose private, personal agenda has not been subject to public scrutiny or democratic debate. Moreover, as a proportion of building costs, sponsors' financial contributions are ludicrously low for the powers conferred on them. Third, the sponsors' Trust funds risk creating two tiers within the state-funded system, with children in academies receiving benefits that are unavailable to other children. Fourth, academies destabilise LAs by distorting provision, for example, for sixth forms, making coherent authority-wide planning impossible. Fifth, local representation and participation are inadequate. At best, LAs are second class partners, not permitted to be lead sponsors with a majority on any governing body, and forced reluctantly to cooperate in commissioning academies by the arbitrary criteria for BSF funding and the government's 14–19 agenda. Parental representation on governing bodies is nominal, almost invariably less than in LA schools. Sixth, academies have not been true to their mission; disadvantaged children are falling as a proportion of their admissions, and they exclude more children than other schools, thus placing an unreasonable and disproportionate burden on hard-pressed LA services.

The government would have little difficulty in replying. First, academies are only necessary because of failure and/or chronic underachievement in LA schools. Second sponsors are publicly accountable for the quality of education in their schools, and indeed this is much more closely monitored than in LA schools. Third, use of sponsors' trust funds to provide extra resources for students in some of the country's most disadvantaged areas is entirely legitimate. Within LAs, there have always been huge differences, invariably linked to social background, in the sums that parent–teacher and Friends of the School associations could raise. Sponsors' trust funds merely take one small step towards redressing this historic inequality. Fourth, LAs are now central to commissioning academies and to planning 14–19 provision. Far from distorting provision, any rational person would see academies as strengthening it. Fifth, parents may have fewer representatives on governing bodies than LA schools, but their welcome of academies can be seen in the number of applicants per place, which far exceeds that of their predecessor schools. Sixth, it is to the credit of academies that they have succeeded in attracting parents who might previously have sought places in other schools, and that many have succeeded in improving behaviour. Moreover, the DCSF has recently tightened the regulations to ensure the same financial arrangements in academies as in other LA schools when they exclude pupils.

The union leaders and officials we spoke to were pragmatic. They did not like academies, but their job was to look after their members' interests:

> I tend to see them as a bit like the independent sector – in an ideal world we think there shouldn't be any need for them. The local education authority and state education system should provide for everyone. But as long as they're there we've got to live with them and work with them. (Union official)

The extra competition that academies introduce was also regretted, but again with a note of realism:

> The academy is seen by the government as the thoroughbred .... It's driven by a need to have winners and losers .... And that's really why we oppose them so much. We want every community to have a good local school. We want parity of esteem. It's really difficult to maintain that now, but that's not to say it wasn't a problem in the past under the local authority system.

They were also relaxed about funding agreements, realising that academies needed the funds previously retained for services provided by the LA. One union representative's memory of GM schools was that they had to learn the hard way how to manage budgets. Thus, when they no longer paid into a pool for maternity cover they found themselves in difficulties when staff members went on maternity leave. 'We used to tell them, "We told you so"!'

Parents' involvement in planning academies

Pennell and West (2007) looked at parents' role in setting up new secondary schools. Some of their work focused on the processes involved in planning and establishing academies and the extent to which parents' views were taken on board. Campaigners against academies found it particularly difficult to obtain information about proposals for an academy. In relation to parental influence in setting up academies, Pennell and West concluded:

> There was concern amongst campaigners about the process of setting up academies, and in particular the lack of information on the proposals; the speed of the process; the limited nature of the consultation; and what was perceived as the lack of democratic accountability regarding academies, particularly in relation to school governance. (Pennell & West, 2007: 5)

The anti-academies website has a series of case studies that illustrate and document these concerns. However, it should also be noted that some anti-academy campaigns have succeeded and parental influence can be brought to bear on academies in the same way as on LA schools.

Concluding Comments

In his critique of the role of sponsor, Beckett (2007) quoted Clement Attlee's (1920) book *The Social Worker:*

> (Charity) is apt to be accompanied by a certain complacency and condescension on the part of the benefactor; and by an expectation of gratitude from the recipients, which cuts at the root of all true friendliness. (Beckett, 2007: 154)

The problem with this view is that exactly the same 'certain complacency and condescension' is apt to become evident when the state, acting through its LAs, holds a monopoly on provision of schools. The best learning is characterised by excitement in and from learning, and is inconsistent with being a passive recipient of charity, whether from a sponsor or a generous LA. Some of the opposition to academies may have been modified by recognition that education was not as good as it should be in LA schools, though with an accompanying fear that an unknown sponsor and a distant government in Westminster could not be trusted. Yet opposition must also have arisen from the insensitive way that some academies were introduced. This is well illustrated in Smith's (2007) Isle of Sheppey Review.

Sheppey is an island off the north coast of Kent, the LA with the largest number of schools in the National Challenge list for failing to meet a target of five GCSE A*–C passes including Maths and English. Almost certainly, this must have something to do with the fact that Kent remains one of the few wholly selective LAs, with selection at 11+ for grammar school places.

Unsurprisingly, schools on the Isle of Sheppey were unimpressive, with a long history of poor management. The islanders saw the academy programme as yet another example of meddling by outsiders, at best ill thought out, and at worst a cynical attempt to use them for an educational experiment. Smith wrote:

> There are two camps. Most of the off-island decision makers and advisers are in favour of a one-site Academy solution: this would create the biggest school in England, of 2,700 pupils. Most of the on-island recipients I spoke to preferred not to have a one-site solution. (Smith, 2007: 4)

Smith agreed with the islanders and proposed two academies. He was scathing about the insensitivity behind the outside experts' and sponsors' preference for the 2700 pupil academy. He was equally scathing about the victim culture on the island, and the 'woefully inadequate' leadership provided by church, community and business groups on the island. He saw their failure to recognise the 'stunningly attractive' coastline and nature conservation area adjoining one of the two sites as an opportunity rather than a problem as 'evidence of deeply rooted lack of aspiration' (Smith, 2007: 25). He concluded:

> If islanders take a Private Fraser approach to secondary education – 'we're doomed' – in their homes, schools and communities on the island, it will inevitably become a self-fulfilling prophecy . . . Education is a collaborative relationship between giver and receiver, teacher and pupil, provider and recipient, described by D'Israeli as a 'conversation between generations'. To assure educational excellence for future generations, which is the task of this review, that conversation needs to be a positive one, not dampened by bickering, apathy or a victim culture, but ignited by energy, passion, involvement. Now. (Smith, 2007: 26)

Two things can be said about Smith's conclusions. First, it is possible to dismiss him for showing the same insensitivity he criticises in sponsors. It is easy for an ex-HMI to arrive, judge, criticise and depart. But second, Smith's analysis implies that for too long education has been part of the problem of low aspiration rather than part of the solution. Sponsors of academies, and Design Companies, *can* behave with indifference to local feelings. So can LAs. Sheppey illustrates this with respect not only to the LA but also to the sponsors' one-academy solution. But sponsors and design teams *can* work with local groups, including parents. So can LAs.

The question should not be whether one structure is better than the other, but how each can work effectively.

Looking ahead

The Conservative – Liberal Democrat coalition government's intention to allow all schools to become academies, with schools rated 'outstanding' by Ofsted fast tracked without the need for a sponsor (DfE, 2010a, b) must create an interesting challenge for opponents of the original academies. The proposals make the Blair government's programme look like an exploratory pilot project. The Labour government never seriously challenged the responsibility of LAs for schools. Now, with the possibility of all secondary, primary and special schools becoming academies, the writing could be on the wall for LAs. Given the extent and intensity of opposition to academies from 2002–2010, it seems unlikely that the new proposals will go unchallenged.

Part 2

Innovation, Governance, Leadership, Teaching and Learning

Chapter 4

'It's Really Down to the Sponsor'
(Academy Principal)

PriceWaterhouseCoopers (2008) identified four types of sponsors: philanthropic, high-achieving schools, chain sponsors and group sponsors. To these one could add universities, LAs and business organisations, though these overlap with the philanthropic sponsorship. Sponsors were central to the thinking behind academies until the Labour government lost power in the 2010 general election to the Conservative–Liberal Democrat coalition but there are important questions about how they exerted an influence. These extend far beyond their potential influence on one curriculum subject, for example, the alleged teaching of creationism in Sir Reg Vardy's academies. Of much greater importance is the extent to which they influence the ethos and culture of their academies and the means they use to do so. These questions are both given added urgency and made much more complex by the near exponential growth in the number of academies in the six years after the first three academies opened in 2002 with 133 in 2008 and a projected rise to 313 open or in preparation by 2010, with the corresponding increase in the number of sponsors, and more important, their backgrounds and the skills, interests and expectations they brought to the task.

We touched on reasons for the increasing varieties in backgrounds in sponsors in Chapter 3. Within two years of the first three academies opening in 2002, it was becoming clear that the number of successful business entrepreneurs willing to contribute their own money to sponsor an academy was finite, and certainly far less than the number needed for the expansion that the government had in mind. The allegations that led to the police 'cash for honours' enquiry were not the cause of a search for new sponsors, but they certainly gave it added momentum.

> The kind of people who want to give something back dried up because they didn't want their private life paraded through the press. He (sponsor) went through absolute hell during that. It was a nightmare.

And all he was trying to do was actually to do something good. (Sponsor's representative)

Possibly of greater importance, though, was the government's gradual recognition of tension between its desire for a countrywide alternative to the traditional LA control of schools and the power given to the early sponsors to run independent schools. There were two problems with the rhetoric of independence. First, it was expensive and some of the mistakes were embarrassing. We discuss some of these in the next chapter on buildings. Second, while a small number of academies (still only 17 by 2004) could be seen as a pilot project with little relevance to overall educational provision in any single LA, that argument could not be sustained as the programme expanded. There was simply no alternative to a closer working relationship with LAs, in which academies were seen as complementary to LA provision rather than in opposition to it. The BSF programme provided the obvious solution, by requiring LAs to consider academies as part of their overall proposals. In addition, the 14–19 agenda (DfES, 2005) with its proposal for 14 diplomas created an explicit requirement of closer cooperation between all local providers, including academies. Without such cooperation, provision at any single institution whether academy, school or college, could legitimately be judged inadequate.

This had implications both for LAs and for sponsors of new academies. Not only did it give LAs a central role in commissioning academies, it also provided a powerful incentive to local sponsorship. This included high-achieving schools, optimistically seen as able to support their lower achieving brethren, universities and local business interests. With their disparate backgrounds, it was inevitable that different sponsors came to the task with different motivations.

The earliest sponsors had links to senior figures in the Labour party, and/or were successful entrepreneurs enthused with the idea of academies by ministers or their advisers. From the outset, though, Blunkett (2000) had recognised the need for sponsors of chains of academies. One of the earliest, ULT, was an offshoot of a charitable trust that saw academies as an opportunity to return to its nineteenth century roots. Sponsors, therefore, came with very different motivations.

Motivation of Sponsors

In this section we summarise five overlapping groups of sponsors. In the next we discuss what they may contribute, and how.

Altruism and philanthropy

The chair of governors at one academy described his outrage at visiting the predecessor school when negotiations were at a very early stage:

> It was really, really shocking. In order to stop the rain coming in through the roof, there were great big tarpaulins over these north windows; the urinals in the loo's were half off the wall; the windows in the class-rooms had been smashed, or whatever, so many times they now had a sort of plastic perspex and when the windows wouldn't open any more, they were drilled shut and graffiti was all over them. The school itself stood and still stands today, on reclaimed marsh land, so during the winter months, there would probably be a couple of inches of water lying across the land. And you had a totally disaffected local community who were very troubled in any event, and an awful lot of people that came from very very challenging circumstances and it needed – it was essential – to have a new building that demonstrated a hope and a faith in those young people and the community – that they weren't just in the dustbin. (Academy chair of governors)

For another representative of the same sponsor, the memory was still vivid, eight years later:

> When he walked round with the minister, he couldn't believe the state of the school. The kids wouldn't look you in the eye, behaviour was absolutely appalling, and teachers in the classroom were just in jeans or scruffy clothes. They were shouting at the kids. The kids were coming and going in the classrooms – the teachers had no control. One kid might come in and talk to some of their friends in the classroom and go out again. And when he (the sponsor) talked to some of the kids about what they wanted to do, their aspiration level was so low, because basically they had been told they weren't ever going to make anything of their lives. (Sponsor's representative)

For another of the early sponsors, the academy met a personal need:

> I was doing a lot of charity bits and pieces. I wanted something to get stuck into. I seem to remember I got in touch with Andrew Adonis. He took me to meet (name of principal). I decided on two projects one was with the disadvantaged. (Sponsor)

One principal said he had been asked by all sorts of people – students, families, colleague heads of LA schools, staff, journalists, local politicians – why such a wealthy man wanted to be involved in schools. He always gave the answer that the sponsor had given him when he himself had asked the same question at their first meeting: he wanted to give something back to his local community.

Other sponsors saw academies as an opportunity to return to their roots. Thus, the UCST, founded in 1888, had a history of educating the poorer members of society. As state funded education developed, their schools, like many others in the private sector, gradually started to cater for children whose parents could afford fees. UCST saw academies, developed through an offshoot, the ULT, as being in the spirit of the original intentions of its founding members. Many independent schools, certainly, offered some scholarships to children whose parents could not afford the fees but there was no question about their changed clientele. This was also the case with well known public schools sponsoring a new academy:

> It was a sense of wanting to reconnect with our past and our origins. In the nineteenth century we had a clear social objective. Between then and now it has changed a great deal ... because it has become a school for those who can afford the fees, like any number of other public schools. (Independent school sponsor)

Faith-based sponsors: serving or proselytising?

The government has supported schools governed by faith groups, mainly but not entirely Church of England or Roman Catholic, since education became free and compulsory. The motivation of faith groups in running academies fall into three categories:

(1) *Academies providing an unconditional service to all children.* Beckett (2007), while generally bitterly critical of faith sponsors, quotes Steve Chalke, founder of the Oasis Chain of academies, with respect:

> You can either have a school only for Christians or a Christian School. You can't have both ... a Christ-Centred School will serve the whole community. (Beckett, 2007: 86)

The sponsor of the largest chain of academies, ULT, is adamant about his Christian roots, but nevertheless insists that its academies are open to pupils of all faiths or none. As principal of a ULT Academy, one of the authors (Phil Hearne) insists that ULT never placed any restrictions on admissions, nor did they impose any conditions with regards to Christian teaching in the curriculum.

(2) *Academies giving priority to children of their own faith.* The basis for admission to all academies is the DCSF code of practice on admissions.

Roman Catholic academies can give priority to pupils from Roman Catholic families in their admission procedures, on the same basis as in Roman Catholic Schools under the LA umbrella. The same applies to some but not all academies sponsored by the Church of England or a diocese. However, when a diocese or the Church of England is co-sponsor with other organisations, no preference appears to be given to Church of England families.

(3) *'The Militants'* (Beckett, 2007: 85). These are the academies sponsored by individuals or organisations with an open and explicit commitment to transmit a strong Christian message. They include Sir Reg Vardy's Emmanuel Schools Foundation and Mr Robert Edmiston, sponsor of Solihull Academy. Vardy's Academies have an open enrolment policy. With reference to the controversial teaching of creationism in his academies, Ofsted (2002) enquiries found that Science teaching met the requirements of the National Curriculum. That verdict, though, did not so much gloss over the teaching of creationism as avoid it.

Independent schools

While our interviews suggest that an altruistic motive is entirely genuine, it is not the sole motivating factor. One sponsor explained that they wanted to:

Support a relatively deprived community and therefore to demonstrate our interest in promoting public good over and above our bursary programme and other things that we do. And of course that coincided with increasing interest in charity legislation on schools for public benefit. We see this as a good way of demonstrating what we are doing. (Independent school sponsor)

The legislation to which this sponsor refers requires charities to show that they are contributing to the public good and hence that their work does not focus solely on the interests of a restricted, narrowly defined group. It would be easy to be cynical about this, concluding that the principal motivation for sponsoring an academy is simply to remove any risk to charitable status, and thus to retain the taxation benefits that this confers. That view is probably too simplistic. There would have been easier ways for UCST to protect its charitable status than setting up the largest chain of academies under ULT. There is no reason to doubt an altruistic desire to return to their roots. Similarly, independent schools who are sole sponsors appear genuinely to see sponsorship of an academy as an opportunity to make a wider contribution to education. Moreover, they recognise the risks to their school's own stability and reputation:

> We looked at the possible objections ... we were worried about finan-cial costs: would that fall on parents who already have paid very heavily? ... We were worried about diverting energy and focus from the internal management of the school into setting up an academy .... We were worried about getting sucked into endless meetings .... And we were worried that parents would be concerned about what we were doing about the academy over there. And we were worried about political uncertainties. We knew that Andrew Adonis was 100% committed to academies, (but) we asked ourselves whether this reflected the attitudes of the government as a whole. We sort of exam-ined the entrails, if you like, and we decided that the risk was worth taking. (Independent school sponsor)

The other significant motivator for independent schools was an assess-ment of the potential benefits for their own pupils

> We felt that we would certainly have something to learn from the state sector for example in the emphasis on classroom teaching and the kind of methods used in classrooms. IT is another area where we thought pupils would probably benefit. We also thought it would help to dem-onstrate to pupils the importance that we attached to the concept of service to the community. In other words, it would actually enrich the quality of education that we offer. And we envisaged contacts between the pupils at the school and the academy, and that, too, is going to serve a purpose to help widen horizons. (Independent school sponsor)

Another aspect of this was the genuine desire to share expertise and bridge the gap between state and independent sectors.

An independent school head teacher had two expectations. First, dis-tinctive features of the curriculum and pedagogy in his own school would be introduced into the academy. Second, the academy would share the school's commitment to service and to achievement. In this way he expected the academy to share the school's DNA.

Universities

The caricature of leisurely academic life is no longer true of universi-ties. Senior management and academic staff are under huge pressure to achieve higher grades in the independent assessments of teaching and of research. In 1998 the incoming vice chancellor at a leading UK university made two announcements: there would be no department achieving less than grade 4 on (then) a five point scale in the independent assessments of research. When the results were announced, one department had failed to meet this injunction and within a week had ceased to exist as a separate entity. (The solution caused more problems than it solved, but that is another story.) And no department would achieve less than 21 points out of a maximum at the time of 24 on the independent assessment of teaching quality. One department failed to meet that target; it was too important to be closed or merged, but the reverberations were felt throughout the university. Given these pressures, why on earth would any university want the hassle of sponsoring an academy? There seem to be three reasons:

(1) *Widening access.* Universities are under pressure to widen access to higher education beyond students with traditional high A level grades. Particularly in the older universities, that can be a challenge, and sponsoring an academy represents one way to demonstrate a commitment to non-traditional students.

(2) *Strengthening contacts with local communities.* One university sponsor explained that a new vice chancellor had been conscious of the university having numerous contacts with local institutions, but not receiving adequate recognition for this. Sponsoring an academy was seen as a high profile initiative that would demonstrate a commitment to one of the more disadvantaged parts of the local community.

(3) *Extending opportunities for students.* A university sponsor explained:

We should be able to add new dimensions to what the school can offer in terms of Music, Science, and a whole range of expertise in other areas. In Science, particularly, we have been using post graduate students in schools. We always thought it would benefit the students but we have found it is also re-motivating the teachers. They thought it was exciting to have somebody else who wasn't a teacher, but could remind them of the excitement they had got from their particular disciplines. I believe the thing that the university can deliver is a great pool of talented people, and I include in that undergraduates, mentoring, chess clubs, and all sorts of other activities including sporting activities; I believe that these activities will be totally embedded within the academies, so that this will be something that doesn't just happen once in a while but happens everyday. (University sponsor)

Local Authorities

LAs are justified in resenting the double standards that successive governments have applied to them. DfE rhetoric emphasises that their role is commissioning schools rather than managing them. Yet they are still held to account for the quality of support that they offer to schools and schools placed in special measures by Ofsted are seen as reflecting badly on them. Given this double speak from the DfE, it is not surprising that some LAs reacted cautiously, even cynically, to the requirements for a closer relationship with academies arising from the BSF programme and the 14–19 agenda.

Two contrasting points were made by an academy principal:

> Since the change of prime minister, I think the current government is trying to position academies as part of the LA. We should be part of the local authority family of schools, and this academy won the chief executive's prize last year for making the most significant contribution to its family of schools of any specialist school, and that included all sorts of aspects of partnership with the LA. But we are partnering as an independent partner, to do things together. I think arguably that makes your partnership stronger. If you are partnering because you are simply told: 'you are part of this and you can't challenge or confront it', then that could be a problem. (Academy principal)

This principal was worried about some LAs, though not his own, taking a bureaucratic approach and expecting schools to go at the pace of the slowest. He contrasted his vision with the weakness that Smith (2008) claimed to identify in Durham. He continued:

> What you need in academies, to be successful, is absolutely restless and relentless ambition, not to be bound by any of the things that either have been done in the past or could in the future hold you back '... I know that what some of the councillors in Durham were trying to do is to make them not really academies, and that's one of the issues'. (Academy principal)

For a minority of LAs, academies have been a way of dealing with intractable problems, albeit not necessarily in a Council meeting:

> A person close to government asked to see me after I became Director and I described to him the most neglected and troubled school in the LA, with a chair of governors who had a very radical agenda. I described this school and this character and said I was on the point of using intervention powers, hopefully to secure changes in the

governing body ... I explained all this and said I was thinking of applying for Fresh Start. He said 'don't waste your time; we are bringing out a new policy', and described it. I said 'Where will I find a sponsor?' He said 'don't worry about that; we will find you one'. So we applied and we got all party support to take this completely stuck community and rebuild it at no cost to the council tax payers in a way that may allow it to start again and recover. (Former Director of Education)

Three things come from this account: first, the power of DCSF patronage; second (though not all the quote is included) the cumbersome process facing LAs in dealing with seriously malfunctioning schools; third, the director's pragmatic willingness, shared by the council's elected members, to use any available strategy to improve the quality of education provided by a problem school.

What Do Sponsors Contribute?

Sponsors of the early academies came from a business background. They created an ethos in which:

Academies tend to be more unbounded in their thinking than most schools. The sponsors are people whose life experiences have been: 'If I see something good I will pick it up and run with it' rather than: 'Why I shouldn't do this, because of this, that, or the other preconceived thinking'. (Academy principal)

Asked about his influence on the academy, one of the early sponsors said

What do sponsors know about schools? Very little! ... I didn't spend much time on it – just certain key things. We wouldn't take no for an answer!

Yet this underestimated his role in setting the ethos for the academy. Asked about the core values he wanted to develop, he replied:

Non-elitist, non-exclusive, no selection. As demand increased we narrowed the catchment area. I would be happy if the affluent want to come – let them! But no priority to anyone. As long as you live in the catchment area it's OK. Don't get over committed to exam results. Some sponsors are driven – they want to get the results up. That's why we need someone like (name of principal) – to resist that pressure! (Academy sponsor)

Again, this sponsor did himself less than justice. He gave two examples of 'key things' on which he had intervened:

> There was a problem over the playing fields, in making land available for the new building. I approached (name) with it. I asked him to talk to the LA. He was paying large sums to projects in the community. They didn't want to upset him. That was how we solved it. (Another time) the party in power on the council was blocking planning permission. I spoke to (an eminent member of the party nationally). He had a word with the chair of the council and it went through.

Later, the principal of this academy said that he could not have resolved either problem himself. He did not have the contacts. Nor do all sponsors. This example illustrates the power of the network on which a powerful sponsor with a business background can draw. The argument that it creates an uneven playing field, and therefore disadvantages other schools, is indefensible. No other school was harmed by this sponsor's influence. More important, this kind of networking is what makes someone effective, whether at local or national level. Historically, only LA schools in affluent areas with influential parents or governors have been able to use the power of patronage. We had evidence of sponsors exercising that power on behalf of the most disadvantaged schools.

Is an Educational Background Necessary? Is it Desirable?

This question goes to the heart of the sponsor's role. As we saw above, the sponsor of an early academy admitted to knowing 'very little' about education. A recently appointed academy principal, in contrast, was sceptical:

> The thing about sponsors of academies is that they are not educationalists. They come from a philanthropic point of view, wanting to make a difference with 100% success and no failure, but they are not actually rooted in an educational background ... They have been to some Charter Schools in America and .... They are fired up with this, but with no thought to how it can work, and they don't speak with people who run schools. (Academy principal)

This excerpt raises an important issue. The concern appears to be less with the sponsor's lack of educational background per se than with ideas introduced from another system without adequate thought about how they might transfer to schools with a very different history and background in this country. A little knowledge, this principal was implying, can be dangerous. As we will see, several principals felt more comfortable with sponsors whose contribution was more explicit:

> He always said 'I don't want anything to do with the curriculum, I'm not going to set the curriculum. All I expect, all I ask, is that you follow my ethos which is about the children and making whole'. He said: 'as long as you do that, whatever you deliver is up to you'. (Sponsor's representative)

The last two quotes raise questions about sponsors' and governing bodies' relationships with principals. In many academies the relationship differs in key ways from that between the head teacher of a LA school and the governors. At one extreme, sponsors and governing bodies can adopt an approach close to venture capitalism, though without the asset stripping; sponsors for whom GCSE results dominate all other performance indicators, and staffing decisions are based largely if not solely on them, illustrate this approach. At another extreme a sponsor's educational agenda can be paramount, seen for example, in a commitment to a particular form of organisation. In either case the principal will need considerable skill in negotiating the relationship.

Relations with principals 1: The non-executive chair model

PWC (2008) quote an academy principal as saying: 'Support on tap, not on top' (PWC, 2008: 114). A principal we interviewed was clear about his responsibilities and about the expectations on him:

Principal:	In an academy model, far more is delegated to the principal, and more clearly, than in most community schools is delegated to the head. The principal has an uncluttered agenda: get it right and you will be supported and rewarded. Get it wrong – good bye!
Interviewer:	So sponsors are essentially non-executive directors?
Principal:	Absolutely.

In this model one of the principal's key tasks is to run a successful school: Another is to establish a relationship with the sponsor:

> I think if you were in the A or B chains of academies and you didn't make a good relationship with (their sponsors) your position would be really rather difficult. So what the principal needs to be able to do is manage (the sponsor) – and the other key people in the governing body, too. You are working with more powerful people in society than

most heads encounter. You need to be able to make a relationship with those people. So you need a degree of self-confidence. You certainly don't need any bullshit because they are extremely good at spotting flannel. (Academy principal)

PWC (2008) quoted the sponsor's representative describing the sponsor's reaction to disappointing GCSE results. He saw them as a 'disaster' but what the principal had to learn was that in working with his sponsor, he had to make predictions correct (PWC, 2008: 107).

PWC (2008) noted that only 9 of 40 principal appointments in the course of their evaluations were female. One wonders whether the chief executive model of sponsorship is a stereotypically male one, and less attractive to people who might achieve the same results through more collaborative, consultative forms of communication. Working with a determined, powerful sponsor requires the principal to work independently, while accepting the sponsor's leadership:

> The principal communicated his passion and knowledge but I put the team (for the new building) together. (Otherwise) we wouldn't have had (name of leading firm of architects). Otherwise I had no personal agenda. Some of the other sponsors have – some of the Christian ones. I am like a non-executive chairman, a bit of advice now and again, turn up to governors meetings .... It has got to add up – make sure the responsible officer is doing the job. (Academy sponsor)

The principal of this academy agreed:

> It is my job to run the school, and so long as he is comfortable with how the school is running in relation to how he originally envisaged it, then he is happy. (Academy principal)

Nevertheless, the sponsor could draw on support. The governing bodies frequently contained a very wide range of expertise and networks. Sometimes quite small things made a difference. In this academy a governor had provided the art department with a high quality printer, and numerous people had commented on the quality of the work that the students were producing.

Relations with principals 2: Sponsors with an educational agenda

The non-executive director model explicitly has no specific educational agenda. He (it usually is he) sets the ethos, for example, 'no goal is beyond our reach' but achieving it is up to the principal. Being a principal of this sort of academy is the ultimate challenge for exceptionally strong, independent minded principals, whose own clear vision is consistent with that of their sponsor. A large part of their motivation is their belief in their own ideas, and their determination to show what can be achieved. Since its launch the academies programme has recognised the importance of strong visionary leadership. The question is whether that is consistent with sponsors who have their own educational agenda.

One quite newly appointed principal described a school in serious difficulties when she arrived. Nobody could tell her who were the most vulnerable children in the school, the child abuse register was not properly maintained, there was no effective monitoring of special education needs, eligible children were not receiving FSM as no one had helped parents fill in the forms, change of address and phone numbers were not being logged on the system, there was no link between pastoral care and the curriculum – and all this was before starting on the quality of teaching and learning. How could such a situation develop, and what is the relevance to a chapter on sponsorship?

The predecessor school had been in difficulties before it became an academy. Perceived weaknesses in leadership, and student behaviour problems had led Ofsted to place it in special measures. That, of course, was why it became an academy. Its sponsor had strong commitments to the small school model seen in some Charter Schools in the United States. The idea behind this model is uncontroversial: Children learn better when teachers know them well and they see themselves as part of a clearly identified group. Nor is the conversion of the idea into practice necessarily controversial. To ensure that every child feels that he or she is a contributing member of a group, and cannot feel lost in a large secondary school, mini 'schools within the school' are created, for example, based on year groups. Yet, however coherent the model is in theory, when applied without preparation to a school in difficulties, turbulence can be the result. Having a small group of teachers for each year group had meant:

> splitting the subject departments. So you already have a weak English department, say, ... you're a teacher in one room teaching key stage 3 and your head of department is right over the other side of the building teaching key stage 4, and only key stage 4. So your line manager is no longer your head of department, so the head of that small school is not an English teacher and doesn't have a passion for the subject .... I put all the departments back together and basically unpicked the model and reinvented it in my own way. (Academy principal)

The sponsor's representative also recognised the problem:

> There are a lot of things to be done in a transition school to stabilise a fragile institution and to work on immediate improvements before you go for structural changes. It's quite difficult, depending on the design of the existing school, to set up a small school structure in existing buildings. If one was looking at policy lessons to be learnt it would be the viability of the clean break between old and new ... but we are morally bound ... to those pupils in year 9 and 10 in the school we are taking over, who will have had a miserable education until now in most cases. (Sponsor's representative)

The excerpt shows changes in the sponsor's thinking as a result of experience in one of the chain's earlier academies. It is not a criticism that two questions remain unresolved at this stage. First, how effective can the model be if introduced into a successful school, or in an academy that is being built up from an initial intake of year seven pupils, or younger? Nobody we met thought it could be introduced successfully into a school with major problems of pupil behaviour or underachievement. Nor, though, did anyone rule it out in other circumstances. Second, would a dynamic, independent minded head, capable of leading a team that turns round a failing school, want to be constrained by a model – any model – imposed by a sponsor?

The academies programme was designed to encourage innovative approaches to school leadership and classroom teaching. The model of a 'school within a school' is potentially an interesting example. If developed in a chain of academies over the next 10 years, its influence on secondary schooling might be substantial. The chain could even start to generate its own leaders both at middle and senior level of management who would in turn develop the model within the chain and extend it to other schools. Yet, although the case for this sort of innovation is straightforward, empirical evidence suggests that it may encounter major challenges in the short to medium term.

Sponsors and Governance

What is needed in a governing body?

It is widely recognised that the supportive and active involvement of the governing body is essential if a school in difficulty is to recover (Mortimore *et al.*, 1988). However, it is also recognised that schools have difficulty in filling vacancies on governing bodies (Phillips, 2008) and that governors can sometimes be less than helpful. We have already noted how a Director of Education used the academy programme to deal with a school and governing body in severe difficulties.

Key attributes of effective corporate boards are summarised by Conger *et al.* (2001: 21–22). These include having experience and understanding in areas such as strategy, succession, finance, governance and how organisations operate, having access to and the capacity to interpret meaningfully the data and information required, having the power to make and influence decisions, opportunity and time to make effective decisions and perform effectively, and finally to find the work rewarding. This is not driven by ideological ideas about democracy and accountability, but by relevance to the goals of the organisation. Boards have a key network building role to play. This can be enhanced by ensuring the right mix of people, providing regular experiences for members to increase their understanding of the organisation's business, and linking members of the board directly to the organisation.

The key point here is that the sponsor appoints a majority of an academy's governing body. This means that a sponsor can construct a governing body to reflect the needs and priorities of the academy. Appointments need not be based on any representational niceties, or on any ideological links to local democracy. In the market place, parents judge a school by its products – or rather the behaviour, attitudes and educational progress of the student 'products' – and it is on helping the academy to demonstrate excellence in its core work that the expertise of the governing body should focus.

Contrasts with governors of LA schools

Superficially, governance of academies has a good deal in common with that of LA schools. Typically, academies have three levels of governance. First, the trustees are responsible for setting the strategic direction, or what more than one person in our study called the 'ethos'. The trustees, or governors, always include the sponsor, usually with some close associates, though numbers can vary. The nearest equivalent in LA schools is the education committee of the LA itself. Second, the governing body is responsible for general policy on day-to-day matters and for monitoring standards. The governors usually include the sponsor, the principal ex officio, and elected representatives of parents and staff. There is also a LA representative. Third, committees are responsible for specific areas, such as SEN, the curriculum, monitoring academic standards. Committees are usually appointed by the governing body and often include trustees.

None of this is likely to sound too unfamiliar to governors in LA schools. The key differences are: (1) that an academy's governing body is generally stronger, and chosen for more specific reasons than in most LA schools; and (2) that it is more streamlined, less tied into the formalities of local representational democracy, and therefore better placed to take difficult decisions more quickly.

> You can't actually push these people around too much. It's going to be a heavy weight bunch. (Independent school sponsor)

> Networking is crucial in constructing the governing body. Business gets things done. Everyone is there for a reason, marketing for example. (Academy sponsor with business background)

Charities commission and company law

A recurring criticism of academies is that sponsors have too much power and, in theory, could use the schools for other purposes, including their own business interests. One principal we spoke to was dismissive of this criticism:

> One of the early criticisms was, 'oh they are going to steal the schools and turn them into hotels!' Of course, the funding agreement makes that absolutely impossible and indeed so does Charities Commission and Company Law. Under Charities Commission and Company law the trustees can only make decisions corporately and severally and they have to be able to demonstrate that their decisions are consistent with the aims of the charity and the Articles of Association of the Limited Company. So, actually, there are much higher and more secure criteria for governance in an academy than in most schools, because it is a registered charity. The manifestation of that is we get fully audited annually and the audit not only checks the money; it also checks the governance. If either of these gives cause for concern the Charities Commission would come down on us like a ton of bricks. And that is a good thing! (Academy principal)

Community schools can have problems recruiting and retaining governors. Phillips (2008) suggested that LAs contributed to these problems as much as the nature of the job itself:

> Governors receive mixed messages from politicians and government officers (both local and national) about the value they place on school governance and school governors. (Phillips, 2008: 20)

She suggested that the continuing practice of the then DCSF of issuing statements, which attribute to head teachers the statutory and legal responsibilities that lie with governors undermines governors, as does the low status attributed to governor training and development in many LAs. It should not be possible to lay these criticisms at the door of academies. In principle, their governing bodies have a clear definition of their function and a clear recognition of the role they play. These latter two points were key issues for Philips in improving the effectiveness of governing bodies.

Does an educational background help? The School Governors One Stop Shop (Adams & Puntner, 2008) provides schools with people willing to be governors. The majority of these people are not educationalists. Whilst governors found it difficult to cope with the jargon, one head quoted by Adams and Puntner (2008) commented:

> The governors we have had from the one stop shop have all been fabulous ... one of their special skills is to apply a non-education context to an issue – taking the steam out of it immediately. (Adams & Puntner, 2008: 16)

How do effective governing bodies add value?

Writing about LA schools Pounce (2008) claimed that effective governing bodies:

- Agree a shared vision for the school.
- Contribute to the self-evaluation of the school.
- Engage with the staff and the community in shaping the development plan.
- Promote genuine community engagement.
- Explore with the school leadership how the budget might be deployed differently to achieve the school's aims.
- Hold the school to account.
- Are themselves accountable.

What factors tend to impede effective governors? According to Pounce (2008) they include:

- Complexity of governing body work.
- Ineffective chairing and clerking.
- Untrained governors.
- The head teacher.

All this raises two questions. First, does the construction of academy governing bodies, with a majority appointed by sponsors, usually with specific tasks or skills in mind, make it easier or more difficult for the governing body to add value to the academy's aims and objectives than the more representational model favoured by LAs? Second, does the academy model encourage or reduce the factors that are likely to impede effective governance? Selecting a majority of governors for their skills and specific contributions rather than for the constituency they represent must tip the first question towards academies. The second is only marginally more difficult. It should help that solutions lie within the control of the sponsor and his or her associates on the governing body.

Tensions in Governance of Academies

Chains of academies

In principle, governance of chains of academies is no different from that of academies with a single sponsor. The trustees set the strategic direction or ethos, and the governing body is responsible for policy within the academy. In theory, an LA has similar responsibilities in LA schools. In practice, the trust may have its own preferences and desired methods, prompting one principal to observe:

> I can see it being a good model, but if I were the head of an academy in (name of chain) I would be wondering what my responsibility was. (Academy principal)

Most chains top slice the schools budget to pay for certain services, including payroll and human resources. This was viewed with alarm in some academies, mitigated only in part by recognition that while LA's typically took 8% of the total budget for central services, most chains were only taking 4%, and at least one takes less than 2%.

Principal:	I'm paying £400,000 of my budget to pay for my sponsor's networks. I've said to them, ' you have to be very careful that you don't become another local authority'. The whole idea of an academy is not that.
Interviewer:	Does your sponsor recognise that danger?
Principal:	I don't think they do. It is a danger, I think it will take away what is so special about academies, that you are independent.

High achieving school sponsors

The opportunities for cooperation between a high-achieving school and the academy it sponsors are equalled only by the potential tensions in their relationship. In the only example in our sample, the independent school head and the academy principal designate were extremely positive, identifying numerous areas for cooperation, from the curriculum to the combined cadet force, to international links and school visits. The sponsoring school appoints the trustees and a majority of the governing body. Yet in practice the key people in leading or coordinating the sponsoring school's influence on the academy will be the two heads; the formal governance arrangements are not likely to play a critical part in the chemistry between them. At the worst one can envisage the academy principal having to negotiate a minefield of relationships: Trustees, many of whom will be linked to the governing body of the sponsoring school, and so have responsibility for monitoring the performance of both heads, the governing body itself, with parent, teachers, and LA representatives, as well as a majority of representatives appointed by the sponsoring school, and the head of the sponsoring school. At best, the governance arrangements will encourage and assist a mutually beneficial relationship.

Group sponsors

As the academies programme has expanded, group sponsorship has become increasingly popular. Thus, business interests may combine with a university, a religious organisation and even the LA to sponsor an academy. The DCSF recognised some of the difficulties with group sponsorship, illustrated in Smith's (2008) critical remarks about bids for sponsorships for academies in Durham (see Chapter 3). At best, group sponsorship can extend the resources and expertise available to the academy. At worst, group sponsorship can be a recipe for confusion and disaster. We heard of one where the lead sponsor was a religious organisation, with a LA and a local business organisation as co-sponsors. There was evidence that the individual who had provided £2 millon in trust funds felt marginalized on the governing body, chaired by a member of the religious organisation. Members of the governing body lacked any clear idea about the strategic direction and ethos being set by the trust. The principal of the academy was in despair from the lack of support from the governors, compounded by chronic problems of student behaviour in the academy. In the middle of all this, the DCSF was encouraging the chair of the governing body to set up another academy.

Decisive action?

PWC noted that 11 of the 27 academies in their five year evaluation had experienced a change of principal, though without giving any detailed reasons. One of the academies that we visited had its fourth principal in four years. One principal described a transition to academy status that, he felt, had not been well handled. The trustees had introduced a new leadership team with a new vertical house system without adequate preparation. As far as we could make out this was partly attributable to trustees who were eager to respond to the innovation for which the DfES was clamouring and partly to a principal who, though successful in a previous headship, did not provide convincing alternative arguments. The current principal felt strongly that the trustees has been right to take decisive action when the academy ran into serious difficulties. That would have been more difficult in a LA school, and it demonstrated a strength of academies. He continued:

> But yes, the principal going is a measure of two things. One, I think, not everyone who has been appointed is, frankly, up to it. Second, we are amongst the highest paid heads in the country so I don't think it's particularly objectionable if we have to fall on our sword if it doesn't work. (Academy principal)

Yet the sponsors' power to dismiss principals did concern the representative of a chain of academies. Having describing the pressure on principals and the risk of burn out, this person continued:

> The other thing is, because the sponsor has control and not the DfES, the sponsor gets fed up with them and kicks them out, and the principal can do nothing about it. The sponsor says : 'I'm getting rid of my head'; no one can do anything about it. So you are reliant on that relationship being right. (Sponsor's representative)

We asked in several interviews how the trustees of an academy appeared to become aware of problems and act upon them so much more quickly than other schools. A principal with a long history of working in LAs explained:

> One of the troubles with local authorities is that little pockets of people may be aware of all sorts of problems. But local authorities are not very good at pulling all that information together and acting on it. And even when local authorities have got a clear view, if a head or a governing body don't want to listen, that's another slowing process.

What happened here was that people working on behalf of the DCFS, advising the people at the school, became worried and they fed stuff through. The chair of the trustees was in the school a lot in the first year .... This large leadership team with everyone responsible for bits of everything and nobody accountable for anything – it didn't work. But also, I don't think it was sustainable financially and somebody pointed that out. (Academy principal)

What this reveals, like other excerpts, is not only the ability of trustees led by the sponsor, to identify and deal with a problem quickly. It also indicates why that can be more difficult within the less flexible, more bureaucratic structure of a LA.

Conclusions

Sponsors were central to the Labour government's conception of the academies programme. Originally, the DfES (now DfE) envisaged sponsors liberating strong, visionary principals from LA control. Less publicly, the DfES also envisaged strong, determined sponsors being more successful than LAs in holding principals to account for their academies' progress, and if necessary replacing them. Our own evidence is consistent with evidence in the PWC reports (2006, 2007 and 2008) that many, if not most, academies experienced turbulence in their early years. At least in our own sample, they seem to have emerged from it successfully, though sometimes the difficult decisions they took included replacing the principal.

That, however, raises two questions. First, how much did sponsors themselves contribute to the turbulence, for example, by pursuing their own educational agenda? Not all sponsors follow the model of the non-executive director who is not involved in day-to-day organisation and decisions. Moreover, difficult questions can be asked about the nature of their involvement. It avoids the issue to argue that idiosyncratic aspects of the curriculum, such as the teaching of creationism, is justified by high demand for places. If LA schools achieve lower results in the mainstream curriculum, parents may feel they have no other option. Second, although entrepreneurs and chains have been able to weather the storms that occurred in the early years of many of their academies, sometimes by taking difficult decisions quickly, it does not follow that all sponsors will be able to do so. Part of the motivation of university sponsors and, to a lesser extent, independent schools, in sponsoring academies is to demonstrate their contribution to their local communities. If the experience of some of the early academies is anything to go by, they could find themselves facing a public relations disaster. A university is an easier and more visible target for local pressure groups and a hostile press than an entrepreneur or a chain with its offices in another part of the country.

To conclude, the success of the programme over the next 10 years will be influenced by its success in dealing with three crucial questions.

Do academies really need sponsors? In May 2010 the new coalition government announced that all primary, secondary and special schools could apply to become academies and that schools rated 'outstanding' by Ofsted would be fast tracked through the application process without the need for an external sponsor or a trust fund (DfE, 2010a;b). Presumably sponsors were deemed unnecessary because outstanding schools would already have a positive ethos and a strong governing body. That, however, is not self-evidently true. An outstanding head can succeed with an unexceptional governing body and in an unexceptional LA. Such schools often deteriorate when the head leaves and neither the LA nor the governing body are well equipped to cope with the new situation.

It remains unclear at the time of writing whether other schools, not rated outstanding by Ofsted, will be required to find a sponsor before seeking academy status, (and if so whether this will create a three tier academy system: the original academies, 'outstanding' academies with no sponsor, and new, but not outstanding academies with a sponsor but no trust fund). More important, although we found unambiguous evidence that sponsors could make important contributions to their academies' ethos and to the strength of a governing body, we also found evidence of tensions, particularly in chains and group sponsorship. Sponsors provide no guarantee of quality but they can act as powerful advocates for the independence of academies. This leads to our other two questions.

Sponsor succession

For a variety of reasons, sponsors may decide not to continue with their sponsorship, not least increasing age and/or failing health. In addition a characteristic of successful entrepreneurs is that they spot new opportunities and move on. It is too early to say whether that will happen with the successful business entrepreneurs who sponsored the early academies. Moreover, sponsors of chains of academies such as ULT, Oasis, Ark, Harris and EduTrust could legitimately say that they are not dependant on an individual, and the way they have set up their trusts guarantees the future. That will be true only to the extent that their successors share their ideals.

New sponsors

If the academies programme is to expand, new sponsors will be needed even if 'outstanding' schools are not required to have one. It is not hard to envisage the university system sponsoring over a 100, nor to see high-achieving schools from both state and independent sectors adding a further 100 or 200. With the projected expansion of the chains and the addition of new ones the Labour government's target of 400 looks achievable. Beyond that the picture is less clear. Ensuring that all the new sponsors have the necessary vision, determination and energy will be a more challenging task.

Chapter 5

Schools for the Future: Trophy Buildings or Learning Environments?

Introduction

An essential feature of the academies programme under the Labour government was the creation of new, and often expensive, buildings. Tony Blair stated the government's commitment:

> A good education depends on many things: teachers, parents, standards, discipline and motivation. But good facilities where young people can learn and grow are a vital foundation. (DfES, 2007: 3)

For Blair, better school buildings were an essential part of the jigsaw of raising standards. This was a sentiment echoed by all his secretaries of state. For Alan Johnson (DfES, 2007: 5), the way schools and colleges were designed supported the government's ambition to create a world-class education system.

For one of the architects we spoke to the rationale for new buildings was simple:

> There are schools where students won't go to the toilet because they are too afraid. That's a pretty basic issue to address. If you say education is very important, and you send your child to school, and you sit them in a leaky classroom, you give a contradictory message. (Architect)

We interviewed architects from three of the firms responsible for the design of the academies that we visited. One concisely expressed the challenge of designing an academy:

> I think the academies programme was special in that it actually called for innovative architectural solutions for innovative educational

concepts, and the two must not be seen as separate. So for us, the architectural concept has its roots in the educational vision. (Architect)

As we shall see, the educational vision had a substantial influence on the design. To illustrate this, a priority in more than one academy was a variety of an organisational model that one architect described as 'being pushed at the time' of home bases for each year group. This was a variety of the small school model described in Chapter 4. Logically, this model implied that there would be less circulation and movement generally throughout the building. If teachers went to the pupils in their home base, rather than pupils going to the teachers in their departmental base, circulation would be hugely reduced, with implications for width of staircases and corridors. Hence, the educational model had implications for design. And if the educational model turned out to be unworkable, the consequences could be serious. It meant that the design of the buildings had to be flexible enough to adapt to different visions. The relationship between the educationists (with their vision,) the reality of design (the architects,) and the reality of constructing the building (the construction company) was crucial. We return to this point later, but must first look at the public face of new academy buildings.

In this chapter we will consider why new buildings were considered an important part of the jigsaw of raising standards, what were the key issues in creating an effective new building, and what the reality has been with academies.

Why were New Buildings Considered to Play an Important Part in the Raising Standards Jigsaw?

Good design ... can make a big difference in very simple ways: imaginatively designed dining halls can encourage healthy eating; wider corridors can help to cut down on bullying; and classrooms with good acoustics and ventilation can improve concentration and behaviour. (Jim Knight, DfES, 2006b: 3)

In the introduction to RIBA's (2006) Education Sector Review Jim Knight affirmed that the government's investment in new buildings for secondary and primary pupils:

supports our drive to raise educational standards, personalise learning and ensure that schools serve the wider community. (RIBA, 2006: 2)

In the official DfES literature (2006a) and in many academy prospectuses, students, staff and governors were quoted. Their (selective) quotes hint at

ɔnship between the buildings they now inhabit and their future
. There are some examples below (quotes from DfES, 2006a):

> The school is always clean and light – you want to learn.
> Year 9 pupil – City Academy Bristol (DfES, 2006a: 46)

> There's a lot of space, which allows us to think.
> Year 10 pupil – City Academy Bristol (DfES, 2006a: 51)

> The building creates a sense of openness which has helped in the inter-action between staff and pupils.
> Chair of Governors – City Academy Bristol (DfES, 2006a: 51)

> I feel a lot safer. There are no dark corridors.
> Student – The Marlowe Academy (DfES, 2006a: 53)

> The use of glass in the walls between classrooms and corridors enables teachers to see a great deal more than in a traditional school building, which has a positive impact on behaviour and discipline.
> Governor – Northampton Academy (DfES, 2006a: 55)

These comments were echoed in statements from DfES publications which suggested the link between buildings and raising standards (DfES, 2003). However, there has been a limited amount of empirical research on the impact of school environments on raising standards and student attainment:

> Not only is the evidence incomplete, particularly in areas such as sys-tems and processes and communications approaches that schools need to underpin their physical environment, but the research that has been done seems to be largely predicated on a traditional view of chalk and talk learning in standardised one size fits all institutions. (Higgins *et al.*, 2005: 3)

And Higgins and his colleagues went on to state:

> Our exploration of the impacts of changes in the physical environ-ment on cognitive and affective measures must be based on an under-standing of the complexity of schools. Schools are systems in which the environment is just one of many interacting pedagogical, socio-cultural, curricular, motivational and socio-economic factors. (Higgins *et al.*, 2005: 35)

There appears to be no straightforward architectural determinism; good school design does not automatically lead to raised standards. Indeed many of the highest achieving and attaining schools in England operate in buildings which were designed for a different age. There are some identifiable impacts regarding ventilation, noise, and so on which, when addressed, create a more pleasant environment in which staff and students can work. This empirical reality is far from the claims made by architects and the DfES about the impact of design. The work of Higgins and his colleagues asks an important, and as yet unaddressed, question as to what extent an environment has to be improved for it to be adequate and have an impact on learning and standards.

Interestingly, reporting on the performance of schools before and after moving into new buildings or significantly improved premises, Estyn (2007) found that in all circumstances there was a strong correlation between new buildings/significant refurbishment and improvements in key performance areas. They raise standards. In particular they found this to be the case in attainment and achievement, quality of teaching, behaviour and the choices that students were offered. However, there is little empirical evidence to suggest that buildings determine behaviour and attempts to link student achievement and the built environment have not been persuasive (Woolner *et al.*, 2007).

There is an obvious tension here. The evidence from Woolner *et al.* (2007) and Higgins *et al.* (2005) is clearly inconsistent with other evidence: The DCSF claims about investment in new academy buildings; the findings of Estyn (2007); comments found in almost all HMI and Ofsted reports on open academies; and the comments of people working in the new academies. Yet empirically there is little to suggest that new buildings have a significant impact in raising standards.

In 'turnaround' models of school transformation there is a direct correlation between 'munificence', or provision of generous teaching resources and new buildings, and improvement. This appears to be borne out by Estyn (2007). However, that view should be seen in a wider context. Munificence is one among many elements which need to be taken into account for effective turnaround/improvement in standards. Munificence alone does not turn failing or under-achieving organisations around. A key element is the human resource one – both in terms of leadership and management and in terms of staff turnover and refocusing. It is the human resource issues that may be key in taking the potential Hawthorne effect of new buildings into the realms of sustainable turnaround. We will address leadership and management issues later but for the moment let us continue to look at the academy buildings in their own right.

Many new academies are imposing buildings, appearing to make a dramatic statement about the future of education. A number are located on the edge of areas of chronic disadvantage, with the obvious implication that they should contribute to urban regeneration, not least in a symbolic way. In our discussion with Andrew Adonis, he would accept this only with an important *caveat:*

> I never talked about them in them in those terms. Shall I tell you why? Its because people associate regeneration with just pouring money in. Now I'm in favour of bigger investment .... I believe that we have under invested in our public infrastructure for generations, and we have under invested in education and our educational infrastructure .... But I have never for one moment believed that simply putting money into these communities alone would produce decent schools .... In fact, academies represent huge investment but I very rarely talked about the money side. I always talked about the change side in terms of quality of schools that you are going to have, how much better the management would be, that these would be good schools with high standards, a really tough approach to discipline, good head teachers, smart uniforms – all those things parents locally look for in schools that they want to send their children to. Now all of that is made possible by the investment, and of course because they are going to be successful schools, this investment is going to have a big regeneration effect, and that definitely was part of the underlying philosophy – that they should have this regeneration effect. But it's the reform that is every bit as important in making a success of academies. (Andrew Adonis)

Andrew Adonis played down the munificence side by emphasising the centrality of reforms in teaching and learning to the academies programme. The turnaround of an organisation is not solely about investment of capital. Effective turnaround has a number of other key elements. Certainly this was reflected in the views of the architects we spoke with who saw their buildings, rather than simply the money invested, as making a contribution to, not delivering, rising standards. So the question is how new academy buildings contribute to the reforms. The less obvious but equally important question is how it fits into the locality and contributes to it.

In some academies the design was intended to convey a message. One site was adjacent to a busy road. The architect explained that the sponsor had suggested how this could be turned to an advantage:

Architect: The front entrance is on a major road and not on the estate side, and that explains the set up: its more outward looking.

Interviewer: There was a criticism of that, wasn't there, that the building was orientated away from the estate .... Whereas the academy's view was that it doesn't belong to the estate but to the wider world.

Architect: The new school was going to be the start of the redevelopment of the whole estate surrounding it. The axis runs straight through the building from the front entrance so that in the long run the surrounding area can link back into the school.

Thus, while the entrance was consciously outward looking, the design made it possible for people from the adjoining estate, home to many pupils, to use the academy in the evening and weekends. The architect acknowledged, though, that the main missed opportunity had been the integration of the academy with the estate. The design could have been linked to the redevelopment of the estate. This could have symbolised more effectively the regeneration of the community. Sadly, neither the LA nor a housing association had the will to do that.

With other academies the challenge was to find a way to make the new building fit into a small plot surrounded by houses. A principal said:

You don't really look at it like a school .... It looks like a building that belongs in this particular space ... with some buildings you can make a statement with the sheer mass of the thing but .... Here you just see glimpses of it as you go along; that really works well in this space. (Academy principal)

In both of these cases, the buildings were viewed with pride by the wider community and those that worked in them – especially those who remembered the darkest hours of the predecessor school.

What is Key to Creating an Effective New Building and How Do You Go About Creating it?

There is general consensus about the importance of teams and consultation at all stages of planning and constructing a new building. The literature review by Higgins *et al.* (2005) shows that the more staff are actually consulted and involved in the process of developing the design of the learning environment the more likely it is to have an impact. This is actively encouraged by the DfES (2007). Higgins *et al.* also noted that design solutions will not last for ever and people who work in a building need to be continually engaged in the process of developing and refining the design to meet the needs of the moment. This iterative process is an extension of the consultation process.

The key issues in making the process of new building design effective were outlined by the DfES (2003). These include:

- 'Focussing on the customer as a key player in the success of the building project' (DfES, 2003: 63).
- Creating a good brief.
- Consultation '. . . to ensure that the objectives and aspirations of the school and its community are turned into reality. . .all potential users should be consulted.' (DfES, 2003: 63).
- Undertaking feasibility studies and options appraisals.
- Cost planning and then procurement.

How is this ideal turned into reality in the academies programme?

Responsibility for the design and construction of the earlier academies rested with the Project Management Company appointed by the sponsor, and sometimes chaired by him, the Design Team Company, or firm of architects employed by the Project Management Company, and the Construction Project Management Company. Describing the construction of one of the early CTC's, a partner in the Design Team Company for that CTC said:

> The key element is that it was sponsored by people who were experts in education. It was sponsored by people who knew all about teaching, and all about the teaching profession, and to put it bluntly, how to run a school. (Architect)

He did not think this had happened in the design and construction of all new academies. He described a CTC where the building was not distinguished from an architectural point of view. In fact, it was deliberately low key, using the same materials as an adjoining building. The LA had been implacably hostile, and it was felt that a building that stood out as a beacon would be a provocation to local vandals. But the CTC, now an academy, had been outstandingly successful. Its success lay in enabling pupils of all abilities (there was a fair banding admissions policy) to lead balanced lives, with music, drama, athletics as well as the usual curriculum. This architect attributed this school's success to four factors: first, the sponsor had advice from 'an absolute expert on education'; second, they knew how to run a school; third, they were able to attract governors of the highest calibre; fourth, they did not want a trophy building. (He told the interviewer to underline the last point three times in red.)

To illustrate the fourth point this architect cited the science laboratories his firm had built at an academy:

> When they were designing (a new, different academy) they heard the laboratories that we had built were rather good – they bloody well should be, I must have done a hundred! ... so about thirteen or fourteen from their team came to have a look, whereas our total team was about five. I knew the project manager and I said, 'Where's the architect?' and he said 'Well they haven't come .... It's not their responsibility to design the laboratories'. So there is an endemic problem in the way these buildings have been put together because central government don't understand the structure of the team that is needed to deliver it ... in this office the education process is holistic – we are involved in everything. (Architect)

The problem, in his view, had been too many consultants and too much involvement at central government level, with nobody ever held responsible for their advice. He described his first meeting at the Department for Education while planning one of the early CTCs. Before the meeting an eminent education professor had explained to him how central government worked:

> It's very simple: everyone you are going to meet today has the right to be consulted. And not one of them needs to make a decision.

The architect contrasted that with meetings with the head of one of the first CTCs: 'you turn up, you know the answers. If not you are sent outside'. The really depressing thing for this architect, though, was that weaknesses in the planning of some of the early academies were not being solved by subsuming the programme in Building Schools for the Future (DfES, 2004; PfS, 2006). Instead of asking experienced people to fix the problems in the previous system, government had designed a completely new system. To see why government considered change necessary, we must look at some projects in the first two years of the programme.

What is the Reality with Academies?

In reality consultation about the design of an academy, though desirable, may be difficult for a range of reasons. Academies were often born in tension, fast tracked or started from scratch with no community to consult about design. It is difficult to consult about design issues with the political tensions that surround the birth of some academies. Some academies were also given their vision and design brief by the sponsor. This is particularly true of those chains which promote a particular model of working.

Perhaps it is not surprising that some new academy buildings have attracted strong criticism. Dismissed as 'trophy buildings' by one architect that we met, PWC's (2005) second report noted:

> new Academy buildings have the appearance of modern office build-ings or universities, and seek to make bold statements in their local communities. (PWC, 2005: 32)

According to this report, feedback on the first three buildings opened was mostly positive, and there was a dutiful acknowledgement of 'inno-vative aspects of design' such as folding walls and partitions to allow more flexible groupings, a purpose built lecture theatre, other areas that permitted more varied teaching styles, and zoning of areas within the building to facilitate access to resources. With only one exception the suggestions for design improvements listed in the report were relatively minor and easy to rectify. The exception was the positioning of sports changing rooms on the first floor, 'requiring often wet and muddy pupils to use internal staircases' (PWC, 2005: 34) (as described in Academy A in the case study below). These somewhat muted concerns hardly seem to justify criticism by some staff that too much emphasis had been placed on the 'bold statement' 'at the expense of some of the more practical requirements of modern teaching and learning spaces'(PWC, 2005: 34).

By the following year (PWC, 2006) criticism had become more robust:

> ... a number of key aspects of the design of new academies that were broadly regarded as unsatisfactory and not fit for purpose. (PWC, 2006: 33)

Of the examples listed, the most serious and therefore the most difficult to rectify were design and size of classrooms too small; changing rooms/facilities not suitable or conveniently located, and 'limited space for full service and school services' (PWC, 2006: 33) (presumably meaning assem-blies of, at least, a full year group). In addition, the report noted aspects of the procurement and delivery process as problematic.

In 2006 the Commission for Architecture and the Built Environment (CABE) published a research report assessing secondary school design quality. While this report was not entirely without self interest from CABE and did not consider the views of end users in its methodology, it is the only study of the suitability of the buildings constructed between 2000 and 2005 undertaken by the industry itself.

CABE (2006) suggested that the design quality of the secondary schools completed between January 2000 and September 2005 was not good enough to secure the government's ambition to transform children's education. Auditing 52 of the 124 completed schools they concluded that not enough were exemplary, inspiring, innovative or flexibly designed. Only 19% of the schools they audited were found to be good or excellent with a further 31% being partially good with weaknesses in build quality. The majority of the schools they audited were considered poor on transformational design. All the good or excellent schools were completed in 2005. The schools audited were a mix of Public Finance Initiative (PFI), non-PFI and city academy builds. CABE's major criticisms were directed at the PFI projects which included all but one of the poor and mediocre schools (CABE's lowest categories). Interestingly the best school audited was a city academy. Academies represented three of the eight good schools and none fell below the half way point of the partially good category (CABE's middle category). No academies were represented in the poor or mediocre categories. Academies represented 25% of the schools in the sample whilst, at the time, only representing 10% of all new builds.

One of CABE's recommendations was the need to have the right team advising and supporting the project. This comment seems an obvious one and supports the guidance CABE had circulated in September 2004. However, it did not arrive on the scene until 2006 (four years after the first academies were being completed). Similar advice from the DFES did not come into the public domain until a year later when advice for leaders was also coming from the British Council for School Environments (BCSE) (2007). Advice was also available from School Works, an organisation of professionals interested in school buildings, though CABE (2006) commented that not many principals will have been aware of it.

Criticisms of Design

In 2007 the independent British Council for School Environments (BCSE) felt the need to publish a 'Call to Action' manifesto because of its concerns about the failure of the new building programme to deliver effective school environments consistently. This sentiment was echoed by CABE (2006) in their guide to developing effective schools. Much of what is written in these two publication reflects the content of various DfES publications including the influential Building Bulletin 95 (DfES, 2007).

Before we built the academy staff at all levels were involved. We had two Saturday sessions which involved them in working up a brief for the architects. The architects then presented this to staff. Students had a say in the design. The design team met weekly to discuss progress. These meetings included the sponsor, DfES representatives, project managers and the architects, as well as me as principal. These meetings continued until well after the building was complete. Ways of working in the new building were trialled whilst we were operating as the academy in the old buildings. (Academy principal)

Building Design (2006) reported that Ofsted was critical of Unity City Academy in Middlesborough:

The nature of the building, while impressive at first sight, means that some students do not feel safe or secure. The layout of corridors is confusing, and high, open balconies and stairwells are daunting.

They further reported that Mossbourne Community Academy in Hackney was criticised for lack of space and acoustic problems, noting that 'the constraints of the building present a challenge for the academy's development'. A spokesman for the architects said that the building was originally designed for classes of 30 pupils but the academy asked for classrooms for 25 pupils. And finally Building Design criticised West London Academy for unsuitable sixth form accommodation.

The representative of one early sponsor described the sponsors as having had

a blank canvas to do what they wanted; there were no rules or regulations to constrain them. (Sponsor's representative)

in the design and procurement processes. This, of course, was consistent with the emphasis on academies as independent schools in the state system, managed by independent sponsors. Yet the DCSF had representatives on the Project Management Company, the Design Team Company and the Construction Management Team Company, presumably with a brief to monitor and if necessary advise on the decisions made. Faced with problems in design and construction, the Department's response to individual academies was: 'but the project team signed it off'. To this, one sponsor's representative responded:

The department were in on it. They are the experts. At the end of the day they should have said (this) is not adequate. (Sponsor's representative)

But civil servants, she thought, came from a world where no one could make a decision. Illustrating his point with reference to an earlier project before the academies programme started, an architect was blunter:

> We built it in 24 months from standing start to finish with almost no controls because nobody could keep up with us. We used to run a book on whether one (representative from the DfE) would make it, and a second book whether they were the same one, and a third book as to the nationality that they might be – and English wasn't on the list – usually South African or Australian ... they were a sop that something was being controlled, but of course it wasn't. (JC: 6)

Faced with criticisms in PWC (2006) that some buildings were not fit for purpose, the Department was in a quandary. They had no wish to upset sponsors, and certainly not to derail the academies programme, (and we argued in Chapter 3 that the decision to expand it was fully justifiable). Nor did they want to acknowledge that they had been remiss in their supervision and monitoring of expensive new projects, let alone in their cost control procedures.

Their response was a civil service masterpiece reminiscent of the gently satirical television comedy 'Yes, Minister'. Two years earlier the department had announced the Building Schools for the Future programme (DfES, 2004). This was an ambitious, wide ranging and overdue programme to replace or upgrade all secondary school buildings. Politically, it signalled the Labour government's commitment to world-class facilities after the neglect of the Tory years (though in fact the Labour administrations of the 1970s had been almost as culpable). Applications under BSF were made by LAs.

This enabled the government to solve two problems at once. First, including academies in BSF ensured that the Department, and thus ministers, would not be associated with expensive building projects that its own evaluators were suggesting might not be fit for purpose. Second, by requiring all LAs to include proposals for academies in their applications for school renovation funds under the BSF programme, ministers ensured the cooperation of the LAs, or at least their reluctant acquiescence. This also provided a straightforward way to expand the academies programme to over 300 by 2010 and 400 at some time thereafter. All LAs were desperate for BSF money for their own schools. If the only way they could get it was to propose new academies, even the most recalcitrant would be brought to heel.

The non-departmental body responsible for delivery of the BSF programme is Partnership for Schools (PfS, 2006). The new arrangement stated that the LA would be the construction client for the academy buildings. As such the LA would be responsible for ensuring that the contractor delivered the building to the agreed specification. That meant the LA was responsible for building standards, quality control and value for money in the same way as for all other schools in the BSF programme. In other words, the LA would be much more accountable to PfS than sponsors had hitherto been to the Department. It was thus possible to clip sponsors' wings while still claiming that they retained a key role:

> The new delivery model will allow the sponsor's vision to be reflected in the academy building, without requiring their personal day-to-day involvement in detailed construction activities. It will also require a more efficient procurement process and better value for money due to the Academy building being part of wider procurement contracts. (DCSF, 2007c: 2)

In developing their vision for an academy, sponsors would:

> ... work with the LA to ensure its effectiveness in achieving educational transformation. They will liaise closely with the LA and PfS design group, to ensure that accurate and sufficiently detailed information about the Academy's requirements are included in the each stage of the design and approval process. (DfES, 2008: 2–3)

It is not hard to read between the lines. Whereas arrangements for the early academies placed sponsors in the driving seat and the Department tried, sometimes ineffectively, to guide or monitor them, the new arrangements placed LAs in the driving seats albeit subject to the BfS traffic police, with sponsors having to negotiate approval for a building that would convert their vision of it to reality. Why LAs, criticised so strongly and often so justifiably for their inability to get to grips with underperforming schools, would be so much better at managing construction projects was not immediately obvious.

The final PWC (2008) report repeated the concerns about the fitness for purpose of some of the earlier academies and about the procurement processes. However, it reported that user feedback on the design of buildings had improved significantly over the previous three years. Cautiously, the report added that it was not yet clear whether the high specification of earlier buildings would be maintained under PfS.

We asked an architect about the new arrangements for greater involvement of LAs. He replied:

> Well, that defeats the whole object that it started out with. It's just barking! (Architect)

Another architect was more tactful but conveyed the same message:

> At the end of the day most of these processes need the clear leadership of a decision maker. If decisions are made by a committee, it can just go round and round, and a project can lose focus. (Architect)

Later in the interview he added that BSF pushed the risk onto the contractor. All buildings were based on a compromise between quality, time and cost. His concern was that a design team could meet with educational staff, but would have to recognise that their client was the contractor, who was tied into a financial contract. If the emphasis were on cost and time, then quality would take a back seat – in terms of both architectural quality and input from the end users. He did, however, suggest that as more academies were built, economies of scale might be possible. For example, identifying around ten basic types would enable sponsors to express a preference for one of them, and this would be adapted for the circumstances of the site. For the first architect the problem with PfS was that it would lead to a 'design and build' approach, with final design delegated to the contractor. This could be successful for straightforward projects such as a detached block of four classrooms, but it was 'utter folly' for a project as complex as an academy. For that, a holistic approach was essential, with as much attention to the classroom furniture as to the architectural features.

> I could walk on to any school campus in this country and I could tell you which were design and build. If you want a science building you sit down with the scientists. Take (name of school): thirteen laboratories, three heads of department; they all have different types of benches and different surfaces .... You give it this unique input from people who have a vested interest in its success – its great and it works! (Architect)

But this, sadly was not the experience of an academy principal who would be moving into new buildings in a few months time. He found it difficult that he had had no involvement in the design or commissioning of the building. Nor, he thought, had the sponsors: 'It's nothing to do with them. It's to do with how it's procured nationally'. He recognised that the sponsors had their own advisors on educational matters, but they had apparently not seen fit to consult him. While he regretted this, he was philosophical:

> I would have configured that building differently for learning. Having said that the fact of the matter is that the building is the way it is. At

the end of the day you have got to do the best you can and to config-
ure the learning around the way the building is. (Academy principal)

Three Short Case Studies

Project management and design: Academy A

This academy replaced one of the lowest achieving schools in the country. The condition of the premises, the children's behaviour and their
attainment and aspirations seemed to have deteriorated together. The
chair of the academy's governors declared himself ashamed to be living in
a country that tolerated such a shambles. The project management team
contained distinguished, experienced educators. The sponsor wanted a
building that was bright, light and airy. The result was impressive by any
standards, with an entrance that was both striking and welcoming. Yet the
avoidable flaws in the building caused huge frustrations to teaching and
non teaching staff, creating obstacles to teaching and, more importantly,
learning that certainly contributed to the academy receiving a highly unfa-
vourable inspection report from Ofsted. The sponsor's representative told
us about four main problems.

(1) The Project Management Company hired a small firm for the IT
system. The system did not work when the academy opened and
never worked properly thereafter. They limped along for three years
with constant failures and constant repairs and eventually the
DCSF helped them to pull out and replace all the cables and infrastructure.

(2) There were only two changing rooms each suitable for a single class of
25–30 pupils. Yet elementary arithmetic would have shown that up to
six classes could have been doing PE at any one time. Moreover, the
changing rooms were on the first floor, so that whenever sports or PE
was held outside pupils would bring mud into the building on their
shoes.

(3) None of the classrooms had walls or doors separating them from the
public areas. The sponsor's representative explained:

In the first year we lost half of our staff because you couldn't teach in
the building. Everybody was competing to teach their kids because
the next classroom down had no wall and there would be kids walking by the classroom on their way to lunch. And no doors or walls on
the restaurant, so basically – noise rising . . . . We managed to get some
money to glass in all the walls last summer.

(4) There was no playground. It is not difficult to envisage a school with
     no playground. It requires staggered lunchtimes, described to us by
     the Principal of Academy B (see below):

> You take the middle part of the day as a double lesson – that's 2 hours
> let's say from 12 noon to 2 pm, but in effect it's a 1½ hour lesson and
> certain classes come down every half hour. That's fine if you come
> down for the first half hour or the last half hour, but some poor souls
> have to bring their classes down after 30 minutes teaching, take 30
> minutes for lunch, and then go back for the 1 hour of teaching left. I'm
> not sure that's the way you are going to get the best out of the kids.
> One of the early CTC's is always held up as a prime example of stag-
> gered lunches. It works brilliantly because they have been doing it for
> ten years and the kids and staff are trained into doing it. Whereas we
> have kids who have been running wild at (predecessor school) and
> totally wild on the streets. And suddenly they are brought in here and
> are expected to behave.

So at Academy A, the lack of a playground created additional noise and
movement inside, which therefore compounded the existing problem of
noise in the classrooms without doors or walls. Yet the project management company had contained experienced educationalists, including one
with headship experience that must have been considered relevant to the
academies programme. The sponsor's representative saw no need for dip-
lomatic niceties:

> They came in with all these wild, mad ideas about how academies
> would work: you know, no bells, constant flow of kids through the
> building – so you would get brunch – lunch, with kids on the move
> from 12 o'clock through to 2 o'clock. No walls or doors, literally open
> plan to everything. It was a nightmare. They basically led (the sponsor)
> down the path of, 'well this is the new model for education'. (Sponsor's
> representative)

Four things emerge from what this sponsor's representative appeared
to regard as close to scandalous. First, educational experts on the project
management team and design team certainly are essential, but just as certainly, they are not sufficient. They also need significant knowledge and
experience in the day-to-day realities of teaching in failing schools, and
the imagination to anticipate what the projected new building will be like
for teachers and children. Second, ideas that may work well in one context will not necessarily work well in another. Third, rather than the input
of external consultants, successful innovation in the planning of new

school buildings is helped above all by the close involvement of the principal and staff responsible for making them work Fourth, when that is not possible, for example, because the principal and senior staff of the new academy are not yet in place, it becomes even more important for the design team to adopt a holistic approach. By that we mean two things: (1) the educational experience to envisage how the different activities in the finished building will interact to create an efficient, effective and humane learning environment; and (2) the knowledge of design, procurement and construction needed to put the different parts in place.

Project management and design: Academy B

The design for this academy was driven by a sponsor who had a background in education. No staff of the predecessor school had been involved, and for various reasons that would have been difficult given the particular circumstances of the academy and the predecessor school. At the request of the design team, the sponsor brought in educationalists who wrote the curriculum requirements for the new building. However, neither sponsor, nor educationalist, nor architect was working with the end user. That created difficulties for the architect:

> You've potentially got a conflict ... or lack of understanding of what's really required. It's one thing for a sponsor to feel that they know what a building should deliver, but ultimately you need your end users. Now, having said that, the sponsor did have a lot of ex heads from various places working with them ... but of course they are all coming from different approaches, backgrounds and the question is how you get a definitive brief. (Architect)

The design brief included a home base for years seven and eight, an idea that was popular at the time. This had implications for the amount of circulation expected in the academy, and that in turn had implications for the widths of staircases. Unfortunately, the home base model quickly proved unworkable for similar reasons to those explained in Chapter 4, when we discussed the sponsor's preference for the model of schools within a school. By the time that was recognised, the stairs could not be altered. As the width did not permit pupils to go upstairs and downstairs at the same time, the academy had no alternative but to introduce a one way system utilising the two staircases. The architect admitted:

> Certainly, the intention was that there wouldn't be as much flow because of the home base scenario, but ultimately a building needs to be able to deal with other organisational models. (Architect)

While that was a realistic, honest assessment the architect could legitimately have added that the design team must work to a budget and to a brief from the project management company. Again we return to the importance of the project management company having educationalists with the experience and the ability to envisage how the building will be experienced by the end users: Children and teachers.

Similarly, the design brief assumed lunches would be staggered as described above. However, the constant flow of children was not a model that was feasible in an academy that was still working to create a sense of stability that had been lacking in the predecessor school. Because it was never intended that all pupils would have lunch at the same time, one of the major points of entry and departure at that part of the building was through the dining room, and could not be used at lunch time. Again, one might have expected a project management company and design team who were sensitive to the likely needs of the end users to have anticipated this problem.

Project management and design: 2. Academy C

The new building for this academy replaced *ad hoc* previous accommodation consisting of a 1950s block with 1970s additions and some mobile classrooms. Notwithstanding the condition of the previous buildings, the academy had been making steady progress in GCSE passes. This was the building with an entrance facing a busy road. By any standards, it was impressive from the outside and no less so from the inside, with wings branching to left and right of the atrium. Classroom walls were of glass, giving a light airy feel, whilst also reflecting a busy working environment. We asked a deputy head how the children reacted to the building:

> This is our third year, but the faces on the children when they walked into the building – there is a big WOW – they are absolutely overcome by that. I think our children were used to living in a school that was falling about their ears. It was really scruffy and dilapidated and I think they still feel proud to be here .... The impact is really, really powerful. Looking around the place, there is just no graffiti. In fact the only bit is here (on a table) in the teachers conference room. These aren't all brilliant quality doors, but they are not damaged, are they? You can't fake that. Kids do like being in this wonderful expensive building. (Deputy principal)

As in Academy B, the original intention had been for each year to have all non-specialist teaching within their home base area. The children, not surprisingly, were happy with this arrangement. Nevertheless, by the end of the year two problems had become apparent. First, having been together in their home base for so much time, some of the more difficult classes started to treat them almost as their own territory. Some teachers found that hard to cope with. As the deputy head remarked, it is better if a teacher welcomes children to a classroom rather than vice versa. Second:

> It didn't respect the needs of teachers to be surrounded by their equipment and resources. Teachers were going round carrying loads of books and equipment from class to class. It is better when children are welcomed into a geography room or science lab – teachers can set up a really good atmosphere within the class.

After one year the academy's leadership decided that each year group would retain a home base for tutor groups. That was where they would go at lunchtime and for registration. Subject departments, though, were also given their own suite of rooms, usually in one year group's home base.

The comparison with Academy B illustrates two important points. First, in Academy B a design feature – width of staircases – created an obstacle to recognition that the original home-base model was impractical, and a solution would require more circulation by students than had originally been anticipated. Academy C faced no similar problem when it, too needed to make changes that necessitated more student circulation as they moved between different subject departments for lessons. Second, and crucially, the design is secondary to leadership. The solution to problems arising from what was essentially a management decision – a particular model of home bases – was more straightforward in Academy C, where the design facilitated use of the new building in different ways. The fact that the solution was less straightforward in Academy B merely illustrates the importance of imaginative leadership.

Assemblies

The principal was not keen on assemblies, having seen them practised too often as control technologies. However, she found herself missing a suitable place to hold assemblies. The original intention had been to hold them in the large atrium in the middle of the academy. That proved impractical, as it was open to the rest of the academy. Thus there were visual distractions such as seeing other pupils in classrooms, or in one of the corridors, and unintentional noise distractions such as a receptionist answering the phone or talking to someone at the front entrance. Given the layout of the building there was no obvious solution to this problem and the principal was hoping to obtain funds for an extension to provide the necessary space.

Visibility

The visibility of all activities in this academy meant that there were no hiding places. Walking round the academy every class could be seen. That meant that the children's responses could also be seen, and no child could leave a class without being noticed. The principal denied that this made the building feel like a goldfish bowl:

> All our evaluations on the children are that they feel safe in this building. There are no hidden areas; the transparency makes them feel secure. The width of corridors … makes movement easier. They don't feel watched. Teachers are used to having a wall and a door, but here much of their classroom is visible as you walk past. That doesn't have appeared to have caused any anxieties. They often welcome people in as they walk past; that's partly because of the building, but partly because of the culture that we have established, where it is open and what teachers do is visible and should be visible. (Academy principal)

The deputy, though, felt that the downside was the inevitable lack of privacy. When a teacher was having a difficult time with a class it was very public, and although the soundproofing was excellent, 'you have got to be very sensitive in dealing with a teacher's feelings'. A more serious problem was a lack of sufficient private rooms in which to see children, either about child protection issues, or the occasional detective work that is necessary in any school: finding out who did what to whom, why and when. In this academy senior staff said that it was difficult to find corners where other students would not notice a teacher talking to a child and later, want to know why.

At this academy, it seemed obvious, the open nature of all teaching, together with the concentration of each department's base in a group of classrooms, should encourage cooperation between teachers, and hence facilitate professional development. Both the principal and deputy said that this had already been established in the old building rather than created by the new one. The new building helped, but the staff had established the academy's professional culture in the old building.

One of the architects we met said that all projects were a compromise between quality, cost and time. 'If you push one, the other will suffer a bit'. At this academy, the quality of some fittings seemed quite poor. Tables and chairs were not robust and the deputy described the toilet fittings as flimsy. They seemed inconsistent with the quality of the main structure. Yet this had not proved a significant problem in the two years since pupils moved into the building. They looked after the buildings and reported damage immediately. Again, the openness of the building ensured that any damage would be noticed immediately.

Conclusions

When Tony Blair opened one of the first academies he declared: 'I have seen the future of education, and this is it'. It's easy to ridicule easy sound bites. But if Prime Ministers get bogged down in detail – in this case some blatantly obvious design flaws that made the building's fitness for purpose questionable – they lose sight of the 'bigger picture'. The 'bigger picture' here, was of a striking new building surrounded by economically depressed former council estates and replacing one of the lowest achieving, and least well cared for schools in the country. It was also of pupils whose behaviour and attendance were starting to improve and whose educational attainments would also improve. In the summer before our visit, 50% of pupils had gained five GCSE passes at A*–C. Even though the academy narrowly missed the National Challenge benchmark of 30% of pupils attaining five passes with Maths and English, this still represents an impressive improvement. The design flaws must have delayed the improvement process by creating frustration for teachers and students. Against that, it represented a huge advance on conditions in the predecessor school and as the original problems were sorted out it became possible to create a positive learning environment.

It would be easy, and legitimate, to criticise design flaws and cost overruns in the early academies. But having committed itself to a major new programme to break the spiral of educational failure, deteriorating behaviour and social exclusion in schools in some of the country's most disadvantaged areas, it was perhaps not surprising that mistakes were made. Throughout the country, school buildings needed replacing or refurbishing. It is hard to see arguments against allocating funds generously to those most in need, just as it was entirely appropriate to link the new buildings with a programme of *educational* improvement.

School improvement is almost invariably multifactorial: the factors include leadership, staffing, teaching resources – and buildings. This is almost certainly why Higgins *et al.* (2005) and Woolner *et al.* (2007) found no significant statistical relationship between new buildings and student performance. Without the possibility of controlling adequately for quality of leadership, both from the principal and from middle management, or for quality and use of teaching resources, it would be surprising if they had found anything else.

A related point in evaluating the conclusions of Higgins *et al.* (2005) and Woolner *et al.* (2007) is that the early academies were all unique designs. That changed with the transfer of responsibility for commissioning new buildings to LAs under BSF (DfES, 2004). The downside to the consequent economies, with much tighter control by LAs of design and expenditure, is the caution and compromise that are likely to characterise the new programme. At worst this is seen in the 'design and build' approach criticised by an architect we interviewed. At best it is seen in the recent new academy buildings being less readily distinguishable from LA schools than the early academies.

The value of Higgins' *et al.* (2005) and Woolner's *et al.* (2007) work lies in demonstrating that, on their own, new and/or renovated buildings are not a sufficient condition for school improvement, let alone the transformation expected of academies. In certain rather exceptional cases they may not even be necessary; improvement can be observed in even the most dilapidated and ramshackle buildings – and not just in the private sector. Thus one academy operated for its first year in portacabins beside a railway line. The main hall doubled as a gym and dining hall and was to all intents and purposes a tent. But behaviour was impeccable and learning purposeful. The crucial factor here was outstanding leadership from the principal and senior staff.

For three reasons, though, this kind of success story is irrelevant to the case for new and/or renovated buildings. First, there can be no moral justification for consigning children from bleak, rundown communities to bleak, rundown schools, irrespective of whether the schools are academies or run by LAs. Second, it is irrational to base policy on the simplistic hope that superheads capable of transforming teaching and learning in the most unpromising conditions will suddenly emerge in large numbers. Third, it is not clear that this academy's success in sub-standard accommodation could have been sustained without the prospect of a new building.

Estyn (2007) provides a more realistic view: While better buildings contribute to improving performance in schools, leadership and management are also major influences. School improvement is a jigsaw and whilst academies are major turnaround projects, like all turnarounds they are dependent upon leadership and management of all aspects – including the (new) buildings in which that improvement is to take place.

We conclude this chapter with quotes from two architects. The first was concerned with the UK's competitiveness in a global economy:

> If you go to the Middle East or China, you can see that if we don't start educating our people, we will just be the poor man of the world. (Architect)

The second was concerned with the opportunities created by well-designed buildings:

> The bottom line is if you've got a really great principal you can do amazing things with kids in bad buildings. If you have good buildings with a rubbish principal you haven't got a chance. If you have a really good principal **and** good buildings, then maybe you'll do something really special. (Architect)

And finally ... . The global recession of 2008–10 led to a change of government in the UK and brought the building programme to an abrupt halt. New academies are no longer likely to enjoy new or refurbished buildings (DfE, 2010b). Politically it would be tempting to cite Woolner *et al.* (2007) or Higgins *et al.* (2005) as evidence that leadership and quality of teaching are more important than bricks and mortar. That is almost certainly true, but it would be disingenuous. To repeat: there can be no moral justification for consigning children from bleak, run-down estates to bleak, run-down school buildings. The challenge for the next decade will be to find ways of helping school leaders to create optimal environments for learning with less funding. That is likely to require principals to focus the available resources more sharply on investments that lead to improvements in learning and achievement.

Chapter 6

Distinctive Features of Academies: 1. Independence, Accountability and Pressure

Introduction

A recurring theme in the debate about academies is whether they have any powers that are not available to LA schools. Their much-vaunted independence is subject to annual audit in financial matters, and their curriculum is constrained by the requirements of public examinations. LA schools, moreover, have been managing their own finances for years and often see no need to seek their LA's permission before introducing curriculum initiatives or reforms. A union official was sceptical about the distinctiveness of academies.

> Schools operate the way they do because that's the way schools operate. If it's got four legs, a tail and it barks, it's a dog. If it looks like a school and operates like a school, then generally no matter what the structures are outside, whether we call it an academy, a Grant Maintained School, a Trust school or an Aided school, they carry on life in much the same way. (Union official)

Nor was this official too worried about the financial arrangements for academies. After initial start up costs, recurrent expenditure was on the same pupil *per capita* basis as LA schools. Retaining the top slice that previously had been allocated to central services was not an issue because:

> ... in the long run they will realise that money needs to be spent for the purposes it was originally allocated by the LA. (Union official)

Thus the academy would need to buy in support services and advisory services. In this official's experience, even poor performance leading to dismissal of teachers was treated in a similar way:

(My union) would be saying: 'you are much more likely to be sacked in an Academy'. I really don't think that's the case. I still think that it is something that is considered seriously by the school .... No, I don't think they have been cavalier about dismissing people – not the ones I've been involved in. (Union official)

So what *is* distinctive about academies? Like all other schools, academies vary, but it can certainly feel different to lead one as a principal or teach in one as a teacher. The same union official referred to burn-out in principals, caused by the exceptional pressures they were under. A principal referred to DfES consultants as being 'all over the school' in his predecessor's last months. A government elected on a mantra of 'Education, Education, Education', had very publicly nailed its colours to the mast of academies as pioneers of secondary school reform. The expectations were huge, with the added pressure of the media submitting every crumb of information to microscopic scrutiny.

Not everyone was as sanguine as one chair of governors:

If we had a problem, whatever it was it became magnified, because not only were you dealing with the issue within the academy, but we were also dealing with any number of journalists, the media and therefore the Department .... So we threw ourselves into public relations mode. Rather than shut the door and pretend there was no one outside, we really tried to embrace it. Sometimes it works and sometimes it doesn't but there you are. (Academy chair of governors)

The Context

A political imperative: 1. Education, education, education

Andrew Adonis was clear from the outset that:

The big issue that academies are dealing with is the systematic replacement of under performing schools in urban areas (Andrew Adonis).

The model, as we saw in Chapter 2, was city technology colleges, but they had to be adapted in four crucial respects. The first was that academies would mainly be replacing existing schools. He continued:

Secondly, (we needed) a model that would work with local authorities rather than against them, but with the local authorities on the basis that these schools would still be independently managed. Third, I needed them focused in areas of disadvantage predominately, because that was where the biggest problem was .... Fourth, we needed to find a way to attract, rapidly, large numbers of good sponsors, particularly sponsors who could set up chains of academies. (Andrew Adonis)

Some LAs might have been surprised to hear that the early academies were working with them. LAs were brought into a sometimes reluctant partnership with academies by the requirement that proposals for academies be included in applications for funds from the school building programme (DfES, 2004) and by the proposals for 14–19 education (DfES, 2005). In retrospect, the early proposals were modest: three academies opened in 2002, and a further nine in the following year. Yet the government's thinking was clear:

> I always thought that if this worked we would need to expand it quite rapidly, and the ability to scale up would crucially depend on our ability to establish chains. (Andrew Adonis)

In the early years, 2002–2004, the media probably did not recognise the intended scale of the academies programme. However, they already had plenty to interest them: transfer of allegedly failing and under-performing schools from LAs to independent sponsors, often with no background in education, large amounts of public money spent on iconic buildings, hostility bordering on fury from LAs and leaders of the teacher unions. The government's credibility in secondary education depended on the success of the earlier academies, and it would do everything possible to nurture and defend its infant project.

A political imperative: 2. Innovation, innovation, innovation

An expensive, high-profile project could not afford to be accused of merely replicating existing practice, even good practice. It would not only need eye catching new buildings. Yet even at an early stage there was evidence of anxiety about the prominence given to innovation as a key theme in academies. Reviewing the experience of Charter schools in the United States, the first PWC report (2005) noted:

> Greater flexibility and autonomy do not automatically ensure innovation; when given greater flexibility and greater autonomy some schools actually return to 'traditional' values and implement a curriculum with a strong emphasis on 'back to basics'. (PWC, 2005: 15)

In contrast:

> The thing about academies (was) it introduced the boldest reforms in the areas of greatest under performance. (Andrew Adonis)

If academies were to be seen as breaking the mould, they would have to be innovative. The government believed that their independence would facilitate innovation. There are two ways at looking at this. PWC (2006) quote an academy principal:

> When you are one of the worst schools in the country you don't have a choice, you have to be innovative or you fail. (PWC, 2006: 24)

Yet a legitimate alternative view would be that the worst performing schools are the last place to experiment with innovation; what they need is stability with well-tried, well-practised methods of teaching, and leadership. (Interestingly this in itself could be seen as refreshingly innovative in some schools.) The school improvement and effectiveness literature offers little evidence of preoccupation with innovation within the most effective schools. They are, certainly, open minded and continually seeking better ways of teaching, but that is not the same thing. A defining characteristic of many academies is the instability of their predecessor schools. The last chapter described problems with innovative designs in new buildings. Chapter 4 identified problems arising from a sponsor's premature introduction of an innovative form of organisation. On this evidence, innovation does not appear to have unlimited benefits. We explore innovation further in the following chapter. First, let us look at issues around independence, accountability and pressure.

Independence

Built on rock or shifting sand?

PWC (2008) identified eight key areas in which the independence of academies distinguishes them from LA schools:

- Academies are not open to the management and scrutiny of their local authority.
- While encouraged to collaborate with neighbouring schools, academies are not required to participate in strategic planning as part of their local authority provision for services for children and young people.
- While subject to employment law, academies have considerable flexibility in staff pay and conditions.
- Academies have different governance arrangements, which provide greater flexibility on the composition of the governing body of the academy.

- Financial accounting requirements differ.
- Academies have certain freedoms from the requirements of the national curriculum.
- Academies within the sample were set up as their own admissions authority; and
- Academies manage their own arrangements for exclusions (PWC, 2008: 66–67).

Individually, none of these provides any guarantee of raising standards. However, combined with an effective model of governance, a clear raison d'etre in raising standards and their greater freedom in use of human and financial resources, academies have an advantage.

The growing role of LAs in commissioning academies, with the consequent emphasis on academies as part of the local 'family of schools', led to some reduction in the level of independence in the second bullet point, and also in the last three. PWC (2008: 69) noted that the introduction of new governance structures, such as those for Trust Schools, had led to some modification of academies' independence in order to ensure coherence in performance and delivery, both locally and nationally. These changes certainly generated both anxiety and resentment in sponsors and principals from some of the earlier academies:

> What has upset (name of sponsor) is that he feels it was a very clear example of DfES officials wanting to clone academies, whereas he thought he had joined a group of leading lights that would be different and independent. (PWC, 2008: 83)

Yet the changes did not seem to have imposed significant restrictions on the sponsors and principals we interviewed, and it is not clear whether that was the government's intention. When we asked Andrew Adonis what pitfalls the academies movement would need to avoid in the future he replied:

> Compromising on the essentials of quality and independence. The moment we start setting them up as a LA school by another means, is the moment that academies will start to fail. They've got to continue to have ambitious and independent sponsors, who are given both the investment, but also the freedom, to manage schools and to be focussed relentlessly and single- mindedly on successful outcomes for students. The moment we start bureaucratising them, seeking to limit their independence, and restricting the capacity of independent

sponsors to manage them, is the moment the academy movement grinds to a halt. (Andrew Adonis)

At the time of the interview Adonis had already moved to the Department of Transport and was no longer involved in policy on academies. Some principals were certainly concerned that academies were being aligned more closely with LAs.

The vision and priorities of a successful academy principal were not unlike those of many head teachers in LA schools:

> Our vision is to provide exceptional opportunities for our students for personal and academic success in the community, delivered through four priorities: **culture for learning** – that's the stuff about students, kind, calm, purposeful school where everyone's valued and known; **resources for learning**, which is about being business like and fit for purpose in the way we use what we have got; **teaching for learning**, which is about the passionate commitment about staff wanting to lead students' desire to learn; and **leading for learning**, which is about being a confident self managing school where everyone is able to take responsibility for self and others. (Academy principal)

This principal was critical of recent DCSF policy on academies, seeing it as a potential threat to their independence. Nevertheless, the essential model of the sponsor and governing body acting as non-executive directors remained. The head of an independent school was adamant that his school was aiming 'to be the most innovative independent school in the country', and expected the academy that they were sponsoring to have the same aspiration. Yet he was equally adamant that appointing the principal was:

> ... by far the most important thing you do, and then it's just trimming it. I have neither the time, nor the will, nor the inclination to interfere. Supporting, encouraging, and being available to be consulted, certainly. (Head teacher of an independent school sponsoring an academy)

Similarly, a principal in a chain of academies quoted the sponsor as saying:

> Well I appointed you and I trust you to get on with it.

He insisted that the sponsor had never interfered with the running of the academy.

We can illustrate the importance of independence by looking at staffing. Every school has three aims in its staffing policy: to attract the best staff, to retain the best staff and to ease out the minority of teachers who do not meet the expected standards. Academies are no different. Where they may have an advantage is in sponsors who expect to take decisions quickly. A newly appointed principal explained:

> Expectations were extremely low, and people thought things were good which were barely satisfactory if not inadequate. But I did manage to catch hold of three or four members of staff and keep hold of them ... I had to make decisions about key posts quickly, and I did. I offered some people jobs that didn't even exist, I'd do anything to keep them ... whatever I did, the sponsor supported me. (Academy principal)

This principal had brought with her, again with the sponsor's support, two key staff. Both were invaluable in the early stages in a volatile climate. Yet even in a volatile climate, with staff who were not even meeting basic requirements, academies have to go through the usual legal processes. A sponsor explained:

> One of the huge frustrations is the amount of time it takes. We have just had a lengthy two day grievance hearing. It was an open and shut case (involving serious professional misconduct) ... in no way do I want to undermine people's rights. But it tends to be the rights of the majority to work in an effective organisation that get overlooked. (Sponsor)

Beliefs that academies are immune to the financial constraints that restrict other schools with respect to staff redundancies and dismissals are wrong. A long serving principal – which in academies in late 2008 when we did our field work meant at least four years and was unusual – explained the decisions that the governing body had made prior to his arrival.

> They grasped the nettle quickly and they threw a lot of money at the redundancies so that they did it without any turbulence. That's had financial consequences for the Trust since. (Academy principal)

This may have been necessary for the academy's development, but it was certainly not sufficient. Equally important, staff development had to take place from within. The same principal explained that 'we had to do an awful lot of growing our own teachers'. Elaborating he continued:

> The work on middle leadership development that we did in years 2, 3 and 4 of the academy took the form of joint work between senior and middle leadership, involving external coaching ... that led to a real

leap forward in leadership from the middle. Also, as staff have left (and we have a high turnover) on the whole we've replaced with better. (Academy principal)

As a measure of the academy's growing confidence and ability to sustain itself he described the situation when experienced and well respected, charismatic members of staff moved on:

> Each time we've lost one of those people we've thought: 'this is going to be difficult!' But actually it's not been difficult at all, because other people (who are) at least as assertive but in a less personality-based way have come up. Its not a breakthrough but in the four years I've been here we've seen the place grow up and seen people take ownership of their own school and recognition that what will make it a great school lies between their fingers. (Academy principal)

It is doubtful whether the same process of organic growth would have been possible if the academy's sponsors and trustees had not been willing to 'grasp the nettle' when things were going bad, by making redundancies. In a LA it would certainly have taken much longer, with the overwhelming temptation of consensual fudge instead of decisive action. Yet decisive action was only one side of the equation. The other was the leadership that stimulated professional development.

Independence has also encouraged academy principals to take risks. One initiative that academies have welcomed is Teach First (Hutchings *et al.*, 2006). As with academies themselves, a key figure was Andrew Adonis. Reflecting alarm at the lack of the best students from the top universities applying for PGCE courses, the scheme enabled them, literally, to teach first, for two years before deciding what to do with the rest of their lives. After a highly competitive selection process these new graduates, all with 2.1 or first class degrees from leading universities spent the summer preparing to teach in an academy or another school in an underprivileged area. Schools could apply to receive these graduates and if accepted would normally receive at least five. Thus the scheme differed from the conventional PCGE route in two crucial ways: first, the preliminary training required three months rather than a full year; second, a group of graduates were placed together in the same school, enabling them to learn from each other as well as from the senior staff mentoring them. Ofsted (2008b) noted that about 50% were planning a career in teaching.

As a way of attracting some of the highest achieving graduates of the year to work in the most challenging schools in some of the most disadvantaged parts of the country, Teach First has been a remarkable success. It has also changed the ideas of some principals and senior staff in academies about professional development, and specifically the case for rapid promotion:

> What we learn from Teach First is that the best people can take responsibility in Year 2, which went against my grain, because I'm a bit old. I thought you needed to learn the trade a bit more at each stage before you took the next stage. I have changed my view about that. I still think you have to be careful to make sure you let people walk before they run, but give them bits of running. (Academy principal)

At another academy one Teach First graduate in her third year of teaching had been promoted to the senior leadership team, and another was being head hunted by a neighbouring school. Rapid promotion has always been possible. In the 1970s, one of the authors worked with a 33-year-old head of a secondary school, appointed after only seven years teaching. If the brightest graduates are to be attracted to teaching, and to remain in the profession, they need to be placed in situations where a lot is demanded of them, and a lot of support is available both from experienced teachers and from their own peers, with opportunities for rapid promotion.

Partnership with the local family of schools

It is not clear how far the independence of academies is being eroded by the DCSF who have moved from seeing them as an essential part of the solution to the failure of LA bureaucracies to address under-performance, to seeing them as an essential part of the 'local family of schools'. Academies are explicitly expected to contribute to their local community and develop innovative links with local businesses. In addition they are expected to contribute to the government's proposals for reforms of 14–19 year education, in partnerships with LA schools and FE colleges.

These are all laudable aims, as desirable for academies as for LA schools. Partnership, though, requires academies to look outwards, and that requires at least a minimum level of internal stability. Given their origins, in many cases, in troubled predecessor schools, together with the open hostility of senior LA officers and other head teachers, it is unsurprising that some academies have taken longer to establish collaborative working relationships than the DCFS might have wished in its more idealistic, but less realistic moments. The principal of an academy that had recently received an impressively positive Ofsted report admitted:

> It's been difficult in the past because our communities have been so disparate . . . I would like to see over the next two to three years that

we work more closely with communities, and centre that around learning, so that the academy truly does become a learning community for families and the people we serve. (Academy principal)

One academy principal had raised £750,000 from local businesses. He had opened two engineering units, outside the academy, both underwritten by local companies, to encourage the sixth form in construction and motorcycle engineering. He saw this as playing an important part in reducing the number of leavers classified as not in employment, education or training (NEET). The year he went to the academy, the NEET figure was a high 9%. He had now reduced it to zero. He had also brought back seven boys who had previously been permanently excluded. He said he had failed with one, but the other six were:

all in the sixth form and are all models of the local society. And in fact they now mentor troublesome pupils down the school. (Academy principal)

Again, this could all have been possible in an LA school. Whether it could have been achieved in less than two years is more doubtful. In some academies collaboration with LA personnel had given rise to opportunities that had not been recognised in the LA schools.

Principal: I have LA personnel doing work in this academy, that they can't do in their own schools.
Interviewer: Why not?
Principal: Because their own schools block them.
Interviewer: Can you give me an example?
Principal: Well then, primary school liaison and transition projects is one area. Data transfer is another area – it just doesn't happen. We actually organise one of the local area partnerships. (Name) takes the minutes and I chair the meeting. Before that it was all over the place – no one did anything; there was no sense of purpose, no sense of organisation .... When I was a head teacher in (another LA) in the last week of August I would have a CD ROM with my entire intake and all their scores to add to my system. Here, I was still waiting in November, which is why this LA itself is in special measures. (Academy principal)

This excerpt makes two points. First, that no academy is necessary for effective primary – secondary data transfer; second, that this rather elementary requirement does not exist in some LAs, and that academies with their faster pace and sense of urgency can be a catalyst for making it happen. More often, the picture was of initiatives that need not necessarily have been difficult for a school to introduce, but might have been less likely to receive much encouragement in schools in some LAs. Two examples in one academy were the selection of up to 10% of students by aptitude for the academy's sports specialism and a 'stage not age' approach to progress throughout the curriculum, In fact these were related. The aptitude tests, had attracted talented athletes to the academy, and their presence provided a stimulus to the others that had come through the ordinary admissions process. Having an athlete in training, for example for the 2012 Olympic team, necessitated a flexible approach to the curriculum.

> These people need a lot of tailored support and help. If they are going to make it at sport, you have to let sport take precedence as you only get that one chance. And if you let them get off the academic track and the sport breaks down, they are stuck. So we have tried very hard not to do that … why should that be available at Millfield, and but not in the state system? (Academy principal)

The relevance of the 'stage not age' approach to the curriculum was that the academy had to think hard about how to personalise learning, so that pupils could choose courses suited to their needs, unconstrained by the their age groups. Thus pupils in year 10 and the sixth form were working together in some vocational areas. Starting with only five or six classes, this was considered a small but significant step to a more personalised curriculum.

Accountability

One of the criticisms levelled at academies from the anti-academies alliance, amongst others, is that academies are not accountable for what they do. Whatever one's perspective on academies, on any rational interpretation of the evidence this claim leaks like a sieve. The starting point must be to ask to whom any school – not just academies – should be accountable, for what they should be held accountable and how.

To whom?

We are not here discussing the accountability of staff to their academy's governing body, though that is important. We are concerned with the interests to which both staff and governors are accountable. Preoccupation with standards and league tables can lead to us overlooking the first level of accountability in any school or academy – to their students. Because children are not generally in a position to hold teachers accountable, it is conventional to regard schools as accountable to parents. This is the basis for the market-driven educational reforms we discussed in Chapter 2. Beyond parents, schools are accountable to their local community and to the government acting on behalf of the tax payer. For government not to accept ultimate responsibility for the quality of education in schools, including its responsiveness to changing conditions, would be negligent. It follows that government must hold schools and academies to account. In no group of schools has government scrutinised performance more closely than in academies.

For what?

As noted above, accountability to students implies an education that enhances the opportunities open to them: at the most superficial level, behaviour and attitudes conducive to learning, progress through the curriculum and evidence of improvement over time at school level. It also implies sensitivity to local conditions including, for example, commitment to students with SEN and cooperation in local responses to 14–19 education initiatives. Again, academies and LA schools are accountable for the same things.

How?

We have already noted one academy principal's view that Charities Commission and Company Law create much higher and more secure criteria for governance than applies to LA schools. The financial audit, certainly, is likely to be more robust. So is scrutiny of students' achievements in annual testing and public examinations, both by the local and national media, and by DCSF officials and ministers. The pre-registration process – equivalent to a full Ofsted inspection – is also as rigorous as the comparable process in LA schools. Similarly, student numbers are monitored locally and nationally at least as closely as in LA schools, including the enrolment of pupils receiving FSM, as a proxy for disadvantaged homes. Ofsted inspection, too, is as frequent as in LA schools. In one case it was carried out at parents' request and resulted in an academy being deemed to require 'special measures'.

Academies are not, of course, accountable to locally elected councillors, nor to members of the local educational establishment, such as LA education officers and inspectors, and other head teachers. It is hard to see why this should be a matter for concern. The rationale for academies was the failure or low achievement of their predecessor schools when they were part of the LA.

Pressure

Media

With academies, even the supposedly quality press sometimes find it hard to resist sensationalism. For example, under the heading:

> The kids were tricky . . . the teachers impossible,

The Sunday Times reported

> Peter Crook was a 'superhead' who could turnaround even the toughest of schools; until he took a job in one of the government's flagship academies.

Nor have reason or facts been allowed to stand in the way of a good story. Thus, two ULT academies achieved substantial improvement in one year, with good Ofsted reports. Yet when, for different and unrelated reasons their principals resigned, the *Daily Mail* wrote under the headline 'Academy system in crisis':

> Critics are blaming the departure of academy heads on school sponsors, claiming that Headteachers are being treated like football managers – under pressure to achieve instant results.

At its annual conference in April 2009, the National Union of Teachers (NUT) released details of a survey into the career prospects of teachers who opt to work in challenging schools. In schools in these circumstances there is a toxic mix of increased stress and workload. It talks of school leaders playing Russian roulette with their careers by opting to work in such schools. In a short piece for the National Council for School Leadership (NCSL) Macaulay (2008a, 2008b) looked at leadership with a focus on academy principals. Her interviews drew a general picture of negative media interest in academies and the consequent need for principals to be media aware and politically astute. Handling the DCSF, though, may be even more challenging.

Sponsors could, and did, say that principals were the experts on education and running a school – and expect them to get on with it. With the high political and media profile of the programme, there was never any chance of the DCSF doing likewise. HMI used to be known as 'the eyes and ears of the Department'. No longer. In academies the DCSF's involvement was much more direct. The *Academy Principals Handbook* (DCSF, undated) described the 'support and challenge' that principals must receive:

(1) *Project Lead*, their first point of contact within the DCSF.
(2) *DCSF Advisor* who will have worked with the academy from the project's inception. He/she provides 'support and challenge' to the principal designate and retains contact with the Project Lead and the principal once the academy opens.
(3) *The Project Management Company's educational adviser*; this person's level of involvement is determined by the principal (if appointed) in liaison with the DCSF.
(4) *The Specialist Schools Advisory Trust* (SSAT) provides up to 90 days bespoke format support in the year before the academy opens and in its first year, based on a 'needs analysis conversation' with the new principal. In addition the SSAT is commissioned by NCSL to broker 'practical leadership induction' and this has to be discussed at the needs analysis conversation and agreed with the DCSF.
(5) *A School Improvement Partner* (SIP) nominated by the DCSF provides 'the main challenge and support'. The SIP is an 'experienced' professional with a thorough understanding of school improvement in challenging contexts. Nearly all those working with academies have broad headship experience. They are accredited by National College for School Leadership (NCSL) and contracted to the DCSF (*Academy Principals Handbook*, undated). The SIP makes at least a termly visit to 'support, monitor and challenge the Academy' and to 'provide high quality support and challenge proportionate to each academy's growth and rate of progress' (Section 1). In addition, of course, they will have contact with the advisor and the project lead.

Academy principals need broad shoulders, combined with a high level of skill and patience to carry so many tiers of support, whilst at the same time under considerable pressure to make rapid improvements. And, a thick skin to withstand so much challenge, combined with exceptional resilience and exceptional clarity in the vision, policies and strategy they deem necessary for success.

Any idea of this plethora of supporters and challengers providing impartial guidance and advice is naïve. They have their own agendas based on their previous professional experience and, crucially, on current DfE priorities. The academies programme was sold to the public, from the start, as pioneering innovative forms of leadership, management and teaching and learning. Under intense pressure from a sceptical media, ministers felt that they had to provide examples of successful innovation. Inevitably, they must have looked to SIPs, advisors and project leads to provide it. These comments should not detract from the success of many SIPs in establishing constructive, helpful relationships with principals. The importance of SIPs providing high quality independent advice and guidance is not in dispute. The question is whether their institutional links with the DfE may sometimes get in the way of this laudable objective.

Conclusions

A politically high-profile programme involving the systematic replacement of under-performing schools in urban areas is bound to attract media interest. It is also certain to receive exceptionally close scrutiny from DfE officials and quasi-governmental bodies. It was therefore predictable that accountability should be as much a defining feature of academies as their independence from LAs. In theory, accountability should focus on outcomes, not on the processes whereby the outcomes are achieved. In practice, the political stakes were so high that SIPs, project leads and advisers were interested in anything and everything that went on in academies, and redoubled their interest at the first sign of failure to deliver rapid improvement.

A principal observed:

> Government was very keen in the beginning to spin every improvement in academies as amazing when it was far too early to tell. We need to be grown up about what we expect from this policy. (Academy principal)

The climate in which they operated must have been experienced as intrusive, and threatening, by some principals, particularly those who resigned or moved on when their academy failed to deliver the rapid improvements expected by their sponsor and DCSF officials. Yet for others, it was stimulating and invigorating. The evidence from our interviews was that 'the challenge and support' provided by outside bodies including the DfE, could too often play a part in destabilising an academy. It is not only necessary to be 'grown up' in what we expect from academies but also in the way that progress is monitored and their principals evaluated. A major challenge in the rapid expansion of the academies programme planned by the Conservative–Liberal Democrat coalition in 2010 will be to avoid the almost obsessive attempts at micro-management that characterised some of the previous government's scrutiny of academies. Yet this must not detract from the evidence of improvements that they have achieved in teaching and learning, to which we now turn.

Chapter 7

Distinctive Features of Academies: 2. Innovation

Introduction

In the beginning was innovation. The DCSF always saw innovation as a key driver of the academy programme's key objective of raising standards. Academies themselves being innovative, they were expected to be innovative in their governance, leadership and curriculum. Innovation was part of the landscape.

> Each term a representative of the DCSF would visit the academy's principal to give the academy a health check. Data was collected and analysed on attendance, behaviour, exclusions, progress towards exam targets, staff turnover and other general issues. The final section of the report that had to be completed was on innovation. The principal would report on new innovations and the progress of current ones. This information was duly passed on to the minister and secretary of state. (Academy principal)

For one DCSF representative the innovation section was the bit that principals disliked the most. Innovation was eventually played down as part of the termly DCSF visit, possibly following one principal's comment that the most innovative thing in the academy compared to the predecessor school was that the children were having lessons that had been planned.

PWC (2008) quote an academy principal as saying:

> We have got to get away from that nonsense of innovation. Innovation might just mean having lesson plans! (PWC, 2008: 174)

Nevertheless, their own questionnaire found, albeit with a low response rate, that the curriculum was more flexible and innovative than in other schools. Yet it is doubtful whether any academies have done anything to enhance pupils' learning that could not in principle have been done in LA schools. It is equally doubtful whether the development of so many academies, and what a number have achieved, would have been possible without the expectation of rapid change and development that the programme generated. The independence of the earlier academies included independence from requirements of the national curriculum. That was later modified to require all new academies to follow the national curriculum in English, Maths, Science and ICT. In practice almost all academies were already following the national curriculum in these subjects. More importantly, although academies had the freedom to diverge from the national curriculum programmes of study, they still had to convince Ofsted that they were offering a broad and balanced curriculum. Moreover, every Ofsted report on an academy was scrutinised in minute detail by the DCSF, SIPs, advisors and even ministers, as well as by the press. We even heard of the Prime Minister phoning a principal to congratulate him on an Ofsted report. That could act either as a powerful constraint on innovation, or as a stimulus to it.

The context

It is not an argument against inspection and accountability to say that in all schools an Ofsted inspection creates disruption and anxiety. In an academy the anxiety is compounded by pressure from the sponsor, DfE and, of course, the media. A chair of governors admitted:

> I hadn't appreciated the stress and strain that the Ofsted inspections and the prospect of Ofsted inspection place on a school. It goes into a different mode. And then we got into this cycle of having one every year, because we effectively had a Notice to Improve. It becomes all consuming and it stops you developing as you have certain tasks to do and achieve ... we then managed to get ourselves past it and that has given us a breathing space to do some housework and get some things sorted out. Quite interesting! (Chair of academy governors)

The more general point coming out of this quote is that narrow objectives can all too easily becomes ends in themselves rather than a means to an end. In the grip of Ofsted, limited objectives are all consuming, and can obscure the broader aims that may be more fundamental to an academy's progress. Yet the principal of another academy identified Ofsted as one of four reforms that had changed schooling profoundly for the better. The other three were the national curriculum, league tables and local management of schools.

Referring to the government's National Challenge (DCSF, 2008b), identifying 673 schools as in need on improvements for failing to meet a benchmark target of 30% of pupils obtaining at least five GCSE passes at A*–C, the sponsor's representative at one academy was relaxed:

> We were 1% below the threshold, which I was delighted about. (Name) from the DCFS less so as he had to go to the Minister and explain that we hadn't hit the floor target. But as I said to him; 'look, it means that we will get the funding, to get us up the 1% we need'. I would rather have 29% than 35%. (Sponsor's representative)

A new principal described a different reaction to the national challenge announcement:

> Lots of political pressure . . . not from the sponsor, from the DCSF. The week of the announcement . . . was the worst week of my life. (Academy principal)

This, presumably, is the 'support and challenge' that SIPs, advisors, and project leads provide. Yet this principal already knew what the problem was – a weak Maths department – and had already taken steps to address it. We hoped that the pressure of national challenge would not affect the other things he was doing, since they were even more fundamental to changing the culture of low aspirations in the predecessor school.

The Mantra of Innovation: Snakeoil, Muddled Distraction – or Necessity?

Academies were not the first initiative in which government encouraged innovation. In their exploration of the impact of innovation in Education Action Zones (EAZ) in London, Halpin *et al.* (2004) argued that they had little impact in raising overall standards. As in the earliest academies, curriculum initiatives included the possibility of disapplication from the requirements of the national curriculum. The problem appeared to be a narrow managerial focus on measurable outcomes such as attendance and examination results. Sustainable improvement in teaching and learning requires more than a narrow focus on examination results. It seems that there was a failure to appreciate the complexity of change.

The Little Oxford Dictionary defines innovation as 'bringing in novelties; making changes'. In education innovation has been described by David Hargreaves (2003) as 'the capacity to re-think existing models of learning, teaching and assessment in ways which create new value for learners'. Because they replaced troubled schools, academies could not succeed without making changes. In some situations, lesson plans were indeed an innovation. Yet in launching an expensive and high-profile programme Secretary of State David Blunkett could hardly announce that the new academies would have lesson plans, nor even that students would start to behave better. Nor could he credibly announce the programme without asserting that academies would do things that existing schools were not doing. It was therefore perhaps inevitable that a realistic expectation of innovations, or changes, in a failing or under-achieving school would elide into a much less realistic expectation of changes with implications for the system as a whole.

It was never logical to think that the changes needed to turn round a failing school would necessarily have wider implications. Under attack from the media and their own backbenchers, the Labour government's ministers and their civil servants were hungry for evidence of success. From seeing transformation in a previously failing school's fortunes, it was a short step to convincing themselves that academies would become pioneers of innovation, extending far beyond lesson plans.

Innovation is an abstract noun. When an abstract noun becomes a mantra, rational thought seldom survives. That is a pity for two reasons. First, it diverts attention from the very real possibility that poorly planned innovation might further destabilise an already unstable situation. Snakeoil, like a placebo in medicine, has no active therapeutic ingredient beyond a belief that it works. Yet ethically, the first responsibility of anyone planning something new is not to demonstrate its value, but to show that it is not harmful. Second, it diverts attention from the equally real possibility that some features of academies may indeed facilitate innovations that could be of value to other schools. And when that happens, the relevant features of academies may be as important as the innovations per se.

Confusion or clarity?

The government saw the independence of academies as facilitating innovation. Two tensions were inherent in this view, though never acknowledged. First, the pressure that the DCSF placed on academies to demonstrate innovation always sat uncomfortably alongside their supposed independence. If academies were really independent, they would neither feel nor be under any obligation to bow to pressure from the DCSF. Some principals were strong enough and skilled enough to resist this pressure, but others were not. Second, even if academies' independence did facilitate innovation, other aspects of the programme arguably did not. In the last chapter we discussed the accountability climate in which academies operate. Faced with intense scrutiny from the DCSF as well as from an often hostile media, it could be tempting to 'play safe', sticking to tried and tested approaches.

In introducing innovation schools face a number of barriers which may be less present in academies. Barriers to innovation have been variously identified (Fullan, 1993; Ofsted, 2008a; Sannino & Nocon, 2008; Silver *et al.*, 1997; Somekh, 2005; Zinkeviciene, 2005). For Ofsted (2008a) there were seven potential barriers to innovation.

- Senior managers had to have a realistic understanding of how far and how fast they could innovate, requiring them to have an understanding of their staff's willingness to participate and the impact of the innovation.
- Managing staff turnover to ensure the momentum of the innovation.
- Managing the anxiety that change brought about.
- A feeling that innovation would only make things worse – results, behaviour, and so on.
- Changes would be too expensive to maintain.
- Fear of external inspection and how Ofsted would view innovative changes.
- Sustaining rigorous and consistent focus and evaluation.

Innovation can mean major shifts in thinking for all involved in the process – staff, students and their families. These stakeholders need to be receptive to the change proposed and it needs to be managed carefully. They need to be motivated to accept the innovation and/or to be innovative themselves, otherwise the well entrenched teaching traditions within the school can sideline the innovation or cause it to stagnate. The culture of the school mediates between the innovation and environment in which it is to be operationalised (Smith *et al.*, 2008; Woolner *et al.*, 2007).

Like Ofsted's checklist, Smith *et al.* (2008) and Woolner *et al.* (2007) fail to address adequately three crucial points:

(1) *The origin of the innovation.* While the selection is doubtless contentious, the largest scale innovations in Britain since 1950 have been: (1) changes in primary school pedagogy and methodology following the Plowden Report (CACE, 1967); (2) comprehensive schools; (3) the national curriculum; (4) a new accountability climate, characterised by changes in testing, examinations and inspection. All but the first of these were imposed on a generally reluctant profession. All became contentious, and key features of academies, such as sponsors and independence from the LA, were also imposed on a generally reluctant

profession. They were also national, system-wide innovations. In demanding a list of innovations from within each academy, or risking the wrath of ministers, DCSF officials and SIPs were looking for 'home grown' innovation with a direct influence on behaviour, teaching and learning. By being at the same time more open ended than externally imposed innovation – 'tell us about anything new that works, anything' – and more narrowly defined – 'but it must improve standards' – this placed unprecedented pressure on some principals.

(2) *The school context.* In a well established school with high standards, resistance to innovation may appear legitimate: if it ain't broke don't fix it! Yet some long-established and successful schools get 'stuck' and resistant to change, or even to rigorous evaluation. In others an iterative process of review leads to constant exploration of ways to improve current practice. Academies are predicated on an assumption of improvement, and hence change. We might therefore expect them to be receptive to change and innovation. That, however, is an over-simplification of the process of changing the culture in a troubled school. The greater the need for change, based on evidence on behaviour and standards, the greater the resistance is likely to be. Earlier, we quoted an academy principal referring to the refusal to accept evidence, and hence responsibility, in a failing school. The most immediate and most demanding task for principals is to change that culture. That said, the fact of setting up an academy with an explicit requirement of rapid improvement helps to create an expectation of change. Perhaps the most favourable context is a new academy, starting only with an intake at Year seven, and growing in size each year thereafter.

(3) *Sustainability.* Whatever its short-term impact, no innovation is likely to have a sustainable impact unless it becomes internalised as part of teachers' day-to-day thinking and classroom practice. That will only happen if teachers recognise that it has helped to make their work more interesting and/or rewarding, without adding significantly to their work load. Even more than in LA schools, teachers in academies already work long hours and feel under pressure. They will try something new, particularly if they think it may help students' progress. But sustainability will depend on it making a positive difference to their working lives.

The implication of our argument is that the culture of the organization mediates the success of the innovation; impacting upon the capacity of the managers to manage, leaders to lead, staff to acquire the necessary knowledge, students and families to respond favourably and supportively and, ultimately, the innovation to bear fruit. Academies offer an opportunity for seeing innovation as a systematic process rather than one-off projects. This may explain why it is possible for a lot of the activity that takes place in academies to happen in LA schools, but it is more fundamental to the culture of academies where the focus on raising standards is key and there are likely to be fewer traditions to contend with. Academies are less burdened with the culture of the past and often have new key personnel; the organisation is established to enable a social infrastructure to be developed, which will support innovation. However, just because all the elements are in place does not mean that innovations will succeed. At the end of this chapter is one case study of innovation in an academy, which was not a success.

Examples of Innovation: 1. Behaviour and Attendance

PWC (2007) in their fourth annual report on academies note, not unreasonably, the importance of systems to track, monitor and reward good behaviour. They also note the need for 'a wide range of structures' and support for pupils with very challenging behaviour. They concluded that:

> Academies generally recognise that this will only be achieved through partnerships with their local authority and their local family of schools. (PWC, 2007: 68)

This was not our impression. One principal had interviewed the education welfare service in four LA areas about providing services to the academy because he was unhappy about the service provided by his own LA. In relation to more general improvement of behaviour LA services were seldom, if ever, mentioned.

Attendance

Low attendance had been a problem in many predecessor schools. One academy linked improvements in attendance to its specialism in business. The four 'business communities' that he had set up, equivalent to house systems in some schools, were used to encourage good attendance:

> So, for instance, we have attendance leagues which are on football lines; Premiership, Division 1, Division 2. We give points each day for attending but the pupil MD's and the Boards summon pupils who are not generating points for good punctuality and attendance ... so the business and enterprise themes are running through, because who is going to employ someone who doesn't attend?

This principal prided himself on excluding few pupils. In his previous post as head of LA schools in a depressed inner city area he had raised attendance from 71% to between 92% and 93%.

Behaviour

The recently appointed principal of an academy was determined to change a culture of low aspirations. The predecessor school had been a comprehensive that had been described as 'sinking fast' but although the pupils came from 'quite a tricky, poor, deprived area' this did not explain their behaviour:

> When I came here someone said to me: 'you can't line these kids up, and you can't have an assembly for year 10, they won't keep quiet'. There were all these low expectations, so what I said was 'of course you can! We are going to do it and let's see if it works'. And everything we did worked! We had assemblies, not a peep, not a sound! And they said: 'It's never been that quiet before!' I said, 'well, that's because I'm expecting them to be quiet' .... In my first week here I was taking so many risks and, I thought: 'Any minute I am going to fall flat on my face and it's not going to work'. It was just a real culture of low expectations. (Academy principal)

The principal of a different academy developed this theme. High expectations were only realistic when children felt a sense of security. Noting that many pupils were acting as carers for parents or siblings with disabilities, she continued:

> For many of our children the academy is their sense of security ... the bit that we needed to strengthen was their sense of belonging ... so if some aspect of their uniform is not correct, we'll correct it and I'll say 'now you look like you belong here'. When we are talking about behaviour, we will say: 'that doesn't belong here; you belong here when you behave'.

This academy too, prides itself on a few permanent exclusions.

The academy mentioned earlier that had set up business communities created a sense of belonging by involving pupils in giving feedback on lessons, described in more detail later. This had largely resolved behaviour problems:

> When last year's Year 11 were saying seventeen boys were disrupting learning we targeted the seventeen boys and we sorted it.

This also could be helpful in meetings with parents. When a parent complained about her son being victimised by teachers:

> I said, well, actually here's what the pupils are saying about your son. Here are thirty accounts of why your son is disrupting their learning, all written and signed. She said: 'well, you've encouraged them to do this!' I said: 'actually, no. Do you want me to get some of these pupils in and they can tell you?'.... Suffice to say we have not had any more trouble. The pupils saying that they are disrupted from learning is more powerful than any teacher saying it. (Academy principal)

The principal of an academy in an industrial but geographically rather isolated area explained:

> We have got four what we call business communities; you would know them as the old house system, but they are all businesses independently run by the pupils and the pupil board and they are all mentored by business people on business principles. This week, National Enterprise Week, we have probably 30 business people in the academy. (Academy principal)

Rather than seeing vandalism as a problem, the same principal used the business communities to create an opportunity for pupils to learn about its costs:

> I gave the vandalism budget, which was £78,000, originally, to the business communities, and said 'right, every item of vandalism comes out of your money'. Guess what happened: vandalism wiped! Even picking up litter – if I have to pay someone to pick up litter, then that comes out of that budget. So the litter's put in the bin. That is how a business would do it, so that is how we do it.

Talking about his priorities over the next two to three years, another principal cited *'remaining a highly student centred school that belongs to the students'* with an 'absolute consistency of expectations'. He continued:

> The shift we have been trying to make in the pastoral system was to get away from a focus on behaviour that we don't want to the behaviour that we do want .... What's really pleasing is that our new sanction and praise system is still recording 3:1 praise to sanctions, although better for the girls than the boys... that came out of our senior to middle leadership work. We have become much closer to becoming a solution-focussed school. So staff now much less frequently identify a problem without first coming up with a solution, and that gives me great satisfaction. (Academy principal)

The interesting thing about this quotation is not the relatively conventional approach to developing positive behaviour, nor even the systematic monitoring and recording of praise and sanctions, though that is too often overlooked. The important point for the academy and its long-term future was that staff at middle and senior management levels were developing a habit of looking for solutions. When the same principal described characteristics of a badly failing school (Chapter 2) he was describing the antithesis of a learning, solution focused organisation. Too often, behaviour problems are accepted as an inevitable drain on energy and morale. The examples in this section have shown that they are not inevitable. More important, creating a more pro-social, positive environment, can lead to initiatives with much wider implications than the problems they solve, helping to create a problem in which learning is the norm.

Inclusion and values

Only two principals mentioned their sponsor's values without a prompt:

That's the thing they put into this academy: its inclusivity.

This principal had rejected a post at another academy because he was not so comfortable with the sponsor's values. The other principal described her sponsor as making the important link with between service to the community and opportunities for students:

He's very highly committed to having an academy that serves the needs of this community. He would see that – and so do I – as ensuring that they have achieved outcomes that give them choices ... so they can do whatever they want ... it's my job to ensure that they get that – those choices and opportunities. And that's his bottom line. (Academy principal)

This meant that neither sponsor nor principal wanted to change the academy's catchment area. The principal pointed out that the deprivation indicators, such as FSM, had shown a small increase and the proportion of students from minority ethnic groups had increased to nearly 62%.

These people had been loyal to the academy and predecessor school and therefore I would want to keep the catchment area as it is.

On the other hand, there would be no bias against those parents who had previously opted out by sending their children to other schools or to the independent sector.

Exclusions

Academies have been consistently reported as having more permanent exclusions than LA schools (House of Commons Committee of Public Accounts, 2007; National Audit Office, 2007; PWC, 2008). This is important for three reasons. First, permanent exclusions increase the chances of some pupils sinking into the criminal justice system, with all the long-term costs and waste of human potential that implies. Second, it places additional pressures on LA resources for children with seriously challenging behaviour. Third, it undermines the credibility of academies. It leaves them open to a charge that their faster rate of improvement compared with LA schools is achieved by rejecting the most difficult pupils. It is important, though, to recognise the wide variation in exclusion rates between academies. PWC (2008) notes that 12 of the 24 academes in their evaluation, excluded three pupils or fewer (and six excluded none). In contrast, eight excluded five or more, two excluded 13 pupils permanently, one excluded 17 and one excluded 20. All six academies that we visited were in the lower exclusion range. One principal admitted to having temporarily excluded 25 students shortly after arriving. The purpose of this was to see their parents, with two objectives in mind: first, to make sure parents knew exactly what their children had been doing in the academy; second, for parents to start a new relationship with the academy.

Another principal, though, was adamant that he would not resort to exclusion, ether permanently or fixed term. He saw it as inconsistent with his sponsor's and his own commitment to inclusion. He felt he had many other options. One was the explicit involvement of pupils in providing feedback on all aspects of the school. A second was the business communities described earlier. A third was an engineering unit set up off site with support from local companies. The engineering unit had enabled him to admit seven pupils excluded before his arrival, six of whom were still there and now making a useful contribution to the academy.

Pupils' voice

Inclusion never exists in a vacuum. It involves relationships. The same principal took the idea of mutual respect between staff and pupils a step further. The predecessor school had formally been a grammar school. He felt it had retained the traditionalist grammar school curriculum and pedagogy and this explained why it was failing its pupils (and had been placed in special measures by Ofsted). Changing this required a cultural shift of emphasis towards greater respect for pupils and, following from that, students started taking more responsibility for everything that happened in the academy, including more involvement in their own learning. This is what lay behind his delegation of the vandalism budget to the students, and the business communities. In addition he enlisted students in selection of staff:

> In every interview we have had, including my own, we have always had two pupil panels. The pupils interviewed the staff, and no member of staff got a job without teaching a class. And the pupils had to approve the lesson.(Academy principal)

If applicants did not like his approach then they did not work in that academy, because it was consistent with how the academy ran on a daily basis:

> In normal lessons, leader–learners/leader–students feed back to the teachers how they are learning. It's nothing to do with me – as good clients they just feed back to the teachers about what's going on in the classrooms in lots of different ways, from behaviour to achievements and learning at home.

And, as we saw earlier, this feedback could be used in meetings with parents, for example, when addressing behaviour problems.

Religion

Two academies we visited were sponsored by Christian faith groups and a third had taken over a Church of England predecessor school. Both were explicit about including pupils of all religions or none. One sponsor had required the design for the new building to include a faith room. When asked whether the faith room was multi faith, an architect from the firm who designed the building read from the design brief:

> While the ethos is rooted in the Christian faith, the beliefs and practices of all faiths will be valued and respected.

However, the design brief also defined Christian beliefs as 'the core principles of the academy in its entirety and the basis of its ethos which will guide and inform decision making policy'. The principal described the faith room as:

> Like a small chapel holding 20 or 30 pupils ... It was meant as a quiet contemplation space and as that it works – it's a lovely space ... the Muslim staff use it for prayers, and sixth formers. Some of the little

ones use it for prayers during the week, but it's not used by any other groups.

This principal had invited local vicars to take prayers for the 10–15% of children who were practising Christians. It led to a rather sad exchange in the interview:

Principal: I invited them in, in the same way that the local Imams come and lead prayers for the Muslim staff and pupils and they just won't do it ... they came and they drank my tea and ate my biscuits, very smiley ... and then just disappeared into oblivion.

Interviewer: Was that because they were on the Evangelical wing of the Church of England and saw their role as gathering in a flock rather than going out into the community?

Principal: They're scared of kids! They don't want to get in amongst them. The trouble with children is that children have views. There's an element of Islam that doesn't allow children to have views. But funnily enough, there's also an interesting conversation about democracy in Islam ... the Imams are quite happy to deal with the kids' views, whereas with the vicars around here, if you challenge their views they run away, they just won't deal with it.

The last two quotes raise two interesting points about the role of faith sponsors and the challenges facing them. First, although this academy's sponsor insisted that its ethos was rooted in the Christian faith, the reality was that Muslim students appeared to be more likely to practise and develop their faith within the academy than Christians. It would probably be true to say that this reflected religious observance outside the academy, but a more important point is that the local imams responded more constructively to the academy's ethos, and the welcome it offered them, than the local vicars. Second, while the ethos of this academy may well have been rooted in the sponsor's Christian faith we could see no evidence that it was distinctively Christian. Two of the three Pauline virtues of faith, hope and love could be defended by atheists as strongly as by people of any faith. And the first, by definition, is specific to no single set of beliefs. Another principal said:

> The number one thing I had to bring from the sponsor was that Christian commitment to believing in people, getting relationships with people right. I put all my energies into making sure this was a relationship establishment, from the youngest Year 7 right up to myself.

Yet this, too, can be seen as a commitment to inclusive education as much as to Christian education. As far as we could tell, the motivation of sponsors and principals was not to proselytise but to ensure that everyone – staff and students – felt safe, respected and able to contribute to the life and work of the academy. The same, of course, could be said of many LA schools.

Tutoring for learning

If our research had taken place in the 1970s or 1980s, every principal would have talked about pastoral care. There were few direct references to this once ubiquitous term, probably because there have been significant advances in the relationship between pastoral care, the curriculum and behaviour. To understand these advances it is worth referring briefly to two earlier controversies on the nature and scope of pastoral care. The first concerns the role of form tutors vis-à-vis heads of year. A large body of literature argued for the importance of form tutors, with the task of heads of year being to lead a group of form tutors. The rationale was simply that if every pupil in a secondary school was to be known well by a least one teacher, it probably had to be the form tutor. They were the only people who saw their tutor group of 25–30 pupils every day and could reasonably be expected to follow their progress across the curriculum. Galloway (1983) showed that all 14 head teachers in studies in Sheffield and New Zealand agreed about the importance of form tutors but the structures in place in a majority of schools made it difficult or impossible for them to play a useful part in pastoral care. For example, they only saw their tutor group for 10 min each day for registration, they did not teach them, and they were expected invariably to refer problems upwards to heads of year or heads of department.

The second controversy of the 1970s and 1980s concerns the focus of pastoral care. It has been likened to the labour of Sisyphus, who in Greek mythology was punished for his sins in this world by being made to push a heavy boulder to the top of a hill, watch it roll down, roll it up again, and so on for the rest of eternity. The similarity to pastoral care was that as soon as a teacher had investigated and acted on one intransigent but terrible problem in a child's home background, another would appear. Hence, the debate centred on how to move the focus of pastoral care from preoccupation with home background to learning in school. The logic was that success and self respect at school could to some extent mitigate the impact of adverse circumstances at home, while negative experiences at school could aggravate their impact.

So how have these debates moved on? The second is no longer contentious. Every school now has a senior teacher with a child protection responsibility, but there is no longer any doubt that the overriding priority is to extend the opportunities open to every pupil by maximising their progress in the curriculum. That is not to say that all schools have effective structures in place that ensure that no pupil is overlooked, nor that all pupils with problems receive attention and support, whether arising from the home or from bullying in school. As we saw in Chapter 4, when discussing problems arising from introduction of a small school model in an already troubled school, pupils could feel uncared for:

> This model, which sounds so pastorally caring, actually had far too many layers in it. Pupils had an advisor who delivered a PSHE program once a week for twenty minutes ... then the small school, which actually had no more than a year group, had a student leader who was a member of staff, a director of learning and a head of small school. So the kids didn't know who was in charge. (Academy principal)

The principal's solution was to upgrade the job of advisor, giving them responsibilities for monitoring pupils' progress across the curriculum. In addition, heads of years were reinstated, with a brief to focus on achievement rather than behaviour. She told the advisors that their groups would be a reflection on them, while simultaneously giving their role status and ensuring 'there was an individual that every child felt was theirs'.

Another principal was sceptical about attaching too much importance to the role of form tutors. He felt that imposing a form tutor on a troubled child or vice versa never worked. It was much better to allow the child to choose a staff member to whom they could relate. A problem arose only when too many children chose the same person. At another academy the principal shared this view but was worried about:

> a group of students that I call 'the invisibles' who sit quietly, who don't raise their hands very much, but, sadly, can go through their entire school year and no one has really engaged with them and no one has really spoken with them. (Academy principal)

This principal's response was to introduce a 'tutoring for learning' initiative:

> Students meet with a tutor once a week, and there are only three other students with them. The tutoring process is not about; 'are you in the right uniform?, have you got your diary?'. That takes place in

registration. The tutoring process is totally focussed on learning – about a learning conversation ... it's about thinking skills and learning skills ... it's definitely not target orientated. It's focussed on getting the students to express their understanding of their learning and the barriers they are facing in their learning, whatever they are, and how to get round them.

The academy had done a lot of work to give tutors the skills to hold these 'learning conversations'. Students were reporting that they enjoyed the personal time, and teachers, too, were enthusiastic about it, valuing the opportunity of getting to know the pupils better, and using the time to discuss their learning with them. An external review team had also given a very positive report.

The explicit decision not to focus tutoring for learning on targets reveals a healthy confidence that this academy had moved beyond a narrow preoccupation with examination results, without in any way ignoring their importance. Indeed, earlier in the interview, the principal had emphasised their importance for her, and for the sponsor, in extending the opportunities available to students. Tutoring for learning was expected to improve students' learning but it was also expected to improve relationships.

In another academy it was felt appropriate to focus on targets. Each Monday, four or five students in a tutor group had one to one sessions with their 'learning advisors':

That's a change we made in September, putting in a regular slot of academic tutoring, working on the student's targets, looking at the outcomes, looking at their records. We have been writing a new reporting system for rewards and sanctions, so that learning advisors have easier access to how much praise or telling off their tutees have had when they see them at the end of each day.

On this evidence, pastoral care is unambiguously about success in the curriculum. That, of course, could apply equally to LA schools. Our point here is simply that academies can provide a favourable climate for 'homegrown' innovation.

Examples of Innovation: 2. Curriculum

National Challenge (DCSF, 2008b) focused principals' and sponsors' attention starkly on the 'basics' of English and Maths. Previously it had been possible to mask low A–C pass rates in these areas with steadily increasing percentages of students gaining five GCSE passes by including

GNVQ, which can count as four. In an academy in which 53% of pupils obtained five passes in English, but only 23% in Maths, only 17% gained passes in both subjects. The principal remarked wryly that publication of National Challenge had given him the worst week of his life, but he had already recognised the need 'to pay the money' to recruit a stronger Maths team. Whatever else the academy did, the benchmark of 30% A–C GCSE passes of English and Maths would take precedence. This is the context in which we discuss distinctive features in the curriculum.

Curriculum choice

Within these constraints, the academies' approach to the curriculum was shaped by what they saw as their mission and core values. Thus, in the academy in which sponsor and principal had both emphasised the overwhelming importance of extending the opportunities on offer to young people – which, of course, meant they had to achieve the necessary public examination passes – the principal's response to a question about the curriculum was immediate:

> Oh, the breadth, we have an extraordinarily broad curriculum. It gives our students real choices. When we set up the curriculum the one thing we did not want was a two or even three tier curriculum in which we made a decision what pathway students took on our per- ceived ideas of what students could achieve. Now, they choose for themselves, ... so GCSE is fully open. So if a child wants to choose hairdressing they can choose hairdressing. The only discussion that takes place after that is 'well what are you going to do with it?' And then after GCSE if they want to do it as a post 16 course they can. Similarly with construction and engineering ... we look at their current attainment levels and might suggest that it may be a difficult subject for them, but if they want to do it, they do it. (Academy principal)

A quick win

The above excerpt illustrates confidence in the curriculum and in the pupils, at a well-established academy in which standards had been rising steadily. That confidence had not had time to develop in an academy in which the incoming principal had encountered open hostility from the LA, the staff of the predecessor school and the parents. He decided that a 'quick win' was needed to convince the children and the families that they could do something they believed was almost impossible. So he decided to go for Year nine students gaining a GCSE pass in one year:

> We had a great music and drama department and a very good art department ... I just analysed the results and thought they would come on board. And they were ready to be released ... I got them together and said: 'this is what I want you to do'. And it was music to their ears as they suddenly realised that they were being valued for what they could do. (Academy principal)

14–19 Agenda

Sixth form provision in some early academies attracted strong criticism from Ofsted. In one case an eminent educationalist on a project management company persuaded a sponsor, who had no background in education that the International Baccalaureate (IB) should be offered. The IB is widely recognised as an excellent alternative to 'A' level, and has the added value of catering to a wide ability range. However, it is expensive to teach and requires a level of independent learning skills that were never realistic in this particular academy with its predecessor school's low aspirations and achievements. The result was an entirely predicable disaster, and was abandoned in a blaze of bad publicity when Ofsted rated the sixth form inadequate. This was yet another example of turbulence arising from advice from experts approved by the DCSF, though perhaps not formally appointed by them.

The government's 14–19 agenda (DfES, 2005) has had two consequences for academies. First, it has concentrated attention on what can realistically be offered at this level. Second, it had provided strong incentive to work more closely with LAs. One principal explained:

> The way it has been set up you cannot operate independently. I have to work with the local authority or local authorities. (Academy principal)

But this principal was also clear that she was not restricted to just one LA: she could negotiate with other LAs if attempts to develop a constructive working relationship with the authority of her predecessor school were to fail. Another principal had reservations about the number of proposed diplomas, but realised that if all 14 were to be made available there would have to be partnerships with numerous schools and colleges to facilitate exchange of students. Nevertheless:

> But of course, if the majority of your children are likely to want access to four or five of the diplomas, and you are willing radically to mix the ages, it's much more possible for one school to offer that range itself.

Because you will then be getting the numbers through pupils doing it as appropriate and as ready rather than trying to do it all in one locked step across a range of institutions. (Academy principal)

The mixing of traditional age divisions had previously been mentioned as one way of creating greater curriculum flexibility for elite athletes who needed to concentrate on their sports specialisms at centres away from the school without damaging their academic progress.

A Short Case Study on the Perils of Innovation

The DCFS expectation that academies would develop innovative models of teaching and learning could be liberating. Without doubt it makes a lot of academies stimulating places in which to work. But it could also create turbulence.

We visited an academy in which a contract for a new building had encountered substantial delays. As a result, the staff and students had had to spend much longer than expected in old, substandard and over crowded accommodation. In itself this would have been dispiriting for staff and students expecting to move to an impressive new building. The principal had been appointed from another school. There was every expectation that she would do as well in the academy. Sadly that did not happen and after less than two years the sponsor decided that a change in leadership was needed. What went wrong?

The incoming principal bought into the DCSF pressure to innovate. As noted already, any idea of the plethora of supporters and challengers listed in the last chapter providing impartial guidance and advice is naive. They had their own agendas based on their previous professional experience and, crucially, on current DCSF priorities. The academies programme was sold to the public, from the start, as pioneering innovative forms of leadership, management, and teaching and learning. Under intense pressure from a sceptical media, ministers felt that they had to provide examples of successful innovation. Inevitably, they must have looked to SIPs, advisors and project leads to provide examples, and in turn these people looked to principals.

At the academy we are discussing, the situation was compounded by the creation of a large new management structure, which did not have clear line management responsibilities and had inexperienced people in key places. The sponsor and principal, though, necessarily relied on advice from educationalists in the DCSF and the project management company. The management team was large, and was doubtless intended to ensure strong leadership. Unfortunately the structure did not include subject leaders, or heads of year who might have led a pastoral and guidance team. That was presumably due to the original commitment to the home base, or small school model. As a result a largely inexperienced staff lacked leadership in the subject specialism on which their sense of professional identity depended. Worse, the pupils realised that no teacher had specific responsibility for them as individuals.

Thus, the incoming principal operated in a lethal combination: Insistent pressure from powerful DCSF personnel to demonstrate innovation, and a management structure that provided security neither to staff nor to students. The principal also put in place a new curriculum which was largely being written as the year of its operation progressed. The situation on the first day of the opening of the academy was that the students and staff did not know each other and the staff did not know what they were to be teaching. Furthermore, there was no effective timetable and everyone was working in a building they had never been in – with no ICT and no telephones. Unsurprisingly, the academy went into a spiral of deteriorating behaviour and educational progress. Within two years the principal had been replaced. One of the key factors that influences the success or otherwise of innovations is leadership and management's capacity to know what to do, and when and how far to push.

The incoming principal's solution was instructive. He restructured the management team, with the departure of all members apart from two deputy principals, and created a management structure that had lines of responsibility and recognisable post holders. Promising members of the existing staff were appointed to senior and middle leadership roles. He halted all innovative curriculum development and began the planning for the curriculum innovations to start the following year. The new slimmed down leadership team provided very explicit leadership and guidance to these middle management staff. He made clear to the sponsor and to the DCSF that he would not accept interference. And on the glass partition of his office, facing outwards for all to see, including the SIP and visitors from the DCSF, he put a notice saying 'Retrovation'! Innovation, in other words, was banned until stability and security had been restored.

In the summer before the new principal's appointment 25% of pupils obtained five GCSE passes at A*–C. In the summer of his third term, the figure was 70% with 42% passing English and Maths, comfortably above the National Challenge benchmark. It seems likely that a key feature in achieving this change was the opportunity that it gave a young, enthusiastic middle management team. Freed from the pressure to innovate, they could concentrate on what they had been trained for: classroom teaching.

Five questions arise from this short case history of innovation that led to turbulence:

(1) *Would the dramatic improvements in examination results be sustainable?* At the time of writing it is too early to say. However, it is possible that one of the most important outcomes of the academies programme may be a better understanding of the process of school improvement in schools in challenging circumstances.

(2) *How do sponsors and principals make educational decisions?* Some chains have their own philosophy and preferred methods. In some of the academies that we have been describing, the sponsors or trustees put the management team in place before the first principal had arrived. Sponsors who do not have an educational background inevitably rely on advice and guidance when putting systems in place. It is fairly clear that as well as providing 'support and challenge' to the principal, SIPs, advisors and project leads also provide information and guidance to sponsors. However, this advice tends to be influenced by SIP's own experience and by current DCSF policy or pressures, neither of which may be helpful in addressing the problems the academy faces.

(3) *How do sponsors get to know that a change is needed?* A sponsor with a business background simply said 'it's not difficult!' (see Chapter 4). Another, also with a commercial background, explained:

I've no hesitation in ringing someone up in the Department and saying, look, we have this issue ... you get a good feeling from the department if they are worried about your principal or not. And management meetings, or anecdotal evidence of things going wrong, things just not being right. (Chair of Governors)

Although information could have come from the DCSF – whose advice could have contributed to the problem in the first place – it tended to confirm the sponsor's own impression, or that of his representatives. Yet whatever they felt about their responsibility for the problem, the sponsors knew when the DCSF thought a change of principal was necessary, and generally seemed to share that point of view.

(4) *Do sponsors and principals get sound advice?* Referring to SIPs, an academy principal told us:

Just because somebody has been a head, it is neither a necessary nor a sufficient condition for being a good mentor in school. I've met some ex-heads who can't do that for toffee. I've met some old fashioned advisors who left teaching at head of department level who are fantastic evaluators of schools. (Academy principal)

This principal could also have been referring to ex-heads on project management companies advising on the design of buildings. We saw in Chapter 5 how this model could lead to damaging and costly mistakes. The same applies to ex-heads advising on the curriculum and management in academies that have opened.

(5) *How often does advice lead to turbulence and false starts?* In four of the six academies we visited there was evidence of advice from the DCSF or educationalists on the project management company contributing to severe turbulence. We have outlined one in this chapter, a second in Chapter 4 and a third in Chapter 5. The fourth was another academy like the one described in this chapter, in which the sponsor had put in place a management structure that was not fit for purpose; this was compounded by the more general problem of innovation:

> I think what didn't help the academy programme at the beginning was excessive emphasis on innovation and transformation. I think innovation and transformation can very quickly become snake oil ... (what happened here was that) they introduced a vertical management system, with no preparation. And they didn't prepare for what would happen in a brand new building with no outdoor play. The results were pretty chaotic .... I think all the things that went wrong here was to do with poor advice in developing ideas and the project. (Academy principal)

There were also budgetary problems caused by a large leadership team with matrix management, whose lines of accountability were unclear. Yet this principal saw it as a strength of academies that, having realised that they had a problem, the trustees had acted quickly to deal with it.

In all four academies the turbulence arising from poor advice precipitated a change in principal. (One academy is currently on its fourth principal, though the present incumbent's predecessor left for personal reasons, to the regret of the trustees). It nevertheless, raises two questions. The first is about the quality of advice received from DCSF officials or nominees. This was doubtless given in good faith and in different circumstances could have led to improvements. Yet in the circumstances of these particular academies it appears, to say the least, to have been unhelpful.

The second question is whether it was necessary for the principals to fall on their swords. The first priority of any governing body is to the students, not to the staff. The people we talked to were sanguine; if the principal did not deliver, he or she must go, in the interests of students. (However, we did not hear of any SIP, advisor or project lead departing as a result of disruption arising from their advice.) From one perspective it is obviously right for the principal to go: Children only have one chance of secondary school education, quite apart from the academies programme itself needing quick results. From other perspectives, it is more worrying. Ofsted reports show that most academies are well managed. Yet one academy we visited had received only four applications from a national advertisement for a principal. If one of the most highly paid posts in secondary education – to lead a well established academy, which was steadily improving its students' GCSE results – could receive so few applications, one has to ask whether principals can be found to provide the necessary quality of leadership in each of the 400 academies projected by the Labour government, let alone the potentially huge expansion envisaged in 2010 by the Conservative–Liberal Democrat coalition.

The tendency in England has been to assume that serious problems in a school can only be resolved with a change of leadership. That is not self-evidently true. Earlier, we noted that in one academy the percent of pupils obtaining at least five GCSE passes at A*–C had risen in one year from 25% to 70%. The improvement coincided with a change in principal, but it was not achieved directly by the incoming principal. It was achieved by teachers responding to strong leadership with clear expectations. If teachers can pick themselves up so quickly after a period of turbulence, one has to ask whether the same could be true of principals. Obviously the buck stops with the principal, and there is no one on the staff to lead him or her. However, it does not follow that the only available advisors are the SIPs or other advisors put in place by the DCSF or the SSAT. Indeed, their advice may be a poisoned chalice for two reasons. First, they follow an agenda aligned to that of the DfE, formerly DCSF. Second, they are expected to feed information back to the DfE and to the sponsor; hence, principals could legitimately feel that they a have good reason for caution in fully trusting them. Some SIPs, certainly, have a deep understanding of school improvement processes and provide a service that principals value highly. Nevertheless, there is an urgent need for alternative, more impartial and more confidential sources of advice, chosen by principals themselves. For example, there are clear examples of support from universities yielding important outcomes in professional development and pupil achievement (Leo & Barton, 2006).

Conclusions

So, have academies been the centres of innovation that Ministers intended? We asserted earlier that ethically the first responsibility of anyone planning innovation is not to demonstrate its value but to show that it is not harmful. Unfortunately, there is evidence from our interviews that the programme failed this test. In four of the six academies we visited, poor advice or poor decisions at the planning stage played a major part in destabilising the academy in its early days. It would be difficult for the DCSF to argue that the project management companies were not their responsibility, since no other government department could have had responsibility for the public money put into them. We also heard evidence that the innovation agenda could be at best stressful and at worst destabilising.

We visited academies that were emerging from a period of severe turbulence, but none that were currently in one. It became clear in the course of our meetings that if one key task for principals was to manage the relationships with their sponsors successfully, another was to manage SIPs and other personnel from the DCSF or SSAT. Inevitably, principals had different strategies, ranging from close and willing cooperation, to making themselves unavailable. The latter strategy would only work for as long as the academy was perceived as running smoothly, with steadily improving results. We also heard of a principal and deputy hurriedly getting together to produce a list of 'innovations' for the SIP to write on his clipboard before returning to the DCSF.

This, nevertheless, is only half the picture. The other half is less bleak. A paradox of academies is that they encourage risk taking in a climate that theoretically should discourage it. The single-minded emphasis on driving up standards, particularly to meet the National Challenge benchmark, should, in theory, lead to a narrowing of the curriculum and extreme caution about anything that might divert attention away from this priority. In other words, it should lead to 'teaching to the test'. That, certainly, is what has happened in the final year of primary schools in response to the high stakes SATs (Beverton *et al.*, 2005). Yet at their best, academies remain lively, stimulating places in which creative responses to challenge are not overwhelmed by fear of league tables.

The examples of successful innovation that principals described were all home grown. They emerged from planning within the academy, sometimes with help from trusted outsider specialists. Combined with effective leadership, the relative independence of academies created a climate in which innovation could flourish.

So there are two answers to our original question: 'Have academies been the centres of successful innovation that Ministers intended?' When innovation is imposed on an academy by its project management company and/or pressure from DCSF officials, the answer is unambiguously: No. But if it is home grown, nurtured and made possible by the climate that principals and staff have created, the answer is: Yes, probably. The only reason for caution is that our fieldwork was limited to a small number of interviews with key players. A more detailed study of innovation in the academies programme could throw more light on how innovation can be destabilising – and on how it can be an essential ingredient in success.

There was one surprising omission in our evidence on home-grown initiatives. Although our interviews with principals were wide-ranging, SEN was hardly ever mentioned. At first sight this is odd because on some conventional criteria for SEN – notably behaviour problems and attainments two years or more below expected levels – no group of schools has more students with SEN than academies. It would not be hard in some academies to justify regarding over 50% of students inherited from predecessor schools as having some form of SEN. Behaviour, certainly, was mentioned, but seldom in the context of provision for SEN. We suspect that the explanation is straightforward. Academies were never seen primarily as an initiative to improve provision for SEN. They were seen as a turnaround initiative for the neediest schools in the most troubled areas. The expectation was not that they label pupils as having SEN, but that they create a climate in which their students would no longer show the problems of behaviour and educational achievement that might justify that label. If this argument is correct, it raises some important questions about how schools develop inclusive practices. It seems possible that academies could have some valuable lessons for policy and provision on SEN. Sadly, that opportunity will be lost without more intensive study.

Nothing we saw could be seen as distinctive to academies. An extended day, for example, operated in most academies, if not all, and certainly created some flexibility in the timetable and curriculum. Yet this, too, is available in LA schools. Innovative methods of self-evaluation such as the Balanced Score card (a planning and management system for monitoring performance against strategic goals) were used in one academy, and are also available in LA schools. There is no doubt that many academies have created stability from the most troubled inheritance, and high aspirations from a culture of resigned acceptance. The question for the final three chapters is what can be learnt from them.

Part 3

Futures

Chapter 8
A Coherent Policy?

Introduction

Academies attracted more controversy than most New Labour education policies. They divided opinion within the Labour party itself, yet were supported by the Conservatives and never vigorously opposed by the Liberal Democrats. Following the 2010 general election, the new coalition government decided to extend the programme to allow all secondary, primary, and special schools to apply to become academies. Under the previous Labour government there had been intense opposition to academies from the media, 'Old Labour' traditionalists and local groups opposed to removal of schools from LAs. One reason may have been that academies were a more radical and therefore better understood initiative to raise standards in areas of social disadvantage and low educational achievements. Evans *et al.* (2005) listed some of the previous initiatives: Education Action Zones, Excellence in Cities, Excellence in Clusters, 'Hard' and 'Soft' innovations, Fresh Start and Diversity Pathfinders. Each of these featured quite prominently in the education press, with some rather limited attention in the national dailies and Sunday papers. None of them captured the public imagination, and none of them received sustained critical attention similar to the academies programme.

The key features of academies were always clear: a fresh start for failing or under-achieving schools, independence, sponsors, strong leadership, innovation and high expectations. These were combined in a policy that was a partial reconstruction of the Tory initiatives of GM schools and, particularly, city technology colleges. For those familiar with the Times Educational Supplement, academies were also covered in the fingerprints of the figure lampooned by the late Ted Wragg as Tony Zoffis. Academies became a symbol of everything that traditionalist supporters within the Labour party, whether in education or not, feared and loathed: operating outside the mainstream, they were always much easier to attack than, for example, Beacon Schools, Specialist Schools or Leading Edge Schools.

Academies were never a simple reconstruction of Tory policy on CTCs. They differed from CTCs in two crucial respects: first, they were an explicit attempt to raise standards in the most challenging schools and areas in the country; second, change of status was linked explicitly to a change in the culture – and poor results – of the predecessor schools.

This chapter explores the nature of the academies policy initiative. Was it a coherent policy and, moreover, one that has produced results – or at least sufficiently robust green shoots of educational recovery to justify expanding it to include all schools? The key aim was to raise standards in the most troubled schools in the most disadvantaged areas. This was to be achieved by changes in governance linked to appointment of sponsors, and by focusing resources on them.

Outcomes

Admission policies

One of the easiest ways to manipulate academic outcomes is to change admissions criteria. A large majority of academies certainly appear popular with parents, with an average 2.6 applications for every place (PWC, 2008). This contrasts with the situation in predecessor schools, many of which were under subscribed. The proportion of children from socio-economically disadvantaged backgrounds, measured crudely by FSM, had fallen by PWC's (2008) final report by 6% compared with only 2% in comparison schools, and 1% in England as a whole. Nevertheless, the actual number of disadvantaged children had actually increased, due to academies admitting more pupils than their predecessor schools. Unsurprisingly the question of admissions has attracted criticism, as discussed earlier (in Chapter 3). However, it should be recognised that if the proportion of children receiving FSM had not declined, the academies programme would have failed to meet one of its central objectives. The growing polarisation of schools, linked to the middle-class flight from inner cities, was central to the thinking behind academies. With an important proviso, evidence that this was changing should be seen as evidence of success. The proviso is that academies were not becoming socially exclusive, and were not in fact rejecting applications that their predecessor schools would have accepted. We have not been able to find any evidence of that. If, as a consequence of increasing the pupil intake following academy status, the balance of intake becomes slightly less uneven, there is no reason why commitment to families served by the predecessor school should be affected. On other indicators, too, academies continue to serve highly vulnerable groups. For example, the percentage for whom English is an additional language remained above that of the comparison schools in PWC's evaluation.

Behaviour and exclusions

One way to improve educational outcomes is to exclude students who are disruptive. New Labour's inclusion agenda argued that this was wrong and that efforts should be made to ensure that schools were inclusive, had personalised learning and took account of individual needs. The investment in behaviour-improvement plans and learning support units can be seen as commitment to ensuring that even the most challenging students were included as part of their school's mainstream work.

Unfortunately, there is no reliable data about overall pupil behaviour in academies compared with their predecessor schools. This matters because in failing or under-achieving schools, improvement in behaviour is generally evident before improvement in academic outcomes. A socially stable climate with good relationships is a necessary condition for educational progress, though on its own not sufficient. In general Ofsted reports tend to be complimentary about behaviour in academies, commenting on positive relationships and an environment in which children feel safe.

In contrast to the picture on behaviour in general, successive reports note that academies have much higher rates of permanent exclusions than those in other schools (e.g. House of Commons Committee of Public Accounts, 2007; National Audit Office, 2007; TUC, 2007). In addition PWC (2008) expressed concern that families of excluded pupils were less likely to receive information about their rights, and that the appeals procedure represented 'an additional layer of complexity' for parents, particularly those from disadvantaged backgrounds (PWC, 2008: 10).

One of PWC's two possible hypotheses for higher levels of exclusions from academies was that high excluding academies might have had a higher number of pupils with very challenging behaviour. This can safely be discarded as implausible. Apart from explicitly denying the academies' own contributions to their students' behaviour, the research on differences between schools in exclusion rates has provided no evidence that low excluding schools are blessed with a compliant, pro-social intake, compared with their higher excluding counterparts (e.g. Galloway *et al.*, 1985a; Galloway, 1995). PWC's hypothesis is as insupportable as saying that chronic disruption, in say a Maths lesson, is due to a high number of pupils with very challenging behaviour, when these same pupils behave well and are highly motivated in English lessons. One has to ask why some academies have consistently high exclusion rates.

This leads to PWC's second hypothesis, only marginally less implausible: That high excluding schools 'may be applying low threshold approaches to misbehaviour in their early days in order to establish a culture of excellent behaviour and achieve rapid improvements in their academic attainments' (PWC, 2008: 62). This was also suggested by National Audit office (2007) and quoted by the House of Commons Committee of Public Accounts (2007). However, it is contradicted by the committee's own paper on exclusion rates from academies in 2003–2004, and 2004–2005. According to the theory we should expect exclusion rates to be lower in the second year when progress towards establishing the 'culture of behaviour' should be evident. In fact, of nine academies with six or more permanent exclusions in at least one year, five had substantially *more* exclusions in the second year. Only one had substantially fewer, down from 27 to 7, and therefore remained a high excluding academy. It should also have been easy to check for any relationship between rate of improvement in the curriculum and exclusion rates. In both cases, previous research provides little, if any, supporting evidence for PWC's hypothesis. What the research does show, with complete consistency, is that LA schools also vary very widely in their exclusion rates, and that demographic or pupil intake variables account at most for a small proportion of these differences (Galloway, 1995).

Exclusion rates do not invariably reflect the overall quality of relationships or behaviour in a school or academy. In other words, it is possible, though unlikely, for academies with consistently high permanent exclusion rates to have generally positive relationships. It is likely that permanent exclusion rates reflect the values of the principal and, probably to a smaller extent, of the sponsor in relation to inclusive education. In at least four of the academies we visited, the inclusive policies of the principals led them to pride themselves on small numbers of permanent exclusions.

Permanent exclusion rates matter, not only as a measure of an academy's practice of inclusive education, but also because, at best, permanent exclusion places a strain on other LA services, and at worst channels some young people towards the youth justice system. Even though the variation between academies is probably no greater than between LA schools, more information is needed. Specifically, do some academies consistently exclude larger than average numbers over several years? What part does the sponsor play in an academy's use of exclusion? How often is a change of principal associated with a change in exclusion rates? What aspects of practice in some academies enable them to retain their most vulnerable pupils?

It is possible that the turbulence created by developing a new academy is too much for some students. Moreover, it is unrealistic to argue on the one hand that academies must raise standards of behaviour, and on the other that exclusion of students should never be used to enforce high standards. One academy we visited excluded five students in one go because of their involvement in an assault on a member of the public. It is important to balance quantitative evidence on the number of students excluded against qualitative data about the reasons for exclusion in particular circumstances. Many academies inherited predecessor schools with poor behaviour plans. When the academy established clear expectations, an increase in exclusions was likely. Nevertheless, that cannot be the whole story. If it were, we should expect a rise in exclusions in the first year or two of academy status, followed by a drop. As we have seen, there is no evidence of that (House of Commons Committee of Public Accounts, 2007). Rather, academies, like LA schools, vary widely in their use of exclusion and in a fairly consistent way; some consistently make little or no use of their power to exclude and others use it quite frequently. Overall, though, they consistently exclude more students than their LA counterparts, and when this happens LA services have to pick up the pieces, as they do with students from their own schools. However, they are allocated funding for that purpose.

Educational achievements

The overall picture of achievement and progress in the curriculum in PWC's final report is that academies made greater improvements than comparison schools. However, there were variations between subjects and between academies opening in different years. For example, in Science 92% of pupils achieved level five at key stage three in one academy. This was well above the national average of 73%. At another academy only 28% achieved level five (p. 193). Variations between academies, and within an academy between subjects, are entirely predicable from the similar situations in LA schools. In Chapter 6 we recorded an academy principal noting that 53% of pupils had achieved an A*–C GCSE pass in English, but only 27% in Maths. Nor is it particularly surprising that in some cases the overlapping intake schools (LA schools with similar demographic characteristics) out-performed academies. Academy status generally resulted from the predecessor school performing at a lower level than the overlapping intake schools. We know that improvements in educational progress and achievement usually follow improvement in behaviour (e.g. Dean & Galloway, 2008). It is too early to tell how much academy status will 'add value' to students' progress (Whitty, 2008). It may be that the quicker, more robust action that academies are able to take, because of their clear focus on raising standards when a department is under performing, for example, in Maths in comparison to English as in the example above, may give them an advantage over LA schools.

Leadership

PWC (2008) commented that:

> the quality of leadership in academies is generally very good, and in a fifth to a third of Academies rated by Ofsted as outstanding and the number in the good category substantially above the average for England as a whole. Pupils and staff have generally fed back positively on academy principals. (PWC, 2008: 13)

Principals were, however, under pressure to achieve quick results. They worked under close scrutiny and although their job satisfaction was generally high, 11 out of 27 academies studied by PWC (2008) had experienced a change of leadership. The sponsor of a chain of academies told us that he had heard from a high placed source in the DCSF that the average length of service of a principal was 15 months. It is not hard to image Ofsted regarding such attrition levels in a LA's 'family of schools' as unsatisfactory, and as evidence of serious problems. No one we met in academies was prepared to endorse that view. Reasonably, they argued that strong governance required rapid action when any member of staff, including the principal, was failing to deliver results. Yet consistency of leadership over a period of more than 15 months could legitimately be regarded as desirable, at least. PWC (2008) recommended that 'DCSF should examine more closely the reasons for the apparent high attrition rates in the Academies' (PWC, 2008: 14).

A Hawthorn effect?

Should improvement following academy status be seen as a classic Hawthorne effect, or are academies laying solid foundations for educational recovery? Named after the factory in the United States where it was first noted, the Hawthorn effect refers to the tendency of an innovation – any innovation – to have an effect, but only for a short time. The attention of workers, in this case teachers and students, is captured by novelty, leading to improvement in performance. When the novelty wears off, performance typically returns to baseline. At it most depressingly deterministic, the Hawthorn effect denies the possibility of progress. If provision of new school buildings were to be accompanied by no change in governance, leadership or the curriculum, we should expect any short-term improvement to be lost within two or three years, as predicted by the Hawthorn effect. The academies programme was more ambitious, insisting that a new physical environment be accompanied by 'transformation' in standards, with improvements in teaching and learning mediated by improvements in governance and leadership. Ministers claimed that the problems in predecessor schools were transparent. If improvements were to be sustained, and not merely to illustrate the Hawthorn effect, academies would need to be based on a coherent vision. Hence, we need to look critically at the coherence of vision behind the development of academies.

A Coherent Vision? 1. Independence of Academies and Impact on LAs

LA tasks

The rationale for academies was based largely on a view that LAs had not addressed weaknesses in under performing and failing schools. In light of this it seems odd that HMCI (Ofsted, 2004) saw school improvement 'as the most consistently satisfactory area of LA work' (quoted in Evans et al., 2005; 233). Unfortunately, it does not follow that LAs were consistently effective in tackling the shortcomings of their most troubled schools. Nevertheless, LAs' 'satisfactory' work in school improvement cannot have been helped by academies. The reduction in resources – approximately 8% of the total income per pupil in academies – could only weaken them. Far from building on LAs' work on school improvement, the DfES (2004) seemed determined to weaken it. LAs were no longer seen as providers, but rather as:

> helping to build up strong independent schools and networks of schools which can drive up their own improvements. Through the school improvement partners, (LA's) will have an important role in holding schools to account, and retain the lead to bring schools to account where schools are under performing. (DfES, 2004: 42)

This, certainly, can be seen as lacking coherence, though with reference to DCSF policy on the role of LAs rather than academies. Stripped of the school improvement responsibilities that had attracted favourable Ofsted comment, LAs were nevertheless, required to hold schools to account and to accept lead responsibility for school failure. Nor is it clear how 'independent schools and networks of schools' that the LA had helped to build up would be able to 'drive their own school improvement'. The LA's role seems to be that of brokering a positive relationship between schools that are in competition with each other.

A more important question is whether it is possible for LAs to intervene with failing schools whose staff from head teacher down believe firmly that the problem lies with the children and their families, and not with leadership, teaching and learning. The question is as much as a political one as an educational one. If intervention requires additional resources and support from advisory staff, LAs should be well placed to provide it, or, since few LAs can now afford to employ many advisory staff, to suggest where schools might obtain it. Indeed, it may be easier for LAs to support a school in difficulty than for the DCSF to support an academy whose transition funding has run out. If, on the other hand, intervention requires staff changes, the governance arrangements in academies are almost certainly better placed to take decisive action before more pupils' education is harmed.

A coordinating role?

In any area, responsibility for ensuring that educational provision is coherent and, in a literal sense, comprehensive has to rest somewhere. Currently in England LAs have a central role. Examples are sixth form provision, behaviour improvement plans (including provision for permanently excluded pupils), provision for children with severe and complex SEN, support services, (including educational welfare and school psychological services) IT services with intranet access across the LA's family of schools, and 14–19 education.

As with their duty to intervene with failing schools, LAs have duties but rather weak powers in relation to 14–19 education. Content is set by a Diploma Delivery Partnership led by employers. That can be seen as logical; a national system for 14–19 education has to be adaptable to local requirements and priorities, but its work needs to be coordinated in light of what is feasible in schools, including academies.

Similarly, provision for permanently excluded pupils and for pupils with severe and complex SEN requires planning and coordination. Again, under the existing system it is logical for LAs to have this role. Again, it has implications for academies.

Logic, then, arguably dictates that academies think of themselves as part of local provision and the DfE expects them to contribute to it. The emphasis, though, is on LAs collaborating with academies, at least as much as the reverse.

Although academies' independence has been substantially weakened, one principal argued that being outside the LA enabled the academy to play a more important part in the LA's planning for 14–19 education than LA schools themselves. For this principal, the erosion of academies' independence was a threat that had not yet materialised, though he recognised the dangers. A former LA director of education expressed the sense of threat:

If you have been at the top of local government, as I have, or if you have been in the medium to top ranks of the civil service, you know what a powerful influence the wish of a leading politician or cabinet minister actually is. At worst, in local or national government, politicians revert to a 'command and control' mode. (Former Director of Education)

It is not clear whether academies will be able to resist such pressure, were it to be exerted. Independence from LA control undoubtedly enables academy principals to withstand pressure from local politicians. Our evidence suggests that pressure from the DfE, previously the DCSF, whether from ministers, civil servants or SIPs can be much more difficult to resist.

A Coherent Vision? 2. Sponsors

Even before the 'cash for peerages' enquiry there was no serious suggestion that individual sponsors could be found for 200 academies, let alone the 400 that Blair announced in 2006. The expansion was always going to depend on chains, universities, independent schools, high-achieving grammar schools and independent schools converting to academy status. We are discounting LAs here because although they can co-sponsor academies, they cannot be lead sponsors. In this section we discuss only the arguments for each of these groups taking part in the academies programme and the practical issues that they may encounter. We discuss the crucial question of the public perception and political presentation of this expansion in the next section.

Independent schools converting to the public sector with academy status

Opponents argue that it is wrong for government to use public funds to bail out independent schools that are short of pupils. The obvious answers are that: (1) only successful schools, which can make a useful contribution to the overall provision in their area, will be accepted; (2) some independent schools have always demonstrated a commitment to parents who cannot afford fees through bursaries, and any wish to extend this to all the places they offer should be welcomed. For example, the Belvedere Girls School in Toxteth Liverpool, had a socially mixed intake before becoming an academy. From 2000 to 2007 it ran an open access scheme under which the Sutton Trust charity paid all or part of the fees for academically able girls from poor homes (Stothart, 2008).

The criteria for independent schools seeking to become academies are, to say the least, broad. The DCSF (2007b) prospectus simply refers to 'successful independent schools that want to serve their whole community and broaden their pupil intake' (DCSF, 2007b: 12). Apart from this the only criterion is that there should be 'a need for additional good secondary school places' (DCSF, 2007b: 12). There is a claim that details of 'clear published criteria' are set out two pages later, but in fact the relevant page provides only rather broad details of procedures and support, with no reference to criteria. One imagines that there will be a commitment to social inclusion to ensure that these new academies do not, like many grammar schools, become middle-class enclaves in which a child from a socio-economically disadvantaged area is a rarity. One hopes, too, that there will be a commitment to a 'fair banding' in which the admissions policy ensures the full ability range. Whether these two conditions are applied in practice will need to be monitored closely.

Grammar schools sponsoring failing secondary moderns

The reference in the last section to children from socio-economically disadvantaged homes being a rarity in grammar schools is actually too generous to grammar schools. The position is even worse. Jesson (2008) has shown a clear tendency in the country's remaining grammar schools to discriminate in favour of applicants from the private, fee-paying sector over applicants from the state sector. The evidence for this is that applicants from fee-paying schools tend to be given places with lower KS2 scores than state primary school applicants. The discrimination may not be intended, or even conscious. That is a feature of institutional discrimination (in precisely the same way that people may not be conscious of institutional racism in their workplace).

At a casual glance, it is hard not to see something deeply unattractive about grammar schools sponsoring secondary moderns, to whose failure their existence has probably been a significant contributing factor. It is no coincidence that the LA with the largest number of schools on the National Challenge list is Kent, largest of 15 remaining wholly selective LAs. It is irrational to deny that 'creaming off' able pupils has played no part in the problems of so many Kent schools. So what was the argument for a Labour government committed to equity and equality permitting grammar schools to act as sponsors?

Andrew Adonis expressed it, succinctly:

I was giving the prizes at Skinner's Grammar School in Tunbridge Wells last week. The reason I went there is that Skinner's Company is sponsoring an Academy, a very important one, taking over one of the secondary moderns, which they will run in an integrated way. (Andrew Adonis)

Skinner's school was in fact the first selective state school to sponsor an academy. The school that it sponsored, Tunbridge Wells High School, was by some criteria already successful, though it remained on the government's National Challenge list of schools. In addition to grammar schools, local church schools exerted a further 'creaming off' of more able pupils. However unattractive the Kent system may seem, politically it would have been next to impossible for a Labour government to legislate against it. Government is the 'art of the possible', and for New Labour to challenge a large Tory LA would divert attention from more important battles. Moreover, no Tory administration would wish to destabilise successful grammar schools, however malign other people might consider their effect on the much larger number of mainly lower middle and working class pupils.

In this light, using the academies programme to link grammar with secondary modern schools can be seen as an imaginative, constructive response to an intractable problem. It could start to break down the socially destructive isolation of the two sectors. It holds out the possibilities of active cooperation, breaking down the barriers between pupils and opening the doors to a sixth form that had been previously been barred and locked (Garner, 2008). Converting the vision to reality will not be easy, but the argument behind the vision is clear enough.

Independent schools

Labour's target of 400 academies was never going to be achievable without a substantial number of independent schools agreeing to sponsor one. As we saw in Chapter 4, they had two main motives. First, there was genuine altruism. UCST, for example, saw academies as an opportunity to return to their 19th century roots in education of children whose parents could not otherwise afford it. Second, changes in charity law require charities to show that they have a wider public benefit. These two motives raise different questions for independent sponsors.

In the medium term the new Tory–Liberal Democrat government might be tempted to remove questions about the charitable status of independent schools. That would be a powerful test of the rhetoric of altruism. A more important question concerns the mechanisms and procedures for establishing a two-way partnership between successful independent schools and historically low-achieving schools in the state sector. The opportunity exists to bridge a socially destructive divide, with benefits to both sides, but the obstacles should not be underestimated. It is easy to imagine, for example, local reaction when an independent school sponsor decides to sack a state-funded academy principal – and even easier to imagine how the national media would relish the story.

University sponsors

Like independent schools, universities were central to Blair's target of 400 academies. A conservative 50 universities, each sponsoring two academies, would put the target within easy reach. Universities are currently driven by government pressure to widen access to higher education and to demonstrate that they contribute to the economy of their local region. These aims are entirely consistent with the personal values of many academics. They can, however, come into conflict with other pressures. One of these is the university's position in league tables published annually by leading newspapers. An important performance indicator in constructing these is the 'quality' of students entering the university as measured by 'A' level grades. High ideals easily surrender to the higher imperative of league tables. A leading UK University, for example, opened a new campus in an area of severe social disadvantage some 20 miles from the main site with the explicit aim of extending higher education opportunities in one of England's most impoverished regions. Students with non-traditional qualifications, for example, access to HE courses from FE colleges, and low 'A' level grades, were welcomed. They did well. On one course, taking the same examinations, they out-performed students at the university's main site, who had some of the highest 'A' Level grades in the country in their subject. Sadly, this policy changed soon after a change of leadership in the university. The course with the largest proportion of local students was targeted for closure. Pressure was placed on admissions tutors to raise entrance criteria, with a consequent improvement in the university's position in the league table, but a reduction in the proportion of students from low-achieving schools in the region.

The implications are clear. Universities may well continue to sponsor academies. They may provide a wealth of contacts, resources and support. Their involvement could lead to important improvements in the academies they sponsor. That in itself is a sufficient justification for their sponsorship. Whether it will go further, particularly in the elite universities, is another question. Some academics (but by no means all) can understand that an applicant from a historically low-achieving school and materially disadvantaged home with an A grade and two B grades at 'A' level may have at least as much potential as a candidate with two A grades and a B grade from a socially privileged home and an elite public or grammar school. For some vice chancellors and professors, preoccupied with league tables, this argument appears to be just too difficult to follow.

As with independent schools, a Conservative government might reduce the pressure to widen access to universities, though that is not a foregone conclusion. More important, academy sponsorship may be subject to changing priorities. With imaginative leadership, universities could make major contributions to low-achieving schools in their regions. Yet, just as with independent schools, they could easily be frightened away by adverse publicity.

Sponsors with a chain of academies

With independent schools and universities, chains were a third crucial link in reaching the Labour government's target of 400 academies. Some of the existing chains, for example, ULT, ARK, Oasis, could grow to around 25 academies each. This raises three questions: First, about the influence they exert on their academies; second, about the leadership and support they provide, (the DCSF's favourite word was 'challenge'); third, about their independence from LAs. A frequent concern about the role of sponsors is that they have their own agendas. Stated baldly, that is an untenable objection. Any sponsor without clear values and vision would be failing to do his job. The same applies to governing bodies of LA schools and indeed to LAs themselves. And, of course, there is no point having clear values and visions if you do not use them to guide your school or academy. The more legitimate concern is that some sponsors might seek to impose their own idiosyncratic or eccentric views. That was the objection to Sir Reg Vardy's academies allegedly teaching creationism. With large chains such as ULT and Oasis the concern could, in theory, be heightened. We did not, however, see evidence to support it. Both Oasis and ULT are explicit in their commitment to admission of children from all faiths or none. Indeed, Oasis' Steve Chalke is one of the few people to appear to win the respect of Beckett (2007) in his polemic against academies.

The leadership and support that chains give their academies varies. There are two main questions. One is that the support comes at a cost. The second is that it may make leading an academy unattractive to the strongest and most independently minded principals when the chain adopts a similar role to that of a LA.

Chains typically top slice around 4% of the resource per student to provide leadership and support. This contrasts with about 8% in LAs. It was nevertheless, a source of some resentment to one principal:

> Because this money is taken out of my budget, I have to buy personnel and several other services from my sponsor, because I can't afford to go elsewhere and be independent. (Academy principal)

It should be noted that sponsors recognised this tension, and were apparently trying to minimise the top slice. Moreover, we did not hear claims that the relevant services could in fact have been purchased more cheaply elsewhere.

The possibility that chains may come to be perceived as similar to LAs is more difficult. We know one highly successful principal who had sought another post because he felt constrained by the restrictions imposed by the chain's sponsor. Superficially, the restrictions might seem unimportant, even eminently sensible, such as central equipment procurement procedures. The problem is that outstanding principals tend to be independent minded, determined to put their own mark on the academy they lead. They may lead a team of team players within the academy, but do not necessarily work comfortably with a team led by a sponsor, especially when that team includes administrative personnel who remind them of LAs.

Recruitment

PWC (2008) noted a potential difficulty in recruiting high-quality sponsors and principals if the target of 400 academies was to be met. Andrew Adonis did not share that concern:

> This isn't a zero sum game. There isn't just a certain number of good principals out there and the question is who can grab them first. Organisations, particularly chains, which are looking to provide managers for a large number of schools will of course grow their own managers. They will nurture talent within their own organisation.... I've lost count how many vice principals to (name of principal) are now managing academies. (Andrew Adonis)

Every organisation needs new blood. If it *only* recruits from within, it will become inward looking, but that is not inconsistent with Adonis's view. A more difficult question is whether the disparate range of sponsors, from business entrepreneurs to grammar schools, public schools and universities can retain the original vision of the academies programme. Will they remain true to mission?

A Coherent Vision? 3. Public Perception

True to mission?

Although there was no suggestion of extending it to include all 638 schools that were originally identified as failing to meet the National Challenge (DCSF, 2008b) benchmark of 30% of pupils gaining five GCSE passes including Maths and English at A*–C, the academies programme had already broadened beyond its original concern with failing and underachieving schools. This broadening took place before a new government proposed a huge expansion in 2010. The most obvious and contentious example is the provision for independent schools to apply for academy status. A university sponsor told us that his university had discouraged co-sponsorship with the local Church of England diocese on the grounds that it would be perceived locally as two elite institutions looking after their own interests. There is no doubt that in the circumstances of that particular university and diocese he was right. The risk to the academies programme is that its opponents will have little difficulty in portraying it in the media as a reintroduction of selection by the back door – and hence as a programme that works against the interests of families with many social problems who have always been a rarity in selective schools. Even if that charge is demonstrably false, the mud will be likely to stick. Evidence lies in the anger that some people in our sample expressed about what they clearly felt was the betrayal of the programme's origins:

> I absolutely do not agree with making grammar schools, independent schools, and CTC's into academies. I'm opposed to it. Vehemently! The academy programme was originally set up to take underperforming schools where everything else had failed and give them that final chance to succeed. It wasn't about converting grammar schools that have already got 95 per cent A*–C into academy status – saying 'if you take over this failing school down the road and – what's the term they use – "use your best endeavours" to work with it' in an indeterminate time scale ... we will give you £30 million pounds to build your new sports hall ... And they go 'oh yes, thanks very much!' So basically they carry on with their same recruitment strategy, same selection

processes. They get a wad of money from the Department and they don't work with the school. What the DCSF is doing is creating a two-tier system. You've got the real academies and you've got those that are not real academies. And as for their prime project, the cathedral school that they have now turned into an academy – they did it because they wanted a cathedral school as an academy. It was an absolute vanity project. (Sponsor's representative)

All these fears may be unfounded. There is in fact a good case, as we have indicated, for grammar schools to sponsor low achieving secondary moderns, as in Kent. It could be the only locally and politically acceptable way to mitigate the continuing corrosive divisiveness of the selective system. There is also a case for welcoming former independent schools into the state sector, with the safeguards indicated above. Yet, faced with vigorous internal dissent the Labour government found the public presentation of these policies difficult. Paradoxically, it may be easier for a Conservative government. They could use it to claim 'one Britain' credentials.

A Coherent Vision? 4. Competition or Collaboration?

PWC (2008) noted examples of cooperation between academies and LA schools, but also noted that there was scope for further development. The logic of academies collaborating with each other is easier to understand than that of them collaborating with their local 'family of schools'. In domestic settings, the reality behind a façade of love and affection can sometimes be what Edmund Leach called 'the tawdry secrets of the western oedipal family'. Similarly, the reality behind the cosy rhetoric of a 'family' of schools can be single minded, ruthless determination in each school to recruit at least its own 'share' of local pupils, and to outperform its rivals. Nowhere is this seen more clearly than in the curriculum. Collaboration is fine, until it threatens a school's supremacy in league tables. The situation is particularly acute in the government's proposals for 14–19 education. No single institution could offer all 14 of the proposed specialised diplomas, at the three levels of General Diploma, Specialised Diploma or Apprenticeship. Yet in taking students from other institutions, a school, academy or college of FE could feel that it was compromising its own position in local league tables. One principal had welcomed involvement in local planning but nevertheless, was also considering how to reduce the need to 'exchange a lot of students' by 'radically mixing the ages' at which pupils took courses offered by the academy itself.

A former director of education saw Ofsted, league tables, local management of schools and the national curriculum as having led to major positive changes in schools. These are the reforms that have driven competition between schools, leading to the 'market' in education in which schools compete for students. It is possible, though, that the power of the market has been over emphasised.

There is little dispute about the flight of the middle class from inner city schools, nor the divisive polarisation of schools between those seen as high quality and those seen as unacceptable by well informed and ambitious parents. How much that has had to do with the market in education is another matter. In 1979, at the tail end of an industrial economy, unemployment was low. Almost every school leaver could expect to find a job, including the 30% with no useful qualifications. That this situation changed so radically in the next 18 years had less to do with the Conservative government than with changes within the national and global economies. Throughout the country, well-informed parents believed that attending a school with 'good' standards of behaviour and educational achievements would be crucial to their children's life chances. Encouraging schools to compete under local management may have accelerated that process, but probably did not cause it.

If this argument is correct, the scope for genuine partnerships between academies and LA schools may be greater than the rhetoric of market competition would imply. It is always difficult for government, or for LAs, to impose cooperation by *fiat*. Partnerships can only flourish in a climate of mutual respect, and in recognition of mutual benefits. Parents and young people, demanding the opportunities envisaged in the 14–19 educational proposals, may demonstrate that mutual benefit lies in cooperation, which in turn should generate mutual respect between academies, schools and colleges. That, at any rate, must be what the government is hoping. Achieving it will require not only political will but also local good will.

A Coherent Vision? 5. Innovation, Innovation, Innovation

An academy principal could not envisage how the government could invest so heavily in academies without requiring innovation. If all it wanted was more of the same, why introduce academies? That view might, presumably, have been shared by Schofield (2006) whose 'Essential Questions for the Future School' challenge many of the well established tenets of secondary school organisation and practice, from their hierarchical structure to their subject departments and pastoral care. These are not new arguments. For example, Schofield contrasts value centred and rule bound communities:

> Value centred communities define what constitutes acceptable atti-
> tudes and behaviours from an agreement about the real purpose of
> the school – from the inside out as far as the individual and the com-
> munity are concerned ... Rule bound communities define what is
> acceptable in terms of lists of do's and don'ts – from the outside in as
> far as the individual is concerned. (Schofield, 2006: 4)

This is close to Dewey's (2004) argument in the early 20th century, sub-sequently taken up by the progressive education movement and special educators in the 1940s and 1950s (e.g. Wills, 1966).

It is easy to assert that there is no problem with the argument; the prob-lems are only that too few people have taken any notice and that succes-sive governments' draconian 'standards and delivery' agendas succeeded only in delivering supine acquiescence in many schools. That may or may not be true, but it overlooks both the context and the process of introduc-ing change. We wish to argue that pressures on academies from the DCSF to demonstrate innovative teaching and learning and innovative forms of leadership and management were profoundly misguided.

A modern rendition of *Beware the Greeks when they come bearing gifts* might be *Beware educationalists when they come bearing their favourite theo-ries*. To repeat: in four of the six academies we visited, ill thought out inno-vation, imposed from the outside, had created severe turbulence. In a fifth academy turbulence had been prevented only by prompt action by the academy's leaders. In three cases it was associated with a 'small school' organisational structure, in one academy with imposition of an over elab-orate management team, and in one with design features that were cer-tainly innovative – and certainly should never be repeated. When an academy's leadership recognised the problems at an early stage, turbu-lence was minimised or prevented. In four academies, though, failure to do so, or to take the necessary remedial action, led to a change of principal, often abruptly.

The rather elementary and obvious point is that innovation requires careful management of change. In 'turning round' a predecessor school the first priority for an academy principal is to create a climate in which teachers, children and parents, believe in what they do. This is what made one principal determined to achieve a 'quick win' (Chapter 7). Innovation requires change, and change necessarily threatens the status quo. To argue that in some circumstances innovation might consist of lesson plans is valid, but both platitudinous and disingenuous. It is platitudinous because it should not need saying that in order to introduce something innovative, and thus by definition untried and untested, teachers and children both need a sense of stability and security. It is disingenuous because ministers never suggested, while presenting academies as pioneers of innovation, that a well-prepared lesson was all they had in mind.

There is no doubt that the emphasis on innovation has created serious instability in some academies. The strongest principals used skilful and careful judgement based on knowledge of their particular academy to decide how to respond to demands for innovations from SIPs and other DCSF officials. They were confident in their relations with SIPs, welcoming their assistance, but not hesitating to use a combination of firmness and guile when they considered a suggestion or request likely to be unhelpful. One principal explained how he had satisfied a SIP by labelling as innovative things that his colleagues were already doing routinely. From our interviews, it is difficult to exaggerate the pressure that DCSF officials and SIPs can put on principals and sponsors when evidence of rapid progress is not immediately visible. Nor is it easy to exaggerate the pressure that ministers and their officials can put on SIPs to provide evidence of innovation. At a time when the overwhelming need was for stability, premature demands from within the DCSF for innovation appeared, in some academies, to be contributing to instability. In these cases, children, teachers and principals paid the price for hubris in high places.

A Coherent Vision? 6. Buildings and Equipment

New or refurbished buildings can have a symbolic value, signalling a change of direction for a failing or under-performing school (Chapman & Harris, 2004). On their own, they are not likely to have a lasting effect. Improvements in leadership, teaching and learning are also essential. The powerful impact of new buildings for the early academies was reduced in the new closer relationships with LAs required by the school building programme and Partnerships for Learning (Chapter 5). And from 2010 onwards, new academies can no longer expect new or refurbished buildings. This has implications both for the independence and for the distinctiveness of sponsors. The sponsor of a chain of academies described the importance he attached to having a single space large enough for all pupils:

> Part of the Local Education Plan (LEP) is that you have to buy what they have in all the other schools because it's the cheapest for them. In

our academies we like to have an assembly hall that you can get the whole school in – you can actually do that if you get a four badminton court sports hall and the ability to cover the flooring ... (there are times when) the principal and senior staff need to get everyone together, that is a very important part of education in our view ... but under the LEP's they say 'you don't need that'. (Sponsor)

Prior to BSF, according to this sponsor, that had been possible but not subsequently. This sponsor understood and sympathised with the need to reduce costs and maximise value for money. Nevertheless, he regretted that the chain of academies that he was now sponsoring would no longer have this distinctive feature. In fairness, we should add that it is hard to see why new academies in this chain could not have had an assembly hall doubling as a four court sports hall. We could see only two explanations. First, the chain might have given priority to other aspects of the building's design, leaving insufficient funds for the sports hall/assembly hall. Second, the chain's officers might have been insufficiently forceful in their negotiations with the LA. The new arrangements under BSF (DfES, 2004) made it more difficult for sponsors to influence the design, but they were still able to do so.

The stronger ties with LAs were obstructing achievement of this sponsor's vision in other areas too. Procurement of IT services was included in the LA's overall application for BSF funds. The sponsor recognised the importance of economies of scale, and also that it linked the academy with other schools within the LA. This sponsor's organisation, though, wanted to create their own 'family' of academies. They wanted an IT system with an intranet that linked academies within the group. That would not only facilitate sharing of teaching and learning. It would also strengthen the professional contacts between teachers within the group and between principals.

There is, of course, a sensible argument that academies should have a quasi-independent status within their *local* 'family of schools'. Yet there is an unavoidable tension between that argument and the view that academies should be developing their own distinctive approaches towards leadership and management, and towards teaching and learning. Similarly sponsors can legitimately expect that within the academies programme, different chains should develop their own distinctive approaches. Nobody wants academies to operate in glorious isolation from other schools within their LA. But they cannot provide an alternative model if their distinctive features are gradually whittled away.

The sponsor quoted above regretted that the DCSF did not allow his chain of academies to form its own LEP for procurement of new buildings, rather than including them in their LA's LEP. That would have allowed economies of scale, within the budget available to the LAs, but would also have allowed him to develop his chain's vision for academies. That opportunity was being lost, and with it the opportunity to achieve some of the stated aims of the academies programme.

Conclusions

With the new coalition government's proposals to allow all schools to apply to become academies, the programme has reached a turning point. With cross party support in Westminster, the turning point is unlikely to affect its survival. The major questions concern the distinctiveness of academies from LA schools and the scope for distinctiveness between academies or chains of academies.

Some academies have been outstandingly successful, with rapid improvements in pupils' behaviour and educational attainments. Others have not. The variation between academies is not surprising. If rapid, sustained improvement in the most troubled schools in the most impoverished areas were easy, there would be no need for academies. The fact that some academies have not been more successful than their predecessor schools is hardly a reason for abandoning the whole programme, as some of its opponents demand.

The expansion of the programme has moved it beyond its original remit with the most seriously failing or under-performing schools. At least until 2010, it nevertheless retained a broad underlying commitment to provision of high quality places where they had previously been in short supply. At first sight the expansion in the range of sponsors looks incoherent. How can grammar schools sponsor low-achieving non-selective schools to whose problems their existence has probably contributed? And how can allowing independent schools to become publicly funded academies be justified? Yet on closer scrutiny both look consistent with the programme's original underlying aims. A partnership between a grammar school and a school for the 80% of pupils the grammar school would not accept could be the best way to start bridging a corrosive social divide. And in principle successful independent schools may bring something valuable to the state funded sector.

Nevertheless, there is a risk of incoherence surrounding the independence of academies and their relationship with LAs. Specifically, academies cannot logically be part of the local family of schools and, at the same time, a radical alternative to that family. On one hand, if they are to develop increasingly close links to their LA, it is not easy to justify their existence.

On the other hand, if they are to develop their own distinctive features, it is hard to justify tying them increasingly closely to LAs. Logically, the new government's proposals in 2010 to allow all schools to apply to become academies implies that LAs could eventually be phased out. LA administration of schools has however, proved remarkably resilient in the face of hostility of successive governments since the 1980s. It will not be possible to ignore the relationship between academies and LAs.

It could be sufficient for sponsors with only one or two academies – 'sole traders' – to aim to use their expertise and networks to provide a higher quality of education than their predecessor schools. Chain sponsors, though, should legitimately hope for something more. They should aim to develop their own distinctive alternative to mainstream LA provision. We referred earlier to the small school model favoured by one sponsor, and in this chapter to another sponsor's wish to use the intranet to develop close links between academies in his chain. There is no reason why allowing chains to form their own LEP should incur additional expenditure. They could be tied to the average for LAs in the region. They could also be required to cooperate with LAs in 14–19 education. It is hard to see why this was not permitted, unless it reflected a decision to appease LAs whose support might have been helpful in the run-up to a general election.

So far, the gradual erosion of their independence has not seriously undermined the distinctive feature of academies. They remain able to set their own agenda in ways that are more difficult, though seldom impossible, in LA schools. Yet, unease remains.

We asked Andrew Adonis what pitfalls this movement would need to avoid in the future. He replied:

> Compromising on the essentials of quality and independence. (Andrew Adonis)

If the independence of academies is to be preserved, the tension between developing their own distinctive features and developing closer links with their local 'family of schools' will have to be a more creative one than currently, seems likely. It will not be made easier by fast tracking schools rated 'outstanding' by Ofsted to academy status, since this could leave LAs with a rump of 'average' or merely 'satisfactory' schools.

Chapter 9
Designed to Deliver?

Introduction

As originally conceived, academies were part of the government's strategy to 'drive up standards' in education. They were seen as a key strategy in driving school improvement in the most challenging schools in the country, located in the most challenging urban estates and inner city districts. As we argued in the last chapter, the clarity of that vision was only slightly clouded by permitting a few independent schools to join the state sector, while retaining their independent status as academies.

Academies were always an outcome-driven reform. The rationale for academies, originating from Blair and promoted in 2010 by the coalition government, was rooted in their independence. While the early academies were also rooted in commitment to innovation, this is no longer a blanket commitment. Rather, the underpinning rationale can be seen as a more subtle recognition of the need for academy principals to be able to act in response to localised needs. Being responsive to the context is a key element in improving learning, achievement and, ultimately, standards. Put simply, it was intended that independence would give academy principals the capacity to innovate in response to the situation and context in which they provided leadership. They would be able to innovate rapidly and without reference to the perceived bureaucracy of a LA. From our interviews it was clear that academy principals thought that their independence made it easier to respond quickly to change.

In so far as there was any model of school improvement, it lay in ministers' conviction that the failure of LAs to get to grips with under-performing schools could be solved by a radical alternative: giving independence to strong sponsors. Unshackled by LA bureaucracy and inertia, strong sponsors would appoint a majority on governing bodies, which would make principals accountable for 'delivery' of rapid improvement. Sponsors would be attracted and principals would be assisted by heavy investment in infrastructure.

After years of neglect, the physical condition of many schools had become a national disgrace – and in some areas still is. There are still children being educated in schools that are damp, vandalised and uncared for, producing examination results that never seem to move in spite of significant external investment. Investing most heavily in the most disadvantaged areas signalled values of which Old Labour traditionalists could have been proud. Logically they might even have brought themselves to approve refusal to allow some LAs to delay improvement in educational opportunities where they were most needed (though Old Labour traditionalists would probably have preferred some – any – alternative to private sector sponsors).

Yet none of the central features of academies provided an educational rationale for improvement and that remains true of the Conservative–Liberal Democrat coalition's plan to expand the programme. There may have been a hope that an educational rationale would somehow emerge from the innovation agenda in academies, but school improvement is a web of interacting processes leading to improved outcomes. Academies were based on a business model of outcomes driven by leadership and accountability. Through consultants, project leads, advisers and SIPs, the DCSF would provide 'support and challenge'. In theory, educational leadership would be provided by the principal. In practice, crucial decisions were taken before the principal's appointment. Without an educational background, sponsors of the early academies were at the mercy of educationalists on the project management company, each coming with her or his favourite and/or fashionable theory. Even when a principal was in place, as potential end-user of the new building, decisions about design could be based on currently fashionable ideas that might not last. Even decisions about professional issues such as the structure of the leadership and management team were taken by sponsors on advice from external experts who were often divorced from the realities of turning round an organisation and establishing a new culture before moving forward with well thought out innovations.

The focus of change and improvement

Knowing that an academy or school has raised the aspiration and attainments of students is interesting, but in itself tells us nothing about *how* it has achieved improvement. Ofsted may rate the leadership of most academies as good or outstanding, but the high attrition rates suggest neither stability nor consistency over time. More important, leadership is an imprecise term, telling us nothing about *what* principals do, *why* they do it, or *how* they achieve their goals. The principal's influence on school improvement, as reflected in children's progress, is necessarily indirect. Children's progress depends on what Schwab (1978) called the four 'commonplaces' of education: Subject matter, lessons, milieux and teachers. The coordination of these by classroom teachers dictates the progress that children make. So how can principals influence the classroom interactions that Ball and Forzani (2007) called the 'instructional dynamic' in the classroom? As important, did the academies programme have an adequate theoretical underpinning in organisational change? In this chapter we examine whether academies are in a strong position to deliver the standards agenda that was demanded of them.

Organisational Failure and Organisational Turnaround

Organisational failure has been defined as decline that threatens the existence of the organisation itself because it no longer appears capable of delivering acceptable outcomes. This decline could be gradual or sudden, caused by internal or external factors. Organisational turnaround can be defined as actions taken to bring about recovery in performance following a period of organisational failure.

The literature on turnaround identifies key determinants of recovery from organisational failure or poor performance. One of these is the environment in which the organisation operates. There appears to be a strong relationship between the level of financial resources (often called 'munificence' in the literature) available to the organisation and successful turnaround. There is also a positive correlation between turnaround and the complexity of the environment. Where the environment is less complex – more focused on core objectives – there is a greater opportunity for successful turnaround. Greater munificence and lower complexity in the environment are not guarantees of success, since other factors also play a part, but they are undeniably important.

Leadership

Unsurprisingly, human resources are a powerful determinant of successful turnaround. The starting point is often a change in leadership. A new principal is often seen as the starting point for changing the culture of an underachieving or failing school. Few academies are created with the same principal or head teacher as their predecessor schools, though one of the authors (PH) was an exception. Perhaps surprisingly, the importance of the head teacher or principal is controversial. Drawing on two large data sets, each of about 500 schools, Searle and Tymms (2007) found no difference in student attitudes, nor in value added measures of curriculum progress in the three years before appointment of a new head and the three years after. Correlations between attitudes and value added measures were higher in secondary schools than primary, leading the authors to conclude that:

> It may be harder for a secondary school head teacher to influence quality across the whole school than a primary school head teacher. (Searle & Tymms, 2007: 25)

An academy principal (Moynihan, 2007) challenged Searle and Tymms' conclusions. He pointed out that large-scale statistical studies have demonstrated that leadership makes an important contribution to students' learning. Moynihan cited Leithwood *et al.* (2004) in concluding that:

> Differences in the quality of teaching in individual classrooms explain more than one third of the variation in student achievement between schools, making head teachers the most powerful in-school influence after classroom teaching. (Moynihan, 2007: 44)

As important, perhaps, Moynihan pointed out that two thirds of schools placed by Ofsted in the failing category of 'special measures' replaced their head teachers. These schools are more likely to improve and sustain their improvement than schools placed in the less serious category as having 'serious weaknesses' (Sammons & Mathews, 2005). Discussing this evidence, Moynihan argued that:

> School failure gives a new head sufficient clout to over-write dysfunctional attitudes and replace them with a new approach. (Moynihan, 2007: 48)

There is increasing evidence that changes in staffing at all levels in the organisation are likely to contribute to successful turnaround. The wider human resources strategy seems to focus on expanding and developing the number of core employees with high expertise in the core business of the organisation. The evidence on leadership appointments followed by successful turnaround is that leaders are often appointed from within the organisation. In other words they have knowledge of the core business of the organisation and are sensitive to its particular needs at this given stage in its fortunes.

In the business literature, two core organisational turnaround strategies feature prominently: retrenchment and repositioning. Retrenchment is about cutting costs and is likely to be necessary where costs are high and output is characterised by low effectiveness. This was seen when an academy had to deal with the fall-out after a project management company had set up an elaborate management system with unsustainable financial implications. Repositioning involves change in how the organisation defines its priorities, presents itself to its clients, and is viewed by the public. It can be achieved by rebranding, but also by a focus on change and innovation to reinvent the organisation in people's eyes. An example was the determination of an academy's principal to do things that the staff had told her were impossible because of the students' behaviour. There is a positive association between retrenchment and repositioning and successful turnaround.

What implications does evidence on turnaround have for academies?

Academies represented an attempt to turn around perceived organisational failure and as such they explicitly embodied features of turnaround strategy. High munificence was available to academies to facilitate change, for example, through new buildings and introductory funding. In addition to the huge capital investment there was sustainable revenue investment in the top slice formerly deducted by the LA for centrally provided services. Academies had a clear requirement to raise standards.

It would be interesting to analyse the background of incoming academy principals in relation to their subsequent success. Salaries, certainly, were often pitched to attract those with experience, (though some chains insisted that they would not offer higher salaries than comparable LA schools). Academies were also well placed to make difficult decisions regarding recruitment and retention of staff.

Change and innovation

The establishment of an academy represents change in itself. The extensive literature on change offers many perspectives on why efforts at transformational change fail. Kotter (1996) summarised these into eight points:

- Not establishing a great enough sense of urgency.
- Not creating a powerful enough guiding coalition.
- Lacking a vision.
- Under-communicating the vision.
- Not removing the obstacles to the new vision.
- Not systematically planning and creating short-term wins.
- Declaring victory too soon.
- Not anchoring the changes in the organisation's culture.

This is not the place to expand on the details of these, but it is clear that attempts to introduce change often do fail. Lack of staff/stakeholder involvement in the change process is probably a further reason why management of change does not succeed in some organisations. Changing the social and learning cultures of schools is indeed 'more than a lick of paint and a well-orchestrated performance' (Thompson *et al.*, 2009).

While the academies programme itself could not change anything, it could help to create an environment in which change was possible. It allowed leaders to address the eight issues that Kotter raised in the context of a new environment with the core purpose of raising standards. Moreover, it provided leaders with the funding and the systems necessary to build their coalitions and engage effectively with staff to move the organisation forward. In their literature review of an organisation's ability to manage innovation, Smith *et al.* (2008) suggested that management of innovation (and by implication management of change) should be seen as a systems based approach, which was rooted in management styles, leadership and a culture focused on change and innovation. Academies sought to offer a fresh start on all levels in developing a culture of change and innovation focused on raising standards.

Understanding Change

Imagine two academies, A and B. Both have replaced consistently low performing predecessor schools in multiply disadvantaged areas. Both have principals with a record as highly successful head teachers of state secondary schools serving similar areas. Both have inherited a demoralised and disillusioned staff from the predecessor school.

Two years after opening, behaviour and relationships at Academy A has changed beyond recognition. In almost all departments staff are working as an effective team and in almost all classes most children appear motivated to learn. There is already sound evidence of improved educational progress and in two more years this will be reflected in GCSE results that lift the academy comfortably above the National Challenge benchmark of five GCSE A*–C passes including Maths and English. The principal is recommended for a knighthood (but government's priorities have changed from education to the economy, so he doesn't get it).

At Academy B nothing much has changed after two years, except that senior teachers in one of the few successful departments have finally given up the unequal struggle and taken a post elsewhere. Children's behaviour still makes teaching an ordeal, and there is no sign of their educational attainments improving. The sponsor is disappointed. The SIP and other DCSF officials share their own disappointment with the sponsor. The sponsor takes the hint and the principal is replaced.

There is no need to identify the academies. The picture is very familiar, repeated many times since the programme started in 2002. The tragedy is not that it has happened, but that so little has been learned from it. In itself, the fact of Academy A's success does nothing to help other academies. It may well be the case that the academy's independence, its sponsor and the principal's leadership helped to 'drive up standards'. But in Academy B's experience 'driving up standards' and indeed the much hyped 'independence' of academies may be perceived as vacuous sound bites.

Neither the sponsor nor the principal nor the independence of academies had any *direct* involvement in 'driving up' the standards in Academy A. The people with direct responsibility were teachers working directly with children. If the academies programme is to have a lasting influence on the practice of secondary and primary schools it will need to show how and why classroom practice changed.

It seems likely that independence from LAs, appointment of sponsors and strong leadership from principals are each important variables, but without a better understanding of how they mediate change in classroom practice, academies will continue to work in the dark. We suggested earlier that the moral justification for the academy programme is its focus on the country's least-privileged schools in its most multiply disadvantaged areas. That seems irrefutable. Another moral justification might have been that it would contribute to knowledge and understanding of the process of school improvement in the most challenging areas. That is something it has scarcely started to do. The PWC evaluations do not even scratch the surface.

To illustrate our argument we cite Ball and Forzani's (2007) view that understanding 'instructional dynamic' is the key task of educational research. They cite Cohen and Hill's (2001) evaluation of an attempt to improve Maths teaching in elementary schools in California. Ball and Forzani note that:

> … although many teachers were enthusiastic about the ideas associated with the reform, they were also deeply reluctant to change their instruction, and when they did adopt new practices, did so in a piecemeal fashion. Others adapted reformers' ideas so that in practice they differed little from conventional forms of instruction. Cohen and Hill's central finding was that the reform succeeded in changing teachers' practice to some degree but only when teachers had significant opportunities to participate in professional development that helped them understand the reform and learn new ways to teach. (Ball & Forzani, 2007: 534)

It would be interesting to know how much the 'hotbed of professional development' to which an academy principal referred focused on understanding the rationale for academies *and* learning new ways to teach. The more important point from Cohen and Hill's work is that it starts to elucidate the complex processes that lie behind change in classroom teaching.

Academies certainly operate in a complex, challenging environment, compounded by high political pressure for quick results. Behaviour change usually precedes attitude change. Hence, changes in classroom practice are likely to come before changes in attitudes and beliefs about children's abilities. That simply means that a quick fix is likely to be a temporary one. If unsupported by an ingrained belief in what they are doing, changes in teachers' classroom practice are likely to be temporary. It is likely that change in attitude – and hence in professional culture – will come from a combination of achieving results year on year, *and* interactions with other teachers, notably subject leaders, the senior leadership team, and those responsible for the academy's governance.

The Holy Grail of Sustainable Change: Contingent Leadership

Capacity to lead depends on a deep understanding of the context and the people in it. This includes understanding what can and cannot be done at a given point in time, and what changes are needed to make something possible. It involves not only creating opportunities, but exploiting them when they arise. In this sense leadership is 'contingent' on the context.

The principal who described herself as having taken risks in the early days of her appointment recognised the need for rapid change in staff expectations and pupils' behaviour. Although she was clear that these were being achieved, she also recognised that it would take time for teachers to internalise high aspirations:

> It's like a big liner. I'm here with this little steering wheel. But its about ten miles before it even appears to turn round. People do feel that it is getting better, but it is going to take a long time before they really notice that it's turned round. (Academy principal)

Another way of understanding this is to contrast behaviour with attitudes and beliefs. Social psychologists have long recognised the lack of significant correlations between behaviour and attitudes. It is quite possible, for example, for a person to have friends of a different ethnicity, yet retain racist beliefs. Similarly, it is quite possible for teachers to achieve high motivation and progress with a class, yet continue to attribute this to factors over which they have no control, such as the pupils' social backgrounds. It can take a long time to internalise new ideas or new practice. Until they are internalised, sustainable change is improbable.

This was recognised by Hargreaves (2001) in an important article in which he contrasted the likely outcomes of initiatives on which teachers are asked to invest a lot of energy with those in which they are asked to invest relatively little energy. A 'high energy' initiative may yield disappointing results. In spite of the effort that teachers put into it, childrens' behaviour remains unsatisfactory and their progress disappointing. This, Hargreaves argued, leads to a feeling of exhausted frustration. On the other hand, a high energy initiative may lead to definite improvement. The progress will not, however, be sustainable for two reasons. First, most teachers are already working hard. They will agree to a request from the principal or their subject leader to try something new, but in the long term the additional workload will not be manageable. Second, as soon as another initiative is introduced – and there has been no shortage of innovation and initiatives since 1997 – the previous one will be consigned to the back burner or, more probably, the dustbin of forgotten initiatives.

Low energy initiatives have a different trajectory. They may have little or no discernible effect. If so, they are likely to be regarded with apathy and cynicism: Just another useless bright idea from people who know nothing about teaching! On the other hand, teachers *may* find them useful. If so, this creates the possibility of levering-up standards through sustainable change. The reason is that low energy initiatives, unlike their high energy counterparts, are more likely to become internalised as part of the teacher's day to day practice, thinking and professional identity.

A further point about low-energy initiatives is that they necessarily take existing practice as their starting point. The message understood by teachers is not 'we're going to have to learn something radically new and different' but 'OK, let's see whether this helps us in our teaching'. The bottom line is that teachers will internalise ideas and practices that make their work more worthwhile and satisfying. The sources of job satisfaction are well-known and rather obvious: Seeing their pupils making progress, relationships with pupils and relationships with colleagues (Galloway *et al.*, 1985b). The relationships, though, are not an end in themselves but a means to achieving the goal of more effective learning.

Critically, the starting point is existing practice. Tempting as it may be for DfE, formerly DCSF, officials and other external experts to issue tabloid sound bites about the need for radical change and innovation, sustainable improvement is achieved incrementally, in small steps. Successful teaching builds on children's *existing* knowledge, understanding and skills. A new initiative or approach may be needed to correct misconceptions, but is only of any value if used in light of current knowledge and practice.

The incremental nature of progress is important, and has obvious implications in timing the introduction of new resources or ideas. A state-of-the-art IT system may, for example, provide a huge boost to teaching and learning in one academy. In another it may further destabilise an already bad situation. Similarly, one academy may be ready for more innovative ways of teaching, such as combining two or more classes for some activities, thus allowing much smaller groups with tutorial support for others. The innovation may enable staff to build on, and develop from, their current practice in ways that enhance children's learning as well as their own professional development. At another academy the same innovation may prove the last straw for an already exhausted and demoralised group of teachers.

In different ways, using different language and examples, all the principals we met described a relentless, uncompromising drive and determination to increase the opportunities open to students by raising their educational performance. Whether they liked it or not, they recognised not only that they themselves would be judged by students' performance, but also that GCSE results would open doors to employment for students, or close them. In other words, they were playing a high stakes game that superficially appears incompatible with Hargreaves' insistence on the importance of low energy input. In fact, there is no inconsistency. Recognising the absolute necessity for rapid improvement is one thing. Identifying strategies for achieving it is another. Focusing sharply, even narrowly, on childrens' behaviour and on their learning in the classroom is entirely consistent with the 'low-energy' incremental approach we are advocating. Anything diverting focus from that is not.

We were able to identify five implications for leadership from our interviews:

(1) *Plan transition* to academy status in light of the changes that teachers and students are likely to be able to accept. In Chapter 6, we reported a principal explaining the chaotic results of innovation without proper preparation. The key point in planning transition to academy status is not necessarily to avoid all innovation, but rather to avoid everything that diverts teacher attention from the core tasks of teaching and learning.

(2) *Model success.* One principal found it necessary, in her own words, to take risks as a way of showing the staff what could be achieved. Told by the staff that an assembly with a full year group was impossible, she demonstrated that it was in fact quite possible. Another principal used a strong department that had previously felt undervalued to

demonstrate that GCSE passes were within the reach of more students than most staff had thought possible.

(3) *Take decisive action* when necessary. The idea of a finite pool of excellent teachers and principals is unsupported by evidence. If a class makes excellent progress, with excellent behaviour in one core subject, but very poor progress with very poor behaviour in another, it is irrational to attribute the latter to lack of ability and/or home background. With effective leadership and opportunities for professional development, most teachers can raise their game, but not all. In academies it is generally easier than in LA schools to take decisive action against poor performance.

(4) *Leadership styles and strategies may need to change as the school develops.* Chapman (2003) argued that firm, directive leadership was needed in the early stages of turning around a school in difficulty, with introduction of more democratic approaches as progress was made. The problem with this suggestion is that changing a leadership style can be extremely difficult. While a leader may want to adopt a more democratic approach, staff who have come to expect firm, directive leadership may find it hard to accept. The possible difficulties for a principal in changing his or her approaches to leadership as a school develops is a neglected topic, both in studies of leadership and of school improvement.

(5) *Principals are accessible to staff and known to children.* PWC (2008) found that a large majority of pupils (73%) thought the principal was really interested in them. Even more said that they often saw the principal around the school, and that he/she made sure the pupils behaved well. Consistent with this, 79% of teachers disagreed with the statement: 'The principal does not encourage teachers to develop themselves professionally' and 91% said that the principal really believed that the academy could make a difference to children's learning, whatever their home background.

Leadership and Strategy: Teaching and Learning

Chapman and Harris (2004) note the rather limited amount of UK based research on turning around failing schools. Drawing on a study of 10 schools facing challenging circumstances (Harris & Chapman, 2002) and another on schools that had shown sustained improvement over five years (Harris *et al.*, 2003) they identified key strategies for school improvement. We list these with examples from the academies we visited.

Improve the environment

Until 2010, new buildings were the most immediately obvious feature of academies, particularly the earlier ones. They showed a commitment to invest in education in communities that, in many areas, had lost confidence in themselves. The long-term consequences of some of the ill-thought-out innovations (classrooms without doors, open to noisy corridors) eccentricities (changing rooms on the first floor) and sheer extravagance (huge atrium with excessive heating bills) remain to be seen. One chain sponsor told us that his organisation had been approached by the DCSF to take over an early academy from the original sponsor. He had declined because the running costs were too high. But none of this should divert credit from the academy programme's achievement in transforming an often dreary environment in the predecessor schools. The new buildings we saw appeared to be well looked after, valued by staff and children.

Generate positive relationships

In three academies the small school model, or an adaptation of it with a home base area for each year group, had failed to generate positive relationships. Indeed, relationships were deteriorating sharply in two cases and led to a change of principal. In all three cases action had eventually been taken to deal with the problem. That involved giving *teachers* a strong sense of professional identity as subject specialists, *and* ensuring that children received tutorial support in very small groups. The emphasis on teachers' professional identity is important. The tutorial 'learning conversations' with children in one academy might have been more difficult if teachers' own learning needs had not been addressed by strengthening subject departments.

Focus on teaching and learning

This overlaps with the generation of positive relationships above. It also includes a continual emphasis on behaviour that helped learning. The principals who prided themselves on low or zero exclusion rates also emphasised that this was achieved by focusing on teaching and learning in the curriculum. Without this, pupils would not attain the GCSE results that would open doors to employment when they left the academy. They could have added that without feeling valued at school and achieving success in the curriculum many students might have had much greater difficulty in coping with adverse circumstances at home.

Building community

One principal took pride in the academy having won an award for its contribution to the schools in the LA. Another described the large sums that local firms had contributed to additional facilities that the academy was providing in and for the local community. In the early years of the programme use of buildings for community use was restricted by the fear that an anomaly in VAT regulations would make the entire construction costs eligible for VAT. That would have been many times the income that could have been achieved by hiring out rooms. After very protracted negotiations, this anomaly was removed. One principal, however, had decided not to charge local community groups for use of the academy in the evening, and continues not to do so.

Continuing professional development

PWC (2008) noted their commitment to continuing professional development (CPD) as a feature of academies, and one principal claimed:

> We've become an absolute hothouse of staff development. Over the four and a bit years that I have been here, each year people walk quicker. There's more energy, more pace and more passion. So developing ... staff leadership, cracking the nut of getting some really powerful leadership from the middle has made a big difference. (Academy principal)

Other principals put it in different ways and were at different stages in staff development, but the message was similar.

Leadership

The architect who told us that if he were a governor he would be 'too bloody scared' to try to tell a well-known principal how to run the school, explained that the leadership that the principal provided was exercised through staff:

> The governors will tell him where they want him to take the ship and then he'll steer it. And he practices the same thing with his departments. He rarely gets involved in disciplinary matters with the children. And if you're with him and ask a head of department: 'who hires and fires in your department', they'll say 'I do'. (Architect)

While this might have been a slight exaggeration in relation to firing staff – legal requirements have to be satisfied – the essential point about leadership being distributed throughout the school remains valid. For one principal, encouraging and facilitating student leadership was possible only because the academy was so actively promoting staff leadership.

Creating an information-rich environment

One principal had been alarmed on taking up the post to find student records in a chaotic state. They could not be used to make informed decisions about vulnerable pupils, nor even about curriculum priorities. Robust and reliable information on behaviour, attendance, exclusions, special educational needs, 'looked after' and other vulnerable children, curriculum achievement and progress by subject and by year group, and so on, are essential features of all well run schools. As so often, there is nothing that is specific to academies. Without baseline data, it is impossible to monitor progress and identify weaknesses at an early stage. More important, data is crucial in identifying priorities for development.

External support

The independence of academies enabled principals to decide where to procure specialist services. In some cases they came from the LA. In others, the principal had decided that better value for money and quality were available elsewhere. Their independence also enabled them to bring in external consultants on an ad hoc basis, for example, a three person team to review the early stages of a tutoring for learning initiative.

The above headings are based on research with schools in difficulty. Chapman and Harris (2004) noted that further work was needed to see whether they applied to schools in more affluent areas. As a list of strategies they have explanatory value, and possibly some predictive value. They do not, however, give any indication of priorities, or *where* to start, nor of *how* to start. For this, the principal's own professional knowledge and experience is needed. Eisner (1991) used the term 'connoisseurship' to describe ability to apply professional knowledge and experience to assess an organisation, weigh up its strengths and weaknesses and identify priorities for change. In some situations little can be achieved without staff changes and structural reorganisation of the leadership team and/or curriculum. In others, fine tuning will suffice.

Conclusions

Is the programme designed to deliver rapid and sustainable improvement in behaviour and educational standards? The organisational rationale is clear with its emphasis on governance, independence and leadership. But these are abstract nouns and improvement results from the concrete actions and strategies of teachers in classrooms. It is unreasonable to criticise the programme for lacking any educational methodology. The Labour government tried to dictate teaching methods in primary schools with results that were at best controversial (Tymms, 2004). With the more complex curriculum in secondary schools they could never play the same card.

The governance of academies seems consistent with the rather limited research-based evidence on school turnaround. For example, it provides greater scope than in most LAs in making new appointments and retaining existing staff. It is also well placed to support retrenchment in non-core areas, and to reposition the academy to focus more sharply on current priorities. Above all it provides a new start with additional funding for a transition period.

The implications for leadership that we identified do not only apply to academies but also to LA schools. Similarly, Chapman and Harris' (2004) school improvement strategies were developed in research with LA schools, though they also illustrate how some academies achieved improvement. Yet neither our own implications for leadership nor Chapman and Harris' improvement strategies are of much help in revealing the part played by the distinctive characteristics of academies. The quick decision making and what one principal called 'restless energy' of academies may indeed facilitate successful and sustained turnaround. Yet they can also facilitate bigger mistakes.

There is a good *prima facie* case for thinking that the distinctive features of academies are indeed 'designed to deliver' improvement. If it is indeed true that the programme contains examples of more rapid and more sustained improvement than many school improvement researchers and many head teachers believed possible, the DCSF should be encouraging their dissemination. They should not be based only on rigorous statistical evidence of improvement. They should also provide qualitative evidence on the processes with which it was achieved. Without such evidence ministerial claims of the programme's success will ring hollow.

Finally, we can only agree with the principal who argued the need for government to be 'grown up' about what it expects from academies. He continued:

> In the end, as with CTCs, some of them will do well after false-starts. But the real proof of the pudding will be in ten, fifteen years. If a school like this is getting 70–80% good GCSE grades in ten years time, that's much more important than where we are now. Because that will be a quantum leap. (Academy principal)

Demonstrating the quantum leap in one academy, or even several, will not be enough. The real challenge will be to throw light on the actions and interactions that mediate it. That is more difficult than it sounds. The core characteristics of governance and leadership needed to turnaround a failing school are not necessarily those needed in helping outstanding schools to continue to develop and improve. It is only if we can understand the processes of *classroom* improvement in schools at different stages in development that there will be a realistic prospect of lasting, sustainable change across the system.

Chapter 10

The Future of Academies: Consolidating a Beachhead?

Introduction

Academies represent high-profile public sector reforms aiming to raise standards for students in some of the most deprived areas of England. They replaced some of the lowest achieving and under-performing schools in these areas. They have had varying success but in many cases can be shown to have made a difference for the better. Loathed by many trade union leaders and LAs, but accepted by both the main political parties, academies have become part of the education landscape. With cross-party support and cautious endorsement of at least some editors and education correspondents in quality newspapers, their future seems assured. With a new government the number of academies looks certain to increase beyond Tony Blair's target of 400 and these could include features that we have not discussed in this book. For example, there are currently only a few 'all through' academies catering for the 3–18 age range. It is too early to say whether this will become an increasingly popular model. Similarly, it is not clear whether the recession that started in 2008, together with a new government, will soften the current ban on 'for profit' organisations as sponsors.

With any high-profile project, whether large or small scale, once the initial impetus declines and, with academies, new buildings lose their lustre, there is a risk of two things happening. First, there tends to be a regression to the mean. Initial hard won improvement in children's behaviour and progress is gradually lost, along with the distinctive features of academies. Drawing on evaluations of anti-bullying programmes, Galloway and Roland (2004) argued that when teachers are overloaded with initiatives and innovation, this becomes almost inevitable. It can be avoided only when the values, expectations and practices associated with a new initiative become internalised, forming part of a principal's or a teacher's identity, and thus practised unconsciously on a daily basis. When enough teachers start thinking in a new way because their values, expectations and practices have changed, there is a cultural shift in the school's climate. When a cultural shift is achieved in a sufficient number of schools, the culture of the profession starts to change. As long as they remained a small scale initiative with only a few academies, there was never any chance of the academies programme exerting an influence beyond academies themselves. The projected growth in the programme, with all schools becoming eligible to seek academy status (DfE, 2010a, 2010b) creates the possibility of triggering a significant cultural shift within the teaching profession.

The second thing that can happen when the initial phase is passed depends on the scale of the project. Small-scale initiatives may simply be incorporated into the wider network. Larger scale projects can become bureaucratised. With the projected large and rapid expansion, that risk is obvious. There is already evidence of chains establishing their own support systems, and the point at which these turn into bureaucracies, similar to LAs, is ill-defined. The greater risk, though, may be that academies cease to be distinctive. One principal explained:

> I worry about the role that local authorities are playing in brokering sponsorship for groups of academies, because we know in some cases what's come with that is: 'Oh, you're not going to be like those other academies, you're going to be much more like a local authority school'. … I see no reason why local authority schools shouldn't be treated just as independently as any other. But if being a local authority school means you can't … say: 'We don't want to do 14 to 19 Diplomas like this' or 'We don't want to be part of your managed services for ICT because we've developed ICT differently and we think it's more fit for purpose,' that could be damaging. (Academy principal)

This principal was worried that with Gordon Brown as Prime Minister, the government was trying to position academies as part of local authorities. The wider question, of course, is whether evaluation data justify the continued expansion.

A Beachhead for Reform?

There is no serious debate over the failure of previous attempts to raise standards in failing and low-achieving schools. Certainly, there is controversy over the reasons for these schools' problems, with some seeing them largely as a symptom of poverty (e.g. Ball, 2009; Gorard & Smith, 2003; Whitty, 2008). We argued earlier that this could not justify government inertia in tackling these schools' problems, any more than the lack of a five year academic evaluation could justify delay in expanding the programme.

While some academies have encountered serious problems, at least in their early stages, others have demonstrated the possibility of rapid improvement in the most unpromising circumstances. As such they can be seen as a significant beachhead for systemic reform. They are clearly innovative in conception, with their independence creating opportunities for more effective governance, leadership, and teaching and learning than sometimes appeared possible under LA control. Together these help to create a change of culture. While most actions taken by principals and governing bodies in academies *could* have been taken in LA schools, it is hard to deny that they were taken more easily and more quickly in academies. Most LA bureaucracies are not well placed to take the decisive action required in turning round a failing or underachieving school.

The risk of bureaucratisation

Innovation has a limited shelf life. Its impact can dissipate over time as the energy needed to sustain it becomes sapped by resistance, absorption or bureaucracy. This is particularly likely when the innovation develops in the face of strong opposition, as with academies. The question, then, is whether the proposed 400 academies, combined with the significant investment in them by DCSF and sponsors, will create the critical mass needed to sustain the programme. It is still a nascent programme and, having had a political birth, is still subject to the vagaries of the political system. Increasing links with LAs, the disbanding of the Academies Sponsors' Trust (AST) and the absorption of academies into the Specialist Schools and Academies Trust (SSAT), along with the vested interests in CPD of the National College for School Leadership (NCSL) all create bureaucratic rocks on which the academies programme could founder. The same applies to the monitoring role of the Young People's Learning Agency and the commissioning role of LAs in courses for students aged 14–19. Academy independence is hard won and fragile.

At least three political and bureaucratic rocks could sink academies, or seriously damage them. The first is the increasingly close relationship with LAs, which we have already discussed. The second is the dilution of academies' separate identity by absorbing the AST into the SSAT. The AST was set up in parallel to the SSAT and its separate identity was diluted when CTCs were, in effect, merged with academies. Absorption within the new SSAT represented further dilution. That might not have mattered if SSAT had been a genuinely independent body. It is not. It has close links with government. It not only acts as a broker for the DCSF in the induction of academy principals; in addition its proposals have to be agreed with the DfE.

The third influence that could potentially damage academies lies in the vested interest in teachers' CPD of the NCSL. Funded by government, the NCSL controls the National Professional Qualification for Headship (NPQH) that is a compulsory pre-requisite for headship of LA schools. The 'one size fits all' approach of the NCSL and the NPQH is inconsistent with the claimed independence of academies. An academy principal told us that when the NPQH was introduced nationwide all applications for head teacher posts followed an identical format. The lack of genuinely independent alternatives to the NCSL in preparing head teachers and principals for academy leadership is unlikely to help academies (or LA schools).

To sustain the original concept of academies as independent organisations, they will have to be free to develop their own independent approaches to teaching and learning. Chains will need to continue to allow their principals to develop academies with individual identities, and where chains themselves have a particular vision they will need to allow principals to develop it in their own way in their own unique institutions. Sole trader academies will need to be aware of their independence from the LA system, while recognising that their contribution to local provision is not confined to some cooperation in 14–19 education. This loose but potentially dynamic mix could stimulate change extending far beyond academies.

The tyranny and corruption of targets

The radical nature of academies within the education reforms of which they formed an important part was their independence. This gave a glimmer of hope to those sceptical of the command and control delivery-led agenda at the heart of the prime minister's delivery unit led, when the first academies opened, by Michael Barber. That delivery-led agenda spawned a seemingly endless number of targets, each with its inspectors to inspect compliance and consultants for principals to consult as to why they had not met them. For Barber (2007: 46) the purpose of the target-led agenda was to remove the 'we've always done it this way' response from the public sector.

For academies to reach their full potential they will need to be freed from the tyranny of targets. That does not mean freedom from national expectations such as the National Challenge requirement of at least 30% of pupils gaining at least five A*–C GCSE grades including English and Maths. It does mean that these should be achievable and should be seen only as part of the education that academies (or schools) provide. *That* means that government directives, initiatives and targets are confined to an absolute minimum consistent with achieving international standards. The question is whether teachers are able to treat targets as a means to achieving wider educational and developmental goals – or continue to see them as a way of avoiding penalties for not satisfying a minister's latest whim.

Targets illustrate the weakness in New Labour's command and control approach to schools (an approach inherited in 1997 from the Conservatives). Two examples illustrate their deeply corrupting influence on teaching quality. First, a logical conclusion from Tymms' (2004) analysis of the improvements claimed by the government from the National Literacy Strategy (NLS) is that they depended on teaching to the test. Moreover, aspects of literacy that were not directly tested in SATs showed no improvement. Desperate to maintain their position in league tables and to keep Ofsted at bay, many primary schools devoted the entire final year to preparation for SATs. Very few primary teachers believed that there was any educational justification for this, nor was there any pretence that the intense preparation would lead to sustainable learning: three months after the tests, when the children arrived in their secondary schools, teachers would insist that many pupils recorded as having met the benchmark were now nowhere near that standard. As anyone who has crammed for a test knows, it takes about 24 hours to forget six months intensive cramming.

Our second example is from the secondary sector. We can only marvel at the money made by one comprehensive school from gaining acceptance of a GNVQ qualification that enabled it to become the first comprehensive with 100% of pupils gaining the equivalent of five A*–C grades in GCSE – creating a stampede from others wanting to follow suit. Again, few people tried to make a serious *educational* case for this. The government's target at the time of five A*–C grades, not necessarily including English and Maths, was what mattered. Eventually even the government realised that acceptable standards depended on rather more than five A*–C grades, and responded with the National Challenge requirement that English and Maths be included.

Mansell (2007) argued vigorously that schools had become examination factories in which intellectual curiosity was stifled. The legacy of this target-led regime was a stifling bureaucracy, creating dysfunctional educational systems. Policies were created and boxes ticked. Experts who had long since left the classroom grew rich: consultants consulting and inspectors inspecting. Meanwhile, the fundamental issues of attitude change that had arisen in some communities over generations were left unaddressed because they were neither measured nor inspected.

To repeat: we are *not* arguing that any school, least of all academies, should be unaccountable. The National Challenge benchmark seems to us quite reasonable. We *are* arguing for alternative approaches within the education system. Academies could provide an alternative, but only if their independence is not undermined by bureaucracy and a suffocating target culture. It may well be the case that other schools might benefit from the governance, leadership and independence that ministers originally claimed would be a defining feature of academies. This was presumably what led the new government in 2010 to encourage outstanding schools to apply for a fast track route, with all other schools eventually becoming elgible to apply for academy status. But much remains to be understood about the apportunities and risks created by the independence that academies offer.

Evaluations

Evaluation data have been equivocal. Ofsted inspection reports praise the leadership and governance in academies much more frequently than in comparable LA schools. On the other hand, turnover of principals has been high. Permanent exclusion of pupils has consistently exceeded the rates in LA schools, though with large variations between academies. Overall, educational progress has been better than in comparable LA schools, though there is controversy over how far this is explained by the success of academies in attracting children whose parents would previously have sought places in other schools. The most consistent point, though, is variation between academies. After a difficult start, some show signs of strong recovery. In a few, progress has been reasonably steady and consistent since acquiring academy status. Ofsted has placed several academies in the 'special measures' category or issued a 'Notice to Improve', indications of a school in sufficiently serious difficulty to justify becoming an academy. In most cases they seem to have recovered.

The variation between academies is important. Differences *within* a system, whether a group of schools or a model of teaching or classroom organisation, are invariably larger than the differences *between* systems. It would be astonishing if differences within a group of academies, and within a group of LA schools in similar areas, were not greater than differences between the LA schools and academies.

Within a secondary school, whether an academy or controlled by the LA, the best principals minimise differences between departments by bringing all to a high standard. Nevertheless, differences remain. Not every department can be outstanding. Similarly, the best and most inclusive principals create a climate in which permanent exclusion of a pupil is rarely or never needed. In any group of schools, levels of competence and commitment to underlying values vary. It was ever thus. Academies are no different.

This is why the averaging of data across academies, as in parts of PWC's reports, is of limited value. If evaluation of academies can tell us anything useful, it will be about the successes and difficulties experienced by individual schools. Nor are the 'enablers to success' in PWC report (2007) a lot more helpful. They tell us that independence, governance, sponsorship, the leadership model, the buildings and curriculum specialisms are all potential enablers to success, [one imagines that the principal quoted as extolling the 'really impressive building that is imminently fit for purpose' (PWC, 2007: 78) was not being ironic] but we are told nothing about the circumstances in which each enabler might contribute to success, nor, more importantly, about the circumstances in which it might contribute to problems. A much deeper level of qualitative data and analysis is required. It is no criticism of statistical analyses such as those of Gorard (2009) to say that they cannot answer such questions.

Three principals believed that academies had shown the possibility of more rapid school improvement than had previously been thought possible. Given the change in pupils' behaviour and in their educational attainments at some academies, compared to their predecessor schools, that does not seem an unreasonable claim. If it can be substantiated, documenting it in detail would be of international significance, not only for understanding school improvement, but for understanding the possibilities and limitations of improvement in schools serving the most challenging areas. The real challenge, though, is to identify the features of leadership that help to transform behaviour and educational achievement.

One principal inherited a one-year-old academy with 25% of pupils gaining five or more GCSE passes at grades A*–C in the summer before his appointment. The following summer this had risen to 70%. Pupils' behaviour had improved, though there had been seven exclusions, five of them at the same time for an attack on a member of the public. Asked how this had been achieved, he replied laconically: 'it's not difficult!' In essence, he had reorganised the senior management team, with the departure of several senior staff. He had appointed promising staff from within the academy as subject leaders and year heads. He and his deputy then explained to these people in middle management leadership posts what they wanted them to do, and how to do it, and supported them through the process. He made it all sound so easy, and therein lies the problem. If it really were easy, everyone would be doing it and the academies programme would be an internationally acclaimed success. A central feature of this academy's achievement appears to have been the appointment of subject leaders and year heads from within. Interestingly, research on organisational turnaround suggests that appointments to key posts from within organisations often have a major positive impact on outcomes. It is not clear whether that was possible because of unusual circumstances in this particular academy, for example, the presence of several talented and promising younger teachers. Nor is it clear whether the improvement will be sustainable. Chapman and Harris (2004) suggest that different leadership styles may be needed at different stages in a school's development, with firm directive leadership giving way to more democratic forms. The empirical evidence for this view is not strong, though the hypothesis seems reasonable. More important, there is little research evidence on the problems the principal may experience in trying to change his or her leadership style.

Academy principals inherited turbulent schools that in many cases had lost the confidence of their local communities and had suffered from chronically ineffectual leadership from their LA. In restoring stability and creating a culture of high aspiration, they had two advantages: first a fresh start, albeit with the same students and most of the same staff, with independence from the LA; second, a new governing body with the majority selected for what they could offer the school rather than the interest group they represented, led by a sponsor with high expectations. To benefit from these advantages, however, academy principals required unusual leadership abilities and interpersonal skills. All head teachers need an understanding of the school environment, and the capacity of people to fill different roles within it. Similarly, all head teachers need an understanding of when and how to innovate. Academy principals need, in addition, both the clarity of vision and the imagination to benefit from their independence of the LA's bureaucracy, rules and regulations. This is what creates the potential for an academy to move faster and more decisively than is often possible within a LA. Academy principals also need the ability to establish a good working relationship with their sponsor and governing body – as one principal put it: 'more powerful people than most head teachers ever meet'.

Since the earliest school effectiveness studies, for example, the classic work of Rutter *et al.* (1979) in London, it has been clear that social background, particularly poverty, exerts a powerful influence on educational achievement. More recently, Reynolds *et al.* (2006) have questioned how much improvement can be achieved by schools facing the most challenging circumstances. Schools make a difference, but it has always been naive to expect them to eliminate the effects of multiple disadvantage. It remains an open question how much can be achieved, for example, whether the government's benchmark of 30% of pupils in all schools gaining five A*–C passes at GCSE including English and Maths is a realistic objective.

Two things, nevertheless, are not in dispute. First, giving children stability and enabling them to achieve success at school is an important end in itself, and may help them to cope with the effects of stress and multiple disadvantage, (and, of course, the reverse is also true: instability and failure at school compound the effect of family disadvantage, at worst tipping young people towards the criminal justice or mental health systems). Second, socially divided schools are socially divisive. If all children in multiply disadvantaged estates go to the same school or academy, and if the school or academy only attracts pupils from these estates, we will create a divided society with the high probability of the school acquiring the estate's reputation. From a middle-class perspective, sink schools serve sink estates. Academies represent an important attempt to break this cycle of despair. If, as the evidence tentatively suggests, they are starting to attract middle-class parents who were previously sending their children to the suburbs or even the independent sector, it represents a notable success, not a rejection of their original aims. The only way to make sure schools become less divisive socially is to make them less divided socially.

The Ethics and Politics of Large-Scale Educational Reform

The first academies opened in 2002 and the programme has been one of the most intensively scrutinised in educational history. As well as the five-year PWC (2004–2008) evaluations, the National Audit Office (2007), TUC (2007), House of Commons Committee of Public Accounts (2007) and the Sutton Trust (Curtis *et al.*, 2008) have all examined it. Responses and conclusions have been fairly predictable, ranging from the DCSF's tendency, in the words of a principal we interviewed, 'to spin every minor success as amazing' to the TUC's (2007) call to return errant academy sheep to the welcoming LA fold. None of these evaluations seriously debated the central aim of academies to focus attention and resources on the most problematic schools in the most multiply disadvantaged areas. Nor did any of them seriously analyse the premise on which the programme was based, namely that many LAs had shown themselves to be unable or unwilling to address the predecessor schools' problems. Nor, finally, did any of them seriously address the core ethical requirement: that the programme should not do harm. (In fairness, PWC [2008] did consider whether academies had adversely affected the social balance of pupil intake of other schools in the area, but the evidence was at best inconclusive. The equally important question is whether aspects of the programme caused harm to children and teachers in academies themselves.)

It would almost certainly be impossible to prove that individual academies, even at their least successful, have done more damage or provided fewer benefits than predecessor schools. It is, however, legitimate to ask whether policies and practices linked to the academies programme have been damaging. The programme was launched with a well-publicised commitment to innovation. That commitment was reflected in DCSF representation on project management companies, and in design team companies. It was also evident in the 'support and challenge' provided by the DCSF and the SSAT.

The evidence we received suggested that the DCSF's innovation agenda was at times profoundly destabilising, at least in the early stages of some academies' development. Details of this innovation agenda were never clearly articulated. Nevertheless, it was made very clear from the outset that academies would be innovative institutions. Ministers demanded evidence of innovation. SIPs visited to demand examples. The destabilising effects were seen in the design of new buildings, in the organisation of pupils' learning and in the structure of leadership teams. In four of the six academies we visited it had been felt that stability and forward progress could be achieved only by replacing the principal, even though he/she had not been responsible for the innovation. In the interests of each academy's pupils the decision may well have been right. Nor can it legitimately be claimed that innovation was the sole reason for the instability that occurred at an early stage of these academies' development. But it certainly played a significant part.

It can be no answer for the government to claim that some academies were helped by innovation. In medicine, if a drug was shown to harm more patients than it helped, could any Minister plausibly resist temptation to cast the first stone at safety procedures and ethics committees? On this evidence, the DCSF would appear to have failed the most basic ethical requirement. A legitimate defence could be that the innovation agenda is no longer pursued with the same single-minded determination. That may be the case, but it has never formally been renounced. More important, there has never been a rigorous, independent analysis of the effects of the innovation agenda. A related example of government practice that may have harmed the development of academies is the relentless pressure for quick results. More than any other group of schools, academies are subject to constant scrutiny from DCSF officials. That is compounded by being in the media spotlight as a direct result of the programme's high political profile and the expectations at the outset of what it could achieve. Sponsors and union officials referred to burnout, and principals themselves referred to the pressure of being under constant scrutiny. High expectations are necessary. So, to use the DCSF's own phrase, is 'high support and challenge'. There is a point, though, at which challenge overwhelms support and destabilises an academy, rather than helping it to improve. A chain sponsor had recently been told by a DCSF official that the average tenure of an academy principal was now 15 months. If so that represents deterioration on the already serious problem of principal attrition identified in PWC (2008) report. We have no way of knowing in how many cases excessive pressure from SIPs or other DCSF officials, as perceived by principals, contributed to their departure. It would be surprising if it were not a significant feature.

We are *not* arguing against innovation. Without innovation there can be no progress. Complacency, apathy and stagnation are the inevitable results. But a self-confident, outward looking profession generates its own innovation. When teachers are constantly looking for new ways to strengthen teaching and children's learning, innovation becomes an organic process, from within.

The best that can be hoped for from the check list of innovations hawked around academies by SIPs and other DCSF officials is a quick burial in the landfill site of forgotten initiatives and innovations. At worst they seriously destabilised some academies before being consigned for burial. In linking academies to an ill-thought-out innovation agenda, the DCSF did not derail the programme, but our evidence suggests that they certainly destabilised it.

Consolidating the Beachhead: The Need for an Academies Development Agency

The DCSF: The LA from hell?

As years pass and budgets tighten, iconic buildings become less distinctive and, in some cases, more expensive to heat and maintain. As chains become longer, the scope for independent, energetic principals to put their own necessarily idiosyncratic stamp on an academy is reduced. The knighted principal (not in our sample) that an eminent architect said he would be 'too bloody scared' to contradict is likely to become an increasing rarity. The danger of drift from Andrew Adonis' core principles of quality and independence is obvious. The temptation to subsume key aspects of academies such as 14–19 education within the commissioning role of LAs is even more obvious, as is the temptation to give all schools academy status, thereby removing their distinctiveness.

We asked a principal whether he thought there was a risk of chains starting to act like LA's he replied:

> I think the biggest danger is that the DCSF is becoming the local authority from hell. (Academy principal)

For this principal, there was an urgent need for a funding agency that placed day-to-day management and decisions about money at arm's length from Ministers. He was clearly right about the importance of placing decisions at arm's length from ministers, but this should go beyond funding and day-to-day management.

Academies have changed since the earliest ones were opened in 2002 and 2003. Their independence has been reduced in relation to the curriculum. Sponsors have far less control over design and procurement of new buildings and LAs play a central role in identifying schools for conversion to academy status. Academies are required to work closely with LAs over provision for 14–19 education. The nature of sponsorship has changed. There is some evidence of chains setting up their own bureaucracies, and it is clear that both universities and successful schools will establish different relationships with the academies they sponsor to the original entrepreneurial business sponsors.

None of this *necessarily* undermines the independence of academies, nor their commitment to the highest possible standards, but it all points in the same direction. It may not be long before the 'support and challenge' provided by project leads, advisers and SIPs is directed at conformity to some predetermined DfE norm. While it may have been politically expedient in the short term for the Labour government to re-attach academies to LAs, it is difficult to justify in educational or policy terms. Academies were given freedom from LA control because LAs were failing to add value to their predecessor schools, and to meet local community needs. Bureaucracies, whether in local or central government, are not designed to deal with the local and turbulent environments of failing and under-performing schools. Nor are they designed to deal with the fast moving environments of academies. Turbulent situations require organisations that are more fluid and more organic than the types of bureaucracy that are starting to be placed around the academies programme.

When the first academies opened there was some truth in the rhetoric of them being independent schools within the state sector and that rhetoric is also evident in the Conservative–Liberal Democrat coalition's plans for expanding the programme. They have struggled to maintain this independence, not always successfully. Yet the principle of an alternative to the LA sector is an important one, as is the necessity for more rapid and decisive action than most LAs are able or willing to take with underachieving or failing schools.

If academies are to provide a valid alternative – and challenge – to LA schools, they will need some protection against the whims of passing Secretaries of State and the resentments of LA politicians and officers. In a democracy no such protection can be absolute, nor should it be. Nevertheless, establishing an Academies Development Agency as an independent body responsible for developing academies as credible, independent alternatives to the LA system would be a powerful declaration of intent, which could not lightly be set aside.

An Academies Development Agency would have 10 tasks:

(1) *Funding.* Academies should have a minimum funding guarantee based on the highest 33% of relevant regional formulae preferably with recognition – as existed until 2010 – of the need for additional resources in the early stages of turnaround.

(2) *Policy.* The academies programme is at risk of policy drift. This could occur when, for example, a new Secretary of State does not share his or her predecessor's views about the importance of the programme and/or the weaknesses of LAs. It will be very easy for ministers to curry favour with LAs by allowing academies, partly through inertia, and partly through developments in other areas such as, 14–19 education, to become increasingly controlled by LAs. The policy is also at risk from arbitrary policy changes as a new Secretary of State strives to create his or her own legacy. Since the average tenure of a secretary of state is less than two years, the scope for instability in policy is almost unlimited. Passing responsibility to an Academies Development Agency, working to an explicit brief to ensure quality and formulate policy, could not overcome this problem, but could provide a more secure future.

(3) *Quality.* Ofsted would have to remain responsible for inspections, but there are other more fundamental considerations, over which Ofsted has less control. One concerns the action to be taken when a sponsor becomes unable or unwilling to maintain a commitment to an academy. A second concerns circumstances in which an academy consistently fails to provide a good quality education, even though it does not meet the criteria for Ofsted's Special Measures. A third concerns appropriate support in the rare circumstances of an academy facing a

high profile but hopefully temporary problem such as a major incident of violence, accidents to pupils or incidents of child abuse. It is not clear that the DfE is well placed to take swift but sensitive action in such circumstances. Swayed by ministerial fear of media headlines, it is all too easy to imagine senior civil servants acting, as the academy principal quoted above suggested, 'like the local authority from hell'.

(4) *Independence.* An Academies Development Agency would insist on independence from LAs and encourage chains to set up their own LEPs. This could also apply to the 'Free Schools' that the DfE is encouraging. These will be 'all ability state funded schools, set up in response to parental demand' (DfE, 2010c). Chains with distinctive features would be encouraged, as alternatives to LA schools.

(5) *Beyond targets and performance indicators.* National standards are important but should be seen as a means to achieving wider educational goals. These are not easily measured, for example, creativity, transferability of skills, desire to learn both within and beyond the formal curriculum. An Academies Development Agency would encourage academies to use their independence to develop and publicise broader personal, social and educational goals.

(6) *Leadership.* To achieve turnaround in the most challenging schools in the most disadvantaged areas, leaders need to be unconstrained by the vested interests of SSAT, NCSL and NPQH. They should be able to use their independence to develop their own leadership programmes, assisted and encouraged by an Academies Development Agency.

(7) *Appointment and professional development of staff.* Through chains, or the creative energy of individual leaders, academies should be able to develop their own staffing and professional development policies assisted and encouraged, again, by an Academies Development Agency. The agency's role would be to monitor, evaluate and publicise developments and innovations.

(8) *Innovations.* Experience suggests that the DCSF's innovation agenda was in general unhelpful to academies. Nevertheless, it is entirely reasonable to encourage academies to become centres for innovation. The ideas and motivation, though, should come from academies themselves. Part of an Academies Development Agency's job should be to encourage and facilitate innovation, and for that it would need a budget.

(9) *Research and publications.* It should be no part of a development agency's job to spin every minor success as an amazing achievement, as at least one principal considered the DCSF to have done. It should

commission and publish high-quality research that throws light on school improvement in the most challenging areas. Work that identifies pitfalls to be avoided should be seen as having as much importance as success stories. It would include rigorous independent evaluation, with a focus on the task of leadership and the process of teaching and learning.

(10) *Monitoring of consultants and SIPs.* We emphasise again that some SIPs and some consultants provide an important service that principals recognise and appreciate. Yet we have argued that the academies programme has suffered from less competent consultants. They were responsible for the almost bizarre decisions on the design of some of the early academies and for the ill-thought-out and insensitive innovations that destabilised others. Some SIPs, too, contributed to destabilisation by their unquestioning obedience to the DCSF's demand for evidence of innovation – *any* innovation. An Academies Development Agency would be well placed to monitor the quality of consultants and SIPs, ensuring that they provide support and, where necessary, challenge, without constraining principals' freedom of action.

Expanding the Programme

Language and logic: the death of innovation. As a matter of language and logic innovation has a short shelf life. After a time – usually quite a short time – an innovation ceases to be innovative. If it is successful an innovation is incorporated into general practice and therefore ceases to be innovative. If it isn't successful it is quietly dropped. The academies experiment, then, cannot expect to remain innovative, even if individual academies do so.

In opposition the Conservative party supported academies. In government they quickly proposed extensions to the programme that will radically change its direction and, possibly, the face of education in England. From being a relatively small programme for underachieving schools in socially disadvantaged neighbourhoods, the government wants academy status to become a coveted accolade. Schools rated outstanding by Ofsted are being encouraged to apply for a fast track route to academy status, and all other primary, secondary and special schools are eventually likely to be offered the opportunity.

The underlying thinking is clear: What was good for problem schools in problem areas must also be good for outstanding schools and, eventually, any school with the courage to seek independence from its LA. The underlying thinking, though, is not necessarily valid. The DfE will need to address two questions. First, *some* academies have shown themselves able to take difficult decisions quickly, either on their own initiative or under pressure from sponsors or DfE officials, and to emerge from the turbulence that characterised their early years. That is not true of all academies. The turnover of principals and the ongoing problems experienced by some academies would undoubtedly be seen as evidence of incompetence if they occurred within a LA. It is not yet clear that group sponsors have consistently produced governing bodies with the necessary clarity of vision and unity of purpose. Nor is it yet clear that universities and independent school sponsors have the clarity of vision and strength of vision to cope with a school in a period of turbulence. Second, it is not clear that the core features required in the governing body and leadership of a failing school are the same as in an outstanding school or a modestly successful one. There is little evidence on how the best LAs and the most successful academies develop the capacity of their governing bodies and their senior leadership teams in schools.

The moral basis for academies. Under the Labour government the moral basis for academies was obvious. First, focus resources on the most problematic schools in the most disadvantaged areas. Help these schools turn around, then extend the programme to other schools. On the assumption that they thought the academy experiment had succeeded, the Conservative–Liberal Democrat coalition decision to extend the programme to outstanding schools also has a clear moral foundation.

Nevertheless, the coalition government has removed one of the programme's strongest moral defences. There is no longer any automatic entitlement to capital investment, nor to the generous start-up funds that were available to academies opening from 2002–2009. These are replaced by a one-off grant of £25,000 to cover everything from legal costs to signage and stationery. Compared to what was previously available, this is insignificant. Schools rated outstanding by Ofsted come disproportionately from more privileged catchment areas, certainly much more privileged than academies opening from 2002–2009. The programme is therefore no longer an initiative for the disadvantaged.

Moreover, the very limited available funding will go disproportionately to schools in more privileged areas. If the new government is serious about helping the most disadvantaged schools in the most disadvantaged areas, it will need to find a more equitable way of distributing limited resources.

Learning from mistakes, not just successes. New academies are expected to be at the centre of their communities and to work with other schools and local partners (DfE, 2010b), Included in this expectation is that they will work with another school to raise its standards. When a successful school is nominated to help an unsuccessful one, the potential for fruitful cooperation is unlimited – as is the potential for discord and acrimony. If this experiment in school improvement is to win the confidence of the profession, the DfE will need to be as open about the problems that will inevitably arise as about the success stories.

Removing the necessity for a sponsor for outstanding schools seeking to become academies raises questions about the sponsor's role on an academy's governing body. The assumption is presumably that a sound governing body does not need a sponsor. There may indeed be no benefit in having a sponsor while the school remains outstanding, but all schools can change. With a downturn in the school's fortunes, the potential value of a sponsor may need to be reviewed.

Conclusions: A Sustainable Cultural Shift?

In the first stage of the academies programme, from 2002–2009, under Labour governments, they could be seen as a necessary irritant within the state system of secondary education: an irritant because they challenged the LA monopoly and made life difficult for it; necessary because every system needs a challenge to avoid complacency. Yet on its own that would be an insufficient justification for academies.

New academy buildings are a powerful symbol of commitment to some of the country's least-privileged communities. Yet, as Andrew Adonis argued, although they are important, probably necessary, on their own they are certainly not sufficient. It needs to be shown *how and in what circumstances* they are most likely to contribute to transformation in teaching, learning and achievement.

The central problem in many failing and low-achieving schools is a culture of low aspiration and low achievement, affecting both pupils and teachers. Principals who thrive under pressure and enjoy responding to the challenge of pupils from multiply disadvantaged neighbourhoods may succeed in turning around an academy's fortunes, but a sustainable cultural shift requires changes in how the teaching profession thinks about itself. That applies not only to what teachers expect of children but also to how teaching in schools in the most challenging areas is perceived by the most promising new teachers: As an ordeal to be endured until a better job can be found, or as a privilege to be sought? The achievement of Teach First is to attract some of the country's best graduates to work in these schools.

Since the 1944 Education Act there has only been one cultural shift in how a large section of the teaching profession thinks about itself. This followed publication of the Plowden Report on Primary education (CACE, 1967). For the first time, primary teachers started to see themselves as specialists in their own right, no longer the under-qualified poor relations of secondary teachers. Freed from the 11+ examination the profession genuinely felt pride in a new, supposedly child-centred curriculum and pedagogy.

It is wrong to dismiss the Plowden revolution as built on sand. Certainly, there were many schools in which dreary Maths and English schemes masqueraded as a child-centred curriculum, and in which tedious, undemanding topics masqueraded as group work. The long tail of underachievement remained unaltered. The best teachers continued to compete for jobs in the best schools in the most privileged areas. Yet two points remain valid. First, Plowden did trigger a profound change in how the primary teaching profession thought about itself. Second, this was a grass-roots movement, not imposed by government, or even receiving much support from it.

The comparison with academies is instructive. Academies are premised on the need for a cultural shift in how teachers in the most challenging schools think of themselves and their students. Unlike the cultural shift triggered by Plowden, academies represent a high-profile political commitment to education of children whom the system has most often failed. A pessimist would argue that the high-profile political commitment is precisely what will prevent the cultural shift that the government wants. By definition, grass-roots movements grow from the ground.

That view may prove correct, but the pessimism is not necessarily justified. We argued in the last chapter that the people directly responsible for raising standards are neither sponsors, nor principals, but ordinary classroom teachers. Some academies are attracting excellent teachers. More important, the sharp improvement in many academies in teaching and learning, at least as judged by Ofsted, suggests that they are also *developing* excellent teachers, who are successful in helping pupils reach the targets they set, based on high aspirations. In two academies we heard of Teach First graduates taking posts with significant responsibility in their second and third years of teaching. For academies to grow their own specialist teachers and their own leaders represents a small but not unimportant step towards the cultural shift in attitude and belief that could transform teaching in the most challenging areas. Academies will not achieve it on their own. Many similar examples can also be found in LA schools. Nevertheless, academies are in the forefront of educational change in these areas. Remaining there is the challenge they face.

A final thought

In her Reith lectures, O'Neill (2002) analysed the corrosive effect of loss of trust in public services. She attributed this to an ever-growing accountability culture. Although her experience was in the Health Service, her arguments apply equally to education. Seddon (2008) argued strongly that the government's misguided belief in targets, incentives and inspections have limited the progress of reform. In an accountability culture, meeting targets can become more important than caring for patients or children. Developing one's professional skills can become less important than record keeping and passing inspections. In this corrosive climate, patients lose trust in healthcare professionals; and healthcare professionals become mere deliverers of the state's demands. (Marxists call this process proletarianisation: the process in which skilled craftspeople lose pride in the skills of their craft, becoming subservient to externally imposed rules and demands.)

Many academies have illustrated O'Neill's ideal, and also what she attacks so eloquently. At worst, constant heavy-handed scrutiny and demands for innovation exposed the DCSF's profound lack of trust in principals and sponsors. The best practice of the best schools was not, apparently, good enough for politicians and civil servants in a hurry. Constant high-profile scrutiny and often unrealistic demands for rapid improvement, too, reveal the same deep-rooted lack of trust.

Yet it is also easy to see O'Neill's ideal in many academies. It can be seen in a climate of mutual trust between teachers and their students – a climate that was rare though seldom, if ever, non-existent in predecessor schools. In such a climate, a teacher has high expectations of students and students are confident that with this teacher, they will achieve success. The same trusting relationships can be seen between principals and their senior leadership teams, and between those teams and subject leaders. They are not unique to academies, but academies still represent the best chance of changing the culture of schools in the most challenging areas.

References

Adams, J. and Puntner, A. (2008) Finding and keeping school governors: The work of the School Governors' one-stop shop. *Management in Education* 22 (4), 14–17.

Adonis, A. and Pollard, S. (1997) *A Class Act*. London: Hamish Hamilton.

Alexander, R. (1992) *Policy and Practice in Primary Education*. London: Routledge.

Alexander, R., Rose, J. and Woodhead, C. (1992) *Curriculum Organisation and Classroom Practice in Primary Schools: A Discussion Paper*. London: Department of Education and Science.

Ball, D.L. and Forzani, F.M. (2007) What makes educational research 'educational?' *Educational Researcher* 36, 529–540.

Ball, S.J. (2009) Privatising education, privatising policy, privatising educational research: Network governance and the 'competitive state'. *Journal of Educational Policy* 24 (1), 83–99.

Barber, M. (1996) *The Learning Game*. London: Victor Gollancz.

Barber, M. (2007) *An Instruction to Deliver*. London: Politico's.

Beckett, F. (2007) *The Great City Academy Fraud*. London: Continuum.

Beckett, F. and Evans, R. (2008) Who's making wishes come true? *The Guardian*, 10th June, Education Guardian, 1–2.

Bennett, N. (1976) *Teaching Styles and Pupil Progress*. London: Open Books.

Beverton, S., Harries, T. and Galloway, D. (2005) *Teaching Approaches to Promote Consistent Level 4 Performance in Key Stage 2 English and Mathematics*. Research Report 699. London: DfES.

Blunkett, D. (2000) Transforming secondary education. *Speech to the Social Market Foundation* (15th March). On WWW at http://www.dfes.gov.uk/speeches. Accessed 23.07.09.

Boyne, G. and Meier, K. (2009) Environmental change, human resources and organisational turnaround. *Journal of Management Studies* 46 (5), 835–863.

British Council for School Environments (2007) *Manifesto for Learning Environments*. London: BCSE.

Building Design (2006) *Academies 'could do better'*. 31st March.

Burgess, R.G. (1983) *Experiencing Comprehensive Education: A Study of Bishop McGregor School*. London: Methuen.

Callaghan, J. (1976) *Speech by the Prime Minister at a Foundation Stone Laying Ceremony at Ruskin College*, 18th October, Oxford.

Central Advisory Council in Education (CACE) (1967) *Children and their Primary Schools*. The Plowden Report. London: HMSO.

Chapman, C. (2003) Leadership in schools facing challenging circumstances: Specialisms and propositions. Paper presented at the _Symposium: School Improvement in Challenging Circumstances_, Sydney: ICSE.

Chapman, C. and Harris, A. (2004) Improving schools in difficult and challenging circumstances. _Educational Research_ 46, 219–228.

Cohen, D.K. and Hill, H.C. (2001) _Learning Policy: When State Education Reform Works._ New Haven, CT: Yale University Press.

Coleman, J.S. _et al._ (1966) _Equality of Educational Opportunity._ Washington: US Government Printing Office.

Commission for Architecture and the Built Environment (2006) _Assessing Secondary School Design Quality._ Research report. London: CABE.

Conger, J., Lawler, E. and Feingold, D. (2001) _Corporate Boards._ San Francisco: Jossey-Bass.

Corrigan, P. (1979) _Schooling the Smash Street Kids._ London: Macmillan.

Cox, C.B. and Boyson, R. (1977) _Black Paper 1977._ London: Temple Smith.

Croll, P. and Moses, D. (1985) _One in Five: The Assessment and Incidence of Special Educational Needs._ London: Routledge and Kegan Paul.

Curtis, A., Exley, E., Sasia, A., Tough,. S. and Whitty, G. (2008) _The Academies Programme: Progress, Problems and Possibilities._ Report for the Sutton Trust. London: Institute of Education, University of London.

Dean, S. and Galloway, D. (2008) Teaching respect: A school and community based approach to improving social and educational climate: Can experience in Canada have implications for practice in England? _Emotional and Behavioural Difficulties_ 13, 217–228.

Department for Children, Schools and Families (2007a) _Delivering Academy Buildings through PfS: The DCSF Project Manager and the Local Authority Project Manager._ London: DCSF.

Department for Children, Schools and Families (2007b) _Academies and Independent Schools: Prospectus._ London: DCSF.

Department for Children, Schools and Families (2007c) _Delivering Academy Buildings through PfS: An Overview for Sponsors._ London: DCSF.

Department for Children, Schools and Families (2008a) _What are Academies?_ On WWW at http://www.standards.gov.uk/academies. Accessed 24.10.08.

Department for Children, Schools and Families (2008b) _National Challenge: A Toolkit for Schools and Local Authorities._ On WWW at http://www.dcsf.gov.uk/nationalchallenge. Accessed 01.07.09.

Department for Children, Schools and Families (2009) _Directory of Academies._ On WWW at http://www.standards.gov.uk/academies. Accessed 03.07.09.

Department for Children, Schools and Families (Undated) _Academy Principals Handbook._ London: DCSF.

Department for Education (2010a) _Michael Gove invites all schools to become academies._ On WWW at http://www.education.gov.uk/news/academies. 21st June, 2010. Accessed 30.6.10.

Department for Education (2010b) _Academies: Frequently asked questions._ On WWW at http://www.education.gov.uk/academies/faqs. 21st June, 2010. Accessed 30.6.10.

Department for Education (2010c) _Free Schools._ On WWW at http://www.education.gov.uk/freeschools. 21st June, 2010. Accessed 30.6.10.

Department for Education and Employment (1998) *The National Literacy Strategy.* London: DFEE.

Department for Education and Employment (1999) *The National Numeracy Strategy.* London: DFEE.

Department of Education and Science (1972) *Teacher Education and Training.* The James Report. London: HMSO.

Department for Education and Skills (2003) *Schools for the Future: Building Bulletin 95.* London: The Stationary Office.

Department for Education and Skills (2004) *Building Schools for the Future: A New Approach to Capital Investment.* London: DfES.

Department for Education and Skills (2005) *14–19 Education and Skills White Paper.* London: The Stationary Office.

Department for Education and Skills (2006a) *Learning by Design: England.* London: Open House Exemplar.

Department for Education and Skills (2006b) *Strategy for Change: Guidance for Local Authorities in BSF Wave 4.* London: DfES

Department for Education and Skills (2007) *Better Buildings, Better Design, Better Education.* London: DfES.

Dewey, J. (2004) *Democracy and Education.* Mineola, NY: Dover Publications.

Doyle, W. (1986) Classroom organisation and management. In M.C. Wittrock (ed.) *Handbook of Research on Teaching* (3rd edn). New York: Macmillan.

Eisner, E.W. (1991) *The Enlightened Eye: Qualitative Inquiry and the Enhancement of Educational Practice.* New York: Macmillan.

Estyn (2007) *An Evaluation of Performance of Schools Before and After Moving into New Premises.* Cardiff: Estyn.

Evans, J., Castle, F., Cooper, D., Glatter, R. and Woods, P.A. (2005) Collaboration: The big 'new idea' for school improvement? *Journal of Educational Policy* 20, 223–225.

Fullan, M. (1993) *Change Forces: Probing the Depths of Educational Reform.* London: Falmer.

Galloway, D. (1983) Disruptive pupils and effective pastoral care. *School Organisation* 3, 245–254.

Galloway, D. (1990) Was the GERBIL a Marxist mole? In P. Evans and V. Varma (eds) *Special Education, Past, Present and Future.* Lewes: Falmer.

Galloway, D. (1995) Truancy, delinquency, exclusion and disruption: Differential school influences. *Education Section Review, (BPS)* 19 (ii), 49–53.

Galloway, D. (2001) Educational reform and the mental health of vulnerable children and young people. *Child Psychology and Psychiatry Review* 6 (iv), 150–158.

Galloway, D., Ball, T., Seyd, R. and Blomfield, D. (1982) *Schools and Disruptive Pupils.* London: Longman.

Galloway, D., Boswell, K., Panckhurst, F., Boswell, C. and Green, K. (1985b) Sources of satisfaction and dissatisfaction for New Zealand primary school teachers. *Educational Research* 27, 44–51.

Galloway, D. and Roland, E. (2004) Is the direct approach to reducing bullying always the best? In P. Smith, D. Pepler and K. Rigby (eds) *Bullying in Schools: How Successful can Interventions Be?* Cambridge: Cambridge University Press.

Galloway, D. and Upton, G. (1990) *Joint Final Report on Special Educational Needs (Primary Education and Secondary Education Consultancies).* Ministry of Education, Barbados.

Galloway, D., Wilcox, B. and Martin, R. (1985a) Persistent absence from school and exclusion from school: The predictive power of school and community variables. *British Educational Research Journal* 11, 51–61.

Garner, R. (2008) First selective school agrees on partnership with failing neighbour. *The Independent*, 28th June, p. 26.

Gonczi, A. (2008) Corporate Australia and the education revolution. *Australian Review of Public Affairs, Digest*. On WWW at *http://www.australianreview.net*. Accessed 23.07.09.

Gorard, S. (2005) Academies as the 'future of schooling': Is this an evidence-based policy? *Journal of Educational Policy* 20, 369–377.

Gorard, S. (2009) What are academies the answer to? *Journal of Educational Policy* 24, 101–113.

Gorard, S. and Smith, E. (2003) What is 'underachievement at school'? *Working Paper Series, Paper 34*. Cardiff: Cardiff University School of Social Sciences.

Gorard, S. and Taylor, C. (2002) Market forces and standards in education: A preliminary consideration. *British Journal of Sociology of Education* 23, 5–18.

Gray, J. and Wilcox, B. (1995) *Good School, Bad School: Evaluating Performance and Encouraging Improvement*. Buckingham: Open University Press.

Hallam, S. (2002) *Ability Grouping in Schools: A Literature Review*. London: Institute of Education, University of London.

Halpin, D., Dickson, M., Power, S., Whitty, G. and Gewirtz, S. (2004) Curriculum innovation within an evaluative state: Issues of risk and regulation. *Curriculum Journal* 15 (3), 197–206.

Hargreaves, D. (1967) *Social Relations in a Secondary School*. London: Routledge and Kegan Paul.

Hargreaves, D. (1982) *The Challenge for the Comprehensive School: Culture, Curriculum, Community*. London: Routledge and Kegan Paul.

Hargreaves, D.H. (2001) A capital theory of school effectiveness and improvement. *British Educational Research Journal* 27, 487–503.

Hargreaves, D.H. (2003) *Education Epidemic: Transforming Secondary Schools through Innovation Networks*. London: DEMOS.

Harris, A. and Chapman, C. (2002) *Leadership in Schools Facing Challenging Circumstances*. Nottingham: National Council for School Leadership.

Harris, A., Muijs, M., Chapman, C., Stoll, L. and Russ, J. (2003) *Raising Attainments in Schools in the Former Coalfields Areas*. London: DfES.

Haviland, D. (1988) *Take Care, Mr. Baker!* London: Fourth Estate.

Higgins, S., Hall, E., McGaughey, C., Wall, K. and Woolner, P. (2005) *The Impact of School Environments: A Literature Review*. London: Design Council.

House of Commons Committee of Public Accounts (2007) *The Academies Programme: Report, together with Formal Minutes, Oral and Written Evidence*. London: HMSO.

Hutchings, M., Naylor, U., Mendick, H., Menter, I. and Smart, S. (2006) *An evaluation of Innovative Approaches to Teacher Training on the Teach First Programme: Formal Report to the Training and Development Agency for Schools*. London: IPSC.

Hutton, W. (1995) *The State We're In*. London: Jonathan Cape.

Jesson, D. (2008) Grammar schools in the twenty first century and 'social mobility'. *Research Intelligence*, November (105), 24–25.

Kotter, J. (1996) *Leading to Change*. Boston: Harvard Business School Press.

Leadbetter, C. (1999) *Living on Thin Air*. London: Penguin.

Leithwood, K., Day, C., Sammons, P., Harris, A. and Hopkins, D. (2004) *Seven Strong Claims about Successful School Leadership*. Nottingham: National College for School Leadership.

Leo, E. and Barton, L. (2006) Inclusion, diversity and leadership: Perspectives, possibilities and contradictions. *Educational Management, Administration and Leadership* 34 (2), 167–180.

Levy, M. (2008) *A Question of Honour*. London: Pocket Books.

Lupton, R. (2004) *Schools in Disadvantaged Areas: Recognising Context and Raising Quality*. CASE Paper 76. London: Centre for Analysis of Social Exclusion, London School of Economics.

Macaulay, H. (2008a) Leadership of academies: Complexity and challenge. PhD thesis, University of Hull.

Macaulay, H. (2008b) *Under the Microscope: Leading in a Climate of Close Public Scrutiny*. Nottingham: NCSL.

Mansell, W. (2007) *Education by Numbers: The Tyranny of Testing*. London: Politico.

McLaughlin, M.J. and Rhim, L.M. (2007) Accountability frameworks and children with disabilities: A test of assumptions about improving public education for all students. *International Journal for Disability, Development and Education* 54, 25–49.

Mortimore, P., Sammons, P., Stoll, L., Lewis, D. and Ecob, R. (1988) *School Matters: The Junior Years*. Wells: Open Books.

Moynihan, D. (2007) Headteachers can and do make a difference. In J. O'Shaughnessy (ed.) *The Leadership Effect*. London: Policy Exchange.

Murphy, J. and Meyers, C. (2009) Rebuilding organisational capacity in turnaround schools. *Educational Management, Administration and Leadership* 37 (91), 9–27.

National Audit Office (2007) *The Academies Programme: Report by the Comptroller and Auditor General*. London: The Stationary Office.

Ofsted (2002) *Teaching of Science at Emmanuel College*. London: Ofsted.

Ofsted (2004) *Annual Report of Her Majesty's Chief Inspector of Schools*. London: Ofsted.

Ofsted (2008a) *Curriculum Innovation in Schools*. London: Ofsted.

Ofsted (2008b) *Rising to the Challenge: A Review of the Teach First Initial Teacher Training Programme*. London: Ofsted.

O'Neill, O. (2002) *A Question of Trust. (BBC Reith Lectures.)* Cambridge: Cambridge University Press.

Partnerships for Schools (2006) Partnerships for schools to deliver future academies. Press release, 31st March. London: PfS. On WWW at http://www.partnershipsforschools.org.uk. Accessed 03.12.08.

Pennell, H. and West, A. (2007) *Parents in the Driving Seat? Parents' Roles in Setting up New Secondary Schools*. London: Research and Information on State Education Trust/London School of Economics.

Phillips, J. (2008) The future of school governance: Educational excellence and community enhancement going hand in hand. *Management in Education* 22 (4), 18–21.

Pounce, M. (2008) Head teachers and governors: A marriage made in heaven? *Management in Education* 22 (4), 8–10.

PriceWaterhouseCoopers (2003) *Academies Evaluation: Annual Report*. London: DfES.

PriceWaterhouseCoopers (2005) *Academies Evaluation: Second Annual Report*. London: DfES.

PriceWaterhouseCoopers (2006) *Academies Evaluation: Third Annual Report.* London: DfES.

PriceWaterhouseCoopers (2007) *Academies Evaluation: Fourth Annual Report.* London: DfES.

PriceWaterhouseCoopers (2008) *Academies Evaluation: Fifth Annual Report.* London: DCSF.

Reynolds, D., Harris, A., Clarke, P., Harris, B. and James, S. (2006) Challenging the challenged: Developing an improvement programme for schools facing exceptionally challenging circumstances. *School Effectiveness and School Improvement* 17, 425–439.

Royal Institute of British Architects (2006) *Education Sector Review 2006.* London: RIBA.

Rutter, M. (1978) Family, area and school influences in the genesis of conduct disorders. In L. Hersov, M. Berger and D. Schaffer (eds) *Aggression and Anti-social Behaviour in Childhood and Adolescence. (Journal of Child Psychology and Psychiatry Book Series,* No. 1.). Oxford: Pergamon.

Rutter, M., Maughan, B., Mortimore, P. and OPuston, J. (1979) *Fifteen Thousand Hours: Secondary Schools and their Effects on Pupils.* London: Open Books.

Sammons, P.A. and Matthews, P. (2005) Survival of the weakest: The differential improvement of schools causing concern in England. *London Review of Education* 3, 159–176.

Sannino, A. and Nocon, H. (2008) Activity theory and school innovation. *Journal of Education Change* 9, 325–328.

Schofield, A. (2006) *Essential Questions for the Future School.* On WWW at http://www.educationforum.ipbhost.com. Accessed 25.11.08.

Schwab, J.J. (1978) The practical: Translation into curriculum. In I. Westbury and N.J. Wilkof (eds) *Science, Curriculum and Liberal Education: Selected Essays.* Chicago: University of Chicago Press.

Searle, J. and Tymms, P. (2007) The impact of head teachers on the performance and attitudes of pupils. In J. O'Shaughnessy (ed.) *The Leadership Effect.* London: Policy Exchange.

Seddon, J. (2008) *Systems Thinking in the Public Sector.* Axminster: Triarchy Press.

Shipman, M. (1997) *The Limitations of Social Research.* London: Longman.

Silver, H., Hannan, A. and English, S. (1997) 'Innovation': Questions of Boundary. Working Paper No. 2. On WWW at http://www.fae.plym.ac.uk/itlhe.html.

Smith, M.J. (2007) *Isle of Sheppey Review: The Best Option for Developing an Academy on the Isle of Sheppey in Terms of Promoting Educational Excellence for the Next Generation.* London: DCSF.

Smith, M.J. (2008) *Independent Evaluation of Bids from Potential Sponsors of Durham Academies.* London: DCSF.

Smith, M., Busi, M., Ball, P. and Van Der Meer, R. (2008) Factors influencing an organisation's ability to manage innovation: A structured literature review and conceptual model. *International Journal of Innovation Management* 12 (4), 655–676.

Somekh, B. (2005) *Information and communication technologies and the culture of schooling: Understanding innovation and building scenarios for radical reform.* Unpublished Paper presented at the British Educational Research Association Annual Conference.

Stothart, C. (2008) Now, young ladies, we've become an academy. *Times Educational Supplement*, 19th December, 18–20.

Thompson, P., McGregor, J., Sanders, E. and Alexiadou, N. (2009) Changing schools: More than a lick of paint and a well orchestrated performance. *Improving Schools* 12, 43–57.

Trades Union Congress (2007) *A New Direction: A Review of the School Academies Programme*. London: TUC.

Tymms, P. (2004) Are standards rising in English primary schools? *British Educational Research Journal* 30 (4), 477–494.

Whitty, G. (2008) Twenty years of progress? English education policy 1988 to the present. *Educational Management, Administration and Leadership* 36 (2), 165–184.

Willis, P. (1977) *Learning to Labaour: How Working Class Kids Get Working Class Jobs*. Farnborough: Saxon House.

Wills, D. (1966) *Throw Away Thy Rod*. London: Victor Gollancz.

Woods, G.J. (2005) Going deep: Adapting the modern leadership agenda. *Management in Education* 18, 28–32.

Woods, P.A. (2000) Varieties and themes in producer engagement: Structure and agency in the schools public market. *British Journal of Sociology of Education* 21, 219–242.

Woods, P.A., Woods, G.J. and Gunter, H. (2007) Academy schools and entrepreneurialism in action. *Journal of Education Policy* 22, 237–259.

Woolner, P., Hall, E., Higgins, S., McCaughey, C. and Wall, K. (2007) A sound foundation? What we know about the impact of environments on learning and the implications for building Schools for the Future. *Oxford Review of Education* 33, 47–70.

Woolner, P., Hall, E., Wall, K., Higgins, S., Blake, A. and McCaughey, C. (2007) *School Building Programmes: Motivations, Consequences and Implications*. Newcastle: CfBT.

Zinkeviciene, N. (2005) *Teachers' receptivity to curriculum change: Possible barriers to the innovation initiation phase*. Paper presented at the European Conference on Educational Research.

Index

Academic Development Agency
– consultants, 205
– funding, 203
– quality, 203–204
– research and publications, 204–205
– tasks, 203–205
academies
– *vs.* CTCs, 153–154
– distinctiveness, 110
– impact on LAs, 159–161
– independence, 112–113, 159–161
– Labour government, 3, 5
– *vs.* LA schools, 112–113
– losing distinctiveness, 192
– moral basis, 206
– pressure, 122
– *vs.* previous reform initiatives, 26
– priorities, 114
– programme launching, 3, 5
– radical focus shift, 3
– turbulence, 83
– underachieving schools *vs.* outstanding schools, 3
– variations within, 196
– vision, 114
academies distinctive features, 109–124, 125–152
– accountability, 109–124
– attendance examples, 131–139
– behaviour examples, 131–139
– context, 110–111
– curriculum examples, 140–142
– independence, 112–120
– innovation, 125–152
– mantra snake oil, 127–130
– muddled distraction or necessity, 127–130
– perils case study, 143–146
– pressure, 121–122
academies future, 191–209
– beachhead consolidation, 201–204
– development agency, 201–204
– educational reform ethics and politics, 199–200
– evaluations, 196–198
– programme expansion, 205–206
– reform beachhead, 192–195
academies rationale, 3–21
– origins, 12–14
– policies stimulus, 15
– primary dream realities and comprehensive utopia, 15
– Sir Keith Joseph's bottom 40%, 16–17
– Tory governments preparing ground for New Labour's academies, 18–21
Academies Sponsors' Trust (AST), 193
accountability, 119–121
– methods, 120–121
– for what, 120
– to whom, 119–120
admissions policies
– outcomes, 154
Adonis, Andrew, 4–5, 12, 31–32, 44
– avoiding pitfalls, 113–114
– buildings, 207
– independence, 174, 201–202
– local representation, 52
– moderns, 163
– munificence, 90
– political imperative, 110–111
– quality, 201–202
– recruitment, 166–167
– social division, 20
– Teach First, 116–117
advice, 145–146
– effectiveness, 146
ambition *vs.* strong government, 50–51
assembly hall, 172
AST. *See* Academies Sponsors' Trust (AST)
Attlee, Clement, 57

Baker, Kenneth, 13
Barber, Michael, 4
– target-led agenda, 194–195
BCSE. *See* British Council for School Environments (BCSE)
behaviour, 25
– attitudes, 182

Blair, Tony, 106
– aspirant parents, 4
– buildings importance, 86
– programme, 59
– secondary school improvement, 3
– target, 190
Blunkett, David, 8–9, 12, 128
– equity, 4
British Council for School Environments
    (BCSE)
– building criticism, 95
building(s), 175–176
– academy principals, 99–100
– CABE, 95
– community link, 91
– creation of future schools, 91–92
– criticism, 94, 95
– decisions, 98–99
– design, 87–88, 90–91, 92–94, 172
– global recession, 108
– importance, 86, 87–90
– improvement, 186
– *vs.* learning environments, 86–108
– in raising standards, 87–90
– responsibility, 92–94
– sponsors, 172
– trophy buildings *vs.* learning
    environments, 91–92
building flaws, 100–106
– classrooms and public areas, 100–101
– home base model, 102, 103–104
– lunchrooms, 103
– no assembly areas, 104–105
– no playgrounds, 101
– privacy, 105–106
– visibility, 105–106
Building Schools for Future, 97–98
bureaucratisation
– risk, 193–194

CABE. *See* Commission for Architecture
    and Built Environment (CABE)
Callaghan, James, 12–13, 21
catholic schools, 4
Certificate of Secondary Education (CSE),
    12
change, 179–180
– focus, 176–177
– recognizing need, 145
– understanding, 180–182
child-centered approach
– curriculum, 14
Christian churches, 49
Christian faith groups, 136–138

Church of England, 66–67
City Academies, 5
City Technology Colleges (CTC), 6–7, 36
– *vs.* academies, 153–154
coherent policy, 153–173
– academies independence, 159–160
– buildings, 171–172
– competition *vs.* collaboration, 168
– equipment, 171–172
– innovation, 169–170
– LAs impact, 159–160
– outcomes, 154–158
– public perception, 167
– sponsors, 161–166
– vision, 153–173
Commission for Architecture and Built
    Environment (CABE)
– building criticism, 95
– secondary school design quality, 94–95
communities
– building, 187
– value centered *vs.* rule bound, 170
Confederation for British Industry, 16
Conservative-Liberal Democrat coalition,
    44, 59, 63
– expansion plans, 203
– radical focus shift, 3
Conservative party, 15
consultants
– Academic Development Agency, 205
continuing professional development
    (CPD), 187
– Academic Development Agency, 204
coordinating role, 160–161
CPD. *See* continuing professional
    development (CPD)
CSE. *See* Certificate of Secondary Education
    (CSE)
CTC. *See* City Technology Colleges (CTC)
curriculum
– child-centered approach, 14
– choice, 141
– examples in innovation, 140–143
– quick wins, 141–142
– stage not age approach, 119

data transfer, 118–119
DCSF. *See* Department for Children,
    Schools and Families (DCSF)
decisive action, 185
Department for Children, Schools and
    Families (DCSF), 30, 38, 123, 167,
    201–205
– admissions, 40, 114

– commitment, 31, 47, 200–201
– innovation, 125, 143–147
– sponsors, 10–12, 81, 96
– Standards site, 9
Department for Education (DfE), 204, 206
– LA, 70
– priorities, 123
Department for Education and
    Employment (DfEE), 35
Department for Education and Skills
    (DFES), 95
Department of Education and Science
    (DES)
– James Report, 14
designed to deliver, 175–190
– leadership, 185–187
– learning, 185–187
– organisational failure and turnaround,
    177–179
– strategy teaching, 185–187
– sustainable change holy grail of
    contingent leadership, 182–184
DfE. *See* Department for Education (DfE)
DfEE. *See* Department for Education and
    Employment (DfEE)
DFES. *See* Department for Education and
    Skills (DFES)
disruptive students, 155–157

EAZ. *See* Education Action Zones (EAZ)
educatholics, 4
Education Act of 1996, 6
Education Action Zones (EAZ), 127
Education Reform Act (ERA) of 1988, 13,
    18–19
– Labour opposition, 19
emotional needs, 27–28
employment
– education impact, 21
environment
– creating information-rich, 188
– improvement, 186
equity, 4
ERA. *See* Education Reform Act (ERA) of
    1988
external support, 188

faith-based sponsors motivation, 66–67
faith groups, 50
financial constraints, 115
14-19 agenda, 142–143
free school meals (FSM), 20, 38, 45, 154
Fresh Start, 7–8
FSM. *See* free school meals (FSM)

funding
– Academic Development Agency, 203
future schools trophy buildings *vs.* learning
    environments, 86–108
– academies reality, 93–94
– case studies, 100–105
– design criticism, 95–99
– new building creation, 91–92
– new buildings importance in raising
    standards, 87–90
– project management and design, 100–104

General Certificate of Education (GCE), 12
global recession
– buildings, 108
GM. *See* Grant Maintained (GM) schools
governance, 76–80
– chains of academies, 80
– Charities Commission and company law,
    78–79
– decisive action, 82–83
– governing boards adding value, 79–80
– governing body needs, 76–77
– group sponsors, 81
– high achieving school sponsors, 81
– *vs.* LA schools governors, 77–78
– *vs.* overconfident ambition, 50–51
– school turnaround, 189
– tensions, 80–83
governing body, 9–10
– adding value through sponsors and
    governance, 79–80
grammar schools
– sponsoring failing secondary moderns,
    162–163
Grant Maintained (GM) schools, 6–7

Harris Trust, 33
Hawthorn effect
– outcomes, 158–159
Her Majesty's Inspectors of Schools (HMI), 12
home base model, 144

IB. *See* International Baccalaureate (IB)
ICT. *See* information and communications
    technology (ICT)
improvement
– focus, 176–177
– multifactorial, 106–107
– strategies, 185–188
incremental change, 182–183
independence, 112–117, 174, 175, 194
– Academic Development Agency, 204
– academies *vs.* LA schools, 112–113

– partnership with local family of schools,
  117–119
independent schools, 163–164
– converting to public sector with academy
  status, 161–162
information and communications
  technology (ICT), 11
initiatives *vs.* academies, 26
inner cities schools
– middle class flight, 3–4
innovation, 29, 111–112, 179–180
– Academic Development Agency, 204
– attendance examples, 130–131
– barriers, 129
– behaviour examples, 132–134
– change management, 170–171
– confusion *vs.* clarity, 128–131
– context, 126–127
– curriculum examples, 140–143
– defined, 127–128
– destabilising, 200–201
– exclusion, 135
– 14-19 agenda, 142–143
– inclusion and values, 134
– management structure, 143–145
– origin, 129–130
– perils, 170
– perils case study, 143–147
– principals' attitude, 125
– pupils' voice, 135–136
– religion, 136–138
– school context, 130
– short time effect, 158–159, 205
– sustainability, 130
– tutoring for learning, 138–140
instructional dynamic, 181
International Baccalaureate (IB), 143

James Report, 14
Johnson, Alan, 86
Joseph, Keith, 17–18

LA. *See* local authority (LA)
Labour party
– 2010 defeat, 3
– buildings importance, 86
– launching academies programme, 3, 5
– sponsors role, 83
LAPP. *See* Lower Attaining Pupils Project
  (LAPP)
LEA. *See* local education authorities (LEA)
Leadbetter, Charles, 5
leadership, 187–188
– Academic Development Agency, 204

– capacity, 182
– change, 147
– designed to deliver, 182–184, 185–187
– principals, 158
– student's learning, 177–179
– styles and strategies, 185
learning
– advisors, 140
– conversations, 140
– designed to deliver, 185–187
– environments *vs.* future schools trophy
  buildings, 86–108
– focus, 186
– from mistakes, 206–207
legitimate concern *vs.* opposition dogma,
  37–62
LEP. *See* Local Education Plan (LEP)
Levy, Michael, 4–5
local authority (LA), 4
– building standards, 98–99
– difficult relationships, 54
– independence, 112–113
– schools *vs.* academies, 5, 112–113
– tasks, 159–160
local education authorities (LEA), 6–7, 38
Local Education Plan (LEP), 171–172
Lower Attaining Pupils Project (LAPP), 17

management, 144–145
media, 121–123
middle class
– flight from inner cities schools, 3–4, 169
– return, 41
middle management, 144–145
mistakes
– learning from, 206–207
model success, 184–185
money
– impact on education, 3–4
moral imperative *vs.* socially divisive
  gimmick, 22–36
Morris, Estelle, 8
munificence, 89

National Challenge, 30, 33
– benchmark, 196
– focus, 140–141
National College for School Leadership
  (NCSL), 193–194
National Curriculum, 13
National Literacy Strategy (NLS)
– teaching to test, 195
National Professional Qualification for
  Headship (NPQH), 194

NCSL. *See* National College for School Leadership (NCSL)
NEET. *See* not in employment, education or training (NEET)
New Labour
– command and control approach, 195
NLS. *See* National Literacy Strategy (NLS)
not in employment, education or training (NEET)
– school leavers, 118
NPQH. *See* National Professional Qualification for Headship (NPQH)

Ofsted report, 20, 24, 31, 89, 147
– 14-19 agenda, 142
– funding agreement, 44
– inspections, 50, 84, 96, 117, 120, 126, 158, 196, 206
– LA, 70, 174
– requirements of national curriculum, 49, 67, 126
opposition dogma *vs.* legitimate concern, 37–62
– expansion justification, 43–46
– local representation, 52–56
– mission truth, 47–49
– pragmatism and ideology, 38–42
– strong government *vs.* overconfident ambition, 50–51
organisational failure, 177–180
organisational turnaround, 177–180, 198
outcomes, 175
– admissions policies, 154
– behaviour and exclusions, 155–157
– educational achievements, 157
– Hawthorn effect, 158–159
– leadership, 158
outliers, 24
overconfident ambition *vs.* strong government, 50–51

pastoral care, 138–140
performance indicators
– Academic Development Agency, 204
perils case study
– innovation, 143–147
PFI. *See* Public Finance Initiative (PFI)
plan transition, 184
Plowden Report, 13–14
– critics, 15
– on education, 208
– reforms, 15
policy. *See also* coherent policy
– Academic Development Agency, 203
political and moral imperative *vs.* socially

divisive gimmick, 22–36
positive relationships, 186
poverty, 25–26, 198–199
pressure, 121–123
primary schools
– critics, 15
principals, 114, 122
– accessibility to staff and children, 185
– educational decisions, 145
– leadership, 158
– management, 148
– recruitment, 166–167
publications. *See also* Ofsted report; Plowden Report; specific name
– Academic Development Agency, 204–205
– National Challenge, 141
Public Finance Initiative (PFI), 50
public perception
– mission, 167–168

quality
– Academic Development Agency, 203–204

realistic expectations, 123–124
rebranding, 179
Reconstituted School programme
– United States, 7–8
reform initiatives
– *vs.* academies, 26
regression, 191–192
repositioning, 178–179
research and publications
– Academic Development Agency, 204–205
retrenchment, 178
Roman Catholic, 66–67

school(s). *See also* specific name or type
– choice, 34
– cultural reform appearance and meaning, 26–29
– leavers, 118
– model, 75–76, 144
– NEET, 118
– performance variance, 23–24
– reform necessity, 22–25
– socially divisive gimmick *vs.* political and moral imperative, 22–29
– trophy buildings *vs.* learning environments, 86–108
School Governors One Stop Shop, 79
School Improvement Partner (SIP), 122, 123, 126, 143–148, 161
– Academic Development Agency, 205
– pressure, 201

– sponsor disappointment, 171
secondary schools
– Blair government and improvement, 3
– critics, 15–16
– design quality and CABE, 94–95
SEN. *See* special education needs (SEN)
SIP. *See* School Improvement Partner (SIP)
Skinner's school, 163
small school model, 75–76, 144
social background, 198–199
socially divided schools, 199
socially divisive gimmick *vs.* political and
    moral imperative, 22–36
– planning academies, 30–32
– school cultural reform appearance and
    meaning, 26–29
– school reform necessity, 22–25
– standards drive and market-driven
    reforms, 33–35
Social Worker (Attlee), 57
special education needs (SEN), 10, 18–19,
    77, 120, 149, 160
Specialist Schools Advisory Trust (SSAT),
    122, 193
sponsors, 9, 47–48, 63–83
– altruism, 65–66
– with chain of academies, 165–166
– Charities Commission and company law,
    78–79
– contributions, 71–72
– with educational agenda, 74–76
– educational background, 72–75
– educational decisions, 145
– governance, 76–79
– governance tensions, 80–82
– governing boards adding value, 79–80
– governing body needs, 76–77
– independent schools, 67–68
– LA, 70–71
– *vs.* LA schools governors, 77–78
– motivation, 64–69
– need for, 84
– new, 85
– non-executive chair model, 73–74
– philanthropy, 65–66
– power to dismiss principals, 82
– recruitment, 166–167
– relations with principals, 73–76
– role in Labour government, 83
– sponsors' contribution, 71

– succession, 84
– types, 63
– universities, 68–69, 164–165
SSAT. *See* Specialist Schools Advisory Trust
    (SSAT)
staffing, 114–116
– Academic Development Agency, 204
strategy teaching, 185–187
strong government *vs.* overconfident
    ambition, 50–51
students
– behavior, 155–157
– records, 188
– teacher symbiotic relationship, 26–27
sustainable change, 182
sustainable cultural shift, 207–208

targets
– Academic Development Agency, 204
task cognitive demands, 26–27
teacher-student symbiotic relationship,
    26–27
Teach First, 116–117, 207–208
teaching
– designed to deliver, 185–187
– and learning focus, 186
Thatcher, Margaret, 13, 15
– gradualism, 18
– popularity, 16
– social division, 19–20
trophy buildings *vs.* learning environments,
    86–108
trust, 209
turnaround
– designed to deliver, 177–179
– implications, 179

UCST. *See* United Church Schools Trust
    (UCST)
ULT. *See* United Learning Trust (ULT)
underachieving schools *vs.* outstanding
    schools, 3
unemployment, 25–26
union, 109–110
United Church Schools Trust (UCST), 49
United Learning Trust (ULT), 33
United States Reconstituted School
    programme, 7–8
university sponsors, 164–165
unqualified school leavers, 16–17